I0888370

# Dismantling Barriers and Advancing the Right of Persons with Disabilities to Participate in Cultural Life

The right to participate in cultural life is profoundly rooted in international human rights law, and, with regard to persons with disabilities, it is enunciated in Article 30 of the UN Convention on the Rights of Persons with Disabilities (CRPD or 'the Convention'). This provision requires States Parties to the Convention to ensure accessibility of cultural materials, services and activities, and cultural heritage, and to support the creative and artistic potential of persons with disabilities. However, people with disabilities continue to face barriers to cultural participation.

On foot of a pan-European empirical study and a socio-legal analysis, this book discusses the normative content of Article 30 CRPD and its implementation. It identifies and categorises barriers to cultural participation, highlighting new paths to operationalise Article 30 CRPD.

This book will be of interest to scholars and students working in disability law, socio-legal studies, international human rights law, as well as cultural studies, disability studies, and cultural policies.

**Delia Ferri** is Professor of Law at Maynooth University (MU) School of Law and Criminology and co-director of the MU Assisting Living & Learning (ALL) Institute.

**Ann Leahy** is a Postdoctoral Researcher with the DANCING project funded by the European Research Council and based at Maynooth University.

## Interdisciplinary Disability Studies

Series editor: Karen Soldatić
*CERC – Health Equity and Community Wellbeing, Toronto Metropolitan University*

Disability studies has made great strides in exploring power and the body. This series extends the interdisciplinary dialogue between disability studies and other fields by asking how disability studies can influence a particular field. It will show how a deep engagement with disability studies changes our understanding of the following fields: sociology, literary studies, gender studies, bioethics, social work, law, education, or history. This ground-breaking series identifies both the practical and theoretical implications of such an interdisciplinary dialogue and challenges people in disability studies as well as other disciplinary fields to critically reflect on their professional praxis in terms of theory, practice, and methods.

**Intersectional Colonialities**
Embodied Colonial Violence and Practices of Resistance at the Axis of Disability, Race, Indigeneity, Class, and Gender
*Edited by Robel Afeworki Abay and Karen Soldatic*

**Deaf People, Injustice and Reconciliation**
Signed Memories
*Hisayo Katsui, Maija Koivisto, Pauli Rautiainen, Niina Meriläinen, Suvi-Maaria Tepora-Niemi, Merja Tarvainen, Päivi Rainò, and Heikki Hiilamo*

**Care and Disability**
Relational Representations
*Edited by D. Christopher Gabbard and Talia Schaffer*

**Dismantling Barriers and Advancing the Right of Persons with Disabilities to Participate in Cultural Life**
A Socio-Legal Analysis
*Delia Ferri and Ann Leahy*

For a full list of titles in this series, please visit:
www.routledge.com/Interdisciplinary-Disability-Studies/book-series/ASHSER1401

# Dismantling Barriers and Advancing the Right of Persons with Disabilities to Participate in Cultural Life

## A Socio-Legal Analysis

Delia Ferri and Ann Leahy

Routledge
Taylor & Francis Group
LONDON AND NEW YORK

First published 2025
by Routledge
4 Park Square, Milton Park, Abingdon, Oxon OX14 4RN

and by Routledge
605 Third Avenue, New York, NY 10158

*Routledge is an imprint of the Taylor & Francis Group, an informa business*

© 2025 Delia Ferri and Ann Leahy

The right of Delia Ferri and Ann Leahy to be identified as authors of this work has been asserted in accordance with sections 77 and 78 of the Copyright, Designs and Patents Act 1988.

The Open Access version of this book, available at www.taylorfrancis.com, has been made available under a Creative Commons Attribution-Non Commercial-No Derivatives (CC-BY-NC-ND) 4.0 International license.

Any third party material in this book is not included in the OA Creative Commons license, unless indicated otherwise in a credit line to the material. Please direct any permissions enquiries to the original rightsholder.

This book is one of the outputs of the project 'Protecting the Right to Culture of Persons with Disabilities and Enhancing Cultural Diversity through European Union Law: Exploring New Paths (DANCING)', funded by the European Research Council (Grant Agreement No. 864182).

*Trademark notice*: Product or corporate names may be trademarks or registered trademarks, and are used only for identification and explanation without intent to infringe.

*British Library Cataloguing-in-Publication Data*
A catalogue record for this book is available from the British Library

ISBN: 978-1-032-60229-5 (hbk)
ISBN: 978-1-032-61935-4 (pbk)
ISBN: 978-1-032-61936-1 (ebk)

DOI: 10.4324/9781032619361

Typeset in Sabon
by Apex CoVantage, LLC

*We would like to dedicate this book to the memory of Dr Damjan Tatić, former member of the DANCING project advisory board, renowned human rights expert and former member of the United Nations Committee on the Rights of Persons with Disabilities. His support and his enthusiasm were important to us, especially in the early stages of the DANCING project. We will always remember his unwavering encouragement of our research. We hope that this book may represent a tribute to him and form a small part of the legacy of his pioneering work and spirit.*

*Delia Ferri and Ann Leahy*

# Contents

# Tables

# About the Authors

**Delia Ferri** is Professor of Law at Maynooth University (MU) School of Law and Criminology and co-director of the MU Assisting Living & Learning (ALL) Institute. Delia is also an affiliated researcher at the DIRPOLIS Institute of Scuola Superiore Sant'Anna (Italy), an international fellow at the Burton Blatt Institute of Syracuse University (USA), and a member of the Royal Irish Academy Ethical, Political, Legal and Philosophical Studies Committee. She has authored several academic publications focusing on the rights of people with disabilities, participatory processes, and cultural diversity. Delia is currently the principal investigator of the project titled 'Protecting the Right to Culture of Persons with Disabilities and Enhancing Cultural Diversity through European Union Law: Exploring New Paths (DANCING)', funded by the European Research Council.

**Ann Leahy** is a Postdoctoral Researcher with the DANCING project funded by the European Research Council and based at Maynooth University. Formerly, she was an assistant CEO of an NGO, Age & Opportunity, with responsibility for policy and public affairs and for the organisation's work on arts and culture. She is also a qualified solicitor. Her academic publications focus on ageing and disability as well as on cultural participation by people with disabilities. Her book, *Disability and Ageing – Towards a Critical Perspective* (Policy Press 2021), based on her PhD research, examines intersections between disability and ageing. Academic awards include postgraduate and postdoctoral awards from the Irish Research Council and a Hume Scholarship from Maynooth University.

# Tables

# About the Authors

**Delia Ferri** is Professor of Law at Maynooth University (MU) School of Law and Criminology and co-director of the MU Assisting Living & Learning (ALL) Institute. Delia is also an affiliated researcher at the DIRPOLIS Institute of Scuola Superiore Sant'Anna (Italy), an international fellow at the Burton Blatt Institute of Syracuse University (USA), and a member of the Royal Irish Academy Ethical, Political, Legal and Philosophical Studies Committee. She has authored several academic publications focusing on the rights of people with disabilities, participatory processes, and cultural diversity. Delia is currently the principal investigator of the project titled 'Protecting the Right to Culture of Persons with Disabilities and Enhancing Cultural Diversity through European Union Law: Exploring New Paths (DANCING)', funded by the European Research Council.

**Ann Leahy** is a Postdoctoral Researcher with the DANCING project funded by the European Research Council and based at Maynooth University. Formerly, she was an assistant CEO of an NGO, Age & Opportunity, with responsibility for policy and public affairs and for the organisation's work on arts and culture. She is also a qualified solicitor. Her academic publications focus on ageing and disability as well as on cultural participation by people with disabilities. Her book, *Disability and Ageing – Towards a Critical Perspective* (Policy Press 2021), based on her PhD research, examines intersections between disability and ageing. Academic awards include postgraduate and postdoctoral awards from the Irish Research Council and a Hume Scholarship from Maynooth University.

# Foreword

In many of my works, I have highlighted the marginalisation and discrimination faced by persons with disabilities in the United States and globally. At different junctures in my career, I have also discussed the importance of addressing systemic issues in the pursuit of human rights policies that improve the social and economic status as well as the lives of people with disabilities. However, while advancements have been achieved, people with disabilities still face barriers and cannot participate as equal citizens of the world. The pandemic, as I contended in my recent works, has raised unprecedented health, social, and economic challenges and exacerbated existing barriers. One of the areas in which those barriers have become even more acute than before – and yet under-researched – is that of cultural life. For this reason, this book provides a timely contribution to knowledge.

While being inherently interdisciplinary, the analysis conducted places the UN Convention on the Rights of Persons with Disabilities (CRPD) at the core of this book. The CRPD, in some ways like the Americans with Disabilities Act (ADA) of 1990, but even more comprehensively, revolves around the requirement that social institutions affirmatively remove attitudinal and structural barriers confronting people with disabilities as they exercise their rights to participate fully in society. As noted elsewhere, the CRPD has established a foundation for equal protection and treatment of people with disabilities across a wide range of basic human rights. Like with the ADA, the CRPD recognised disability as a label applied when people with impairments confront attitudinal and environmental (structural and policy) barriers that hinder full and effective participation in society on an equal basis with others. In that regard, the ADA provided foundational elements for the CRPD's international human rights model of disability and its objective to spur change in the domestic laws of its signatory member nations.

The authors of this book, in line with the approach of the CRPD, flesh out the content of the right to cultural participation, highlighting the barriers faced by people with disabilities in exercising it, but also what facilitates access to cultural goods, services, and heritage and what dismantles such barriers. They develop an original interdisciplinary analysis of cultural participation by people with disabilities. They also point to the concrete legal implications of barriers and facilitators to cultural participation and unveil what best may advance the implementation of Article 30 CRPD. Such a systematic examination has not been undertaken before, and this book thereby offers a rich and intriguing contribution to the disability law and studies literature.

Albeit focusing on Europe, the book presents a socio-legal analysis which is of wider – namely global – relevance. In presenting the lived experiences of persons with disabilities and in engaging with the international legal debate on the CRPD, it makes a contribution that goes beyond the geographical boundaries of the analysis and provides important insights that may support other States Parties to the CRPD in implementing their legal obligations. By examining the role of non-discrimination and accessibility legislation in enhancing cultural participation, this book foreshadows future directions for research on disability law and disability issues more broadly.

Prof. Dr. Peter Blanck
Syracuse (US), 30 June 2024

# Acknowledgements

This book is one of the main outputs of the project 'Protecting the Right to Culture of Persons with Disabilities and Enhancing Cultural Diversity through European Union Law: Exploring New Paths (DANCING)', funded by the European Research Council (Grant Agreement No. 864182). It presents the key findings of Work Package 1 of the project which aimed to advance understanding of the barriers faced by persons with disabilities in participating in culture, the causes of exclusion of people with disabilities from the cultural domain, and also of the elements that facilitate cultural participation.

This book is the product of a close collaboration between us as authors and of three years of intense research. We are grateful to all the DANCING team members that supported the research in different ways and helped us to shape this volume. Special thanks go to Tiarnán McDonough for his help at various junctures in the writing process. We are grateful to the advisory board of the DANCING project for their feedback along the way. Our appreciation also goes to Prof. Dr. Peter Blanck for writing the foreword to this book.

Last but not least, our thanks go to Claire Jarvis, Sullivan Evans, and the publishing team at Routledge for their advice and patience, as well as their efficient management support, to the anonymous reviewers that helped streamline the book, and to all our colleagues, who, at different stages, provided constructive comments and feedback.

Delia Ferri and Ann Leahy
Maynooth, 30 June 2024

The DANCING project has received funding from the European Research Council (ERC) under the European Union's Horizon 2020 Research and Innovation programme (Grant Agreement No. 864182).

# Introduction

*Delia Ferri and Ann Leahy*

## 1. The State of the Art and the Aims of the Book

Cultural participation is a vital part of being a member of society, and opportunities to participate in, and to contribute to, culture are intrinsic to the humanity of all people. As articulated by the former UN Special Rapporteur in the field of cultural rights, humanity dignifies and reimagines itself through creating, performing, preserving, and revising its cultural and artistic life (Bennoune, 2018). Further, culture is recognised as having the potential to promote fuller enjoyment of human rights, including by championing the universality of human rights and dignity, embodying and embracing cultural diversity, challenging discrimination and contributing to reconciliation (Bennoune, 2018). To be excluded from the cultural realm, on the other hand, is not just about the fact that you do not get to go to the theatre or the movies; it is about something more profound – it is about exclusion from full participation in what it means to be human, as articulated by O'Toole (2006). Indeed, without the right to participate in cultural life, individuals fail to develop the social and cultural connections that are important to maintaining satisfactory conditions of equality, which can have consequences for the well-being and even sustainability of the social order (Laaksonen, 2010). For people with disabilities, no less than for people without disabilities, therefore, participating in culture is recognised as an essential dimension of life (Tatić, 2015).

The right to participate in cultural life is deeply rooted in international human rights law. Article 27 of the Universal Declaration of Human Rights (UDHR) states that 'everyone has the right to freely participate in the cultural life of the community, to enjoy the arts and to share in scientific advancement and its benefits'. Article 15(1)(a) of the International Covenant on Economic Social and Cultural Rights (ICESCR) recognises 'the right of everyone to take part in cultural life' (O'Keefe, 1998). Other international provisions guarantee, to various extents, the right to participate in culture and set out the collective cultural rights of minorities and indigenous peoples (Bidault, 2009; Stamatopoulou, 2007, 2012). Article 30 of the United Nations Convention on the Rights of Persons with Disabilities (CRPD or simply 'the Convention')

DOI: 10.4324/9781032619361-1

This chapter has been made available under a CC-BY-NC-ND 4.0 license.

(United Nations, 2006) specifically articulates the right of persons with disabilities to participate in cultural life, alongside the right to participate in sport, leisure, and recreation, while listing a number of obligations to be complied with by States Parties to the Convention (Manca, 2017). As noted elsewhere (Ferri & Leahy, 2023), the importance of this provision lies in its rather detailed normative content, and also in that it sheds light on the need for dismantling barriers that hamper the cultural participation of persons with disabilities.

Notwithstanding being rooted in international human rights law, the right to cultural participation has been depicted as the 'Cinderella of human rights' (Xanthaki, 2015). As recalled by Guibert (2023), there is an enduring stigma surrounding the right to cultural participation, and particularly to artistic expression, as a non-essential 'luxury'. Further, this right is considered 'one of the least studied human rights in the international literature' (Bantekas et al., 2018, p. 865; Veal, 2022). Veal (2022) claims that the right to cultural participation is neither fully endorsed nor implemented, echoing what Symonides (1998, p. 569) had observed in his research. Veal (2022) also argues that literature on cultural participation has generally neglected a human rights approach.

The right to culture of people with disabilities has been discussed only within the remit of commentaries to the CRPD, with very limited scholarship going beyond the analysis of Article 30 CRPD (Ferri & Leahy, 2023; Leahy & Ferri, 2022, 2023). Literature outside the legal remit which examines the barriers to, and the facilitators of, cultural participation has traditionally been limited and is still rather narrow in scope and approach. However, as Chapter 1 will show, the cultural participation of persons with disabilities has become a growing area of focus within disparate areas of scholarship. Data on participation of persons with disabilities in culture are also scant. The report of the Office of the High Commissioner for Human Rights (OHCHR) on 'Data sources for outcome indicators on Article 30 CRPD' indicates that most surveys measuring time spent on cultural activities do not measure disability status (OHCHR, 2020). Often national surveys that do present data on disability aggregate leisure, cultural, and social categories of activities (OHCHR, 2020). Those national studies that address rates of participation in culture by people with disabilities are published in a range of languages and are not always updated.

In Europe, the limited data available are mostly connected to the Eurostat Survey on Income and Living Conditions (SILC). SILC includes annual data on disability (or 'activity limitations' as it is termed in SILC) and ad hoc modules that comprise questions on cultural participation. This data evidences that participation in cultural events tends to be lower on the part of people with disabilities than those without disabilities (Eurostat, 2024). This tallies with recent literature that postulates that persons with disabilities have generally very poor access to culture both as audience and as artists. Such exclusion of people with disabilities from cultural life has contributed to their marginalisation and to discrimination against them and entails a blatant breach of their human right to participate in cultural life.

Against this background, this book aims to advance the state of knowledge by analysing what hampers and what facilitates the cultural participation of people with disabilities, with a view to supporting the realisation and fulfilment of the right to participate in culture provided for in Article 30 CRPD. This book brings a unique perspective by adopting a socio-legal approach and looking at various forms of cultural participation across a wide range of countries and types of impairments. In that regard, it aims to overcome the current limited interaction amongst disciplines that have dealt with cultural participation of persons with disabilities, which has caused conceptual fragmentation and epistemic gaps. From a methodological point of view, the book blends legal-doctrinal research with qualitative research. It is underpinned by the view that, in order to advance the rights of people with disabilities, it is important to keep our focus on how they experience barriers across social and cultural settings (Williams et al., 2018).

On the whole, the book presents three distinctive and novel facets: first, it advances the understanding of the normative content of the right of people with disabilities to participate in cultural life by means of a novel socio-legal analysis; second, it brings together legal analysis, multidisciplinary scholarly work with empirical research examining perspectives of people representing organisations of people with disabilities (OPDs) about what operates as barriers to, or facilitators of, participation in culture, focusing both on attendance as audience and as creators and artists; third, it categorises barriers to, and facilitators of, cultural participation and connects them to the normative content of Article 30 CRPD.

Notably, the book is one of the academic outputs of the academic project titled 'Protecting the Right to Culture of Persons with Disabilities and Enhancing Cultural Diversity through European Union Law: Exploring New Paths – DANCING', funded by the European Research Council (ERC) under the European Union's (EU's) Horizon 2020 research and innovation programme.[1] It brings together the multifaceted research conducted under Work Package 1 of this project, which aims to advance understanding of the barriers to participation in culture, the causes of exclusion of people with disabilities from the cultural domain, and the facilitators of participation.

After having highlighted the core aims and innovative aspects of this book, Section 2 moves on to outline the core features of the CRPD as overarching legal framework. Section 3 presents the human rights model of disability as the theoretical framework of the book and lays out the book's understanding of what disability is, and our choice of terms, both of which are consistent with the CRPD, outlining how the issue of barriers, both attitudinal and

1 ERC Consolidator Grant – Grant Agreement No. 864182.

environmental, are central to how disability is defined in the preamble and in Article 1 CRPD. In that connection, Section 4 focuses on the conceptual scope of the book, delineating the intersection between disability and culture within contemporary disability studies, as well as the meaning of culture and cultural participation for the purpose of the analysis conducted. Section 5 then moves on to discuss the salience of a socio-legal approach and the methodology of the book. Finally, Section 6 briefly outlines the structure of the book to help the reader navigate through its contents.

## 2. The UN Convention on Rights of Persons with Disabilities as an Overarching Legal Framework

Traditionally, disability had been deemed a mere individual deficit, deriving from a disease or condition hampering physiological or cognitive functioning (Bickenbach et al., 1999; Barnes & Mercer, 2010; Tennant, 1997). It was understood as a personal tragedy. This 'medical model' of disability was challenged by activists in the United States and in the United Kingdom (UK) in the 1970s (Blanck, 2020; Sépulchre, 2021, p. 63; Schur et al., 2013, p. 99). They put forward a conception of disability as a societal construction, currently labelled the 'social model of disability' (Oliver, 1983, 1990, 1996, 2013). Activism of persons with disabilities and the broad academic debate around the social model stimulated the international development of disability rights as a key element of UN work (Degener & Begg, 2017; Ferri et al., 2025), as well as national developments in countries like the United States (Blanck, 2020, 2023a).

Degener and Begg (2017) suggest that, from 1945 to 1970, persons with disabilities 'were invisible' in the UN system. With the flourishing of the disability movement, from 1970 to 1980, disabled persons 'became recognised as subjects of rehabilitation', and signs of a rights-based approach became visible, even if rather tentatively (Degener & Begg, 2017, p. 2). The Declaration on the Rights of Disabled Persons (United Nations, 1975) posited that persons with disabilities were entitled to the enjoyment of civil and political rights and encouraged the adoption of measures to support the enshrining of these rights. According to Degener and Begg (2017), it was only around the 1980s that persons with disabilities became 'objects of human rights'. The 1993 (non-binding) Standard Rules on the Equalization of Opportunities for Persons with Disabilities represented a significant political commitment to realising equality for persons with disabilities (United Nations, 1993). The new millennium represented a key turning point as a binding treaty to ensure equal rights to persons with disabilities was indicated as the key objective to be achieved. An ad hoc committee was then created in December 2001 by the UN with a mandate to draft a comprehensive international convention. This committee released the text of the CRPD, which was then approved by the UN General Assembly and formally adopted on 13 December 2006, entering into force on 3 May 2008.

The CRPD is commonly acknowledged to be a ground-breaking treaty, imposing a new disability rights paradigm (Harpur, 2012). Felder (2022, p. 48) suggests that 'the CRPD is visionary, extensive and new compared to existing law'. As will be further discussed in the subsequent section, and as noted elsewhere (Ferri et al., 2023, p. 6), the 'transformative potential of the CRPD is linked to the fact that it recasts disability as a social construct and abandons the outdated medical model of disability'. Skarstad and Stein (2018, p. 2) argue that the 'CRPD precipitated a dramatic sea change in the relative human rights empowerment of persons with disabilities by recognizing their equal dignity, autonomy, and worth, and by ensuring their equal enjoyment of all human rights and fundamental freedoms'. Other authors contend that the importance of the CRPD is also linked to its detailed normative content and to the fact that it requires specific national implementation institutions and monitoring tools. Arbour referred to the CRPD in this respect as a 'catalyst for change' (Arbour, 2006).

Although the CRPD has been sometimes deemed of limited relevance in non-Western contexts and in the Global South (Meekosha & Soldatic, 2011), it is generally considered the global normative point of reference for the implementation of disability rights. As recalled by Degener and Gomez-Carrillo De Castro (2022), the 'CRPD is champion amongst United Nations' human rights treaties with its speedy record of ratifications'. In that regard, there is little doubt that the CRPD represents a global standard for disability rights, including the right to cultural participation of persons with disabilities. For this reason, and although other international and regional instruments will be mentioned (namely, European, in line with the geographical scope of the book), the CRPD represents the key legal framework for the socio-legal analysis propounded here.

## 3. The Human Rights Model of Disability as Theoretical Framework

As will be further discussed in Chapter 2 of this book, the novelty of the CRPD arises from its embedding of the 'human rights model of disability'. Hence, consistent with the choice to refer to the CRPD as the overarching legal benchmark, this book is underpinned by the 'human rights model of disability' as its theoretical framework.

The 'human rights model of disability' had been initially mentioned by Quinn and Degener (2002) and was further elaborated on by Degener (2016a, 2016b, 2017a, 2017b). That model, which builds on the academic elaborations of the 'social model', was then revisited and developed by the UN Committee on the Rights of Persons with Disabilities (CRPD Committee) in 2018 (CRPD Committee, 2018). In that regard, Degener and Gomez-Carrillo de Castro (2022, p. 33) suggest that the 'human rights model emerged from the CRPD Committee's responses to the States parties' difficulties in grasping equality of persons with disabilities'.

Degener (2016a, 2016b, 2017a, 2017b) argues that this model emphasises the human dignity of persons with disabilities and 'encompasses both sets of human rights, civil and political as well as economic, social and cultural rights' (2016b, p. 4). She contends that the human rights model values impairments as part of human diversity, paying attention to intersectional discrimination. Further, the human rights model 'offers room for minority and cultural identification' (Degener, 2016b). In line with Lawson and Beckett (2020), Degener and Gomez-Carrillo de Castro (2022, p. 35) postulate that the human rights model 'does not explain disability; instead, it provides a framework to conceptualize agency, rights and the content of rights', and, while building on the social model 'which exposes structural discrimination', it further recognises different experiences of impairment and disability. They clarify that 'this recognition of diversity in humankind' allows the human rights model of disability 'to house different epistemic and political claims from people with disabilities'. According to the CRPD Committee (2018, para. 9):

> The human rights model of disability recognizes that disability is a social construct and impairments must not be taken as a legitimate ground for the denial or restriction of human rights. It acknowledges that disability is one of several layers of identity. Hence, disability laws and policies must take the diversity of persons with disabilities into account. It also recognizes that human rights are interdependent, interrelated and indivisible.

Degener and Gomez-Carrillo de Castro (2022, p. 43) highlight that the CRPD Committee initially used the terms 'human rights model of disability' interchangeably with 'social model of disability', but lately it refers exclusively to the human rights model of disability. In its most recent Concluding Observations (COs), the CRPD Committee places emphasis on the failure of States Parties to implement the human rights model of disability and identifies this as a root cause of the marginalisation of persons with disabilities.

Neither the CRPD Committee nor Degener articulates the role of the right to participate in cultural life within the human rights model of disability. Nonetheless, this right is encompassed by, and essential for the realisation of, such a model (Ferri & Leahy, 2023). In fact, the recognition of the right to culture is inextricably linked to the recognition of the inherent dignity of persons with disabilities, and the freedom of creative activity implies the expression of everyone's 'layered' identity.

Cognisant of the ongoing debate on the language of disability (Best et al., 2022), but consistent with the human rights model of disability, this book uses people-first (or person-first) language (i.e. 'people/persons with disabilities') and, only occasionally and in an interchangeable fashion, 'disabled person/people'. While recognising the challenges around the language on disability, as noted by Blanck (2023b, p. 177), people-first language emphasises 'the importance of the individual as a "person" who has accompanying rights and responsibilities in law'.

## 4. The Right of People with Disabilities to Participate in Cultural Life: Conceptual Boundaries

### 4.1. *Disability and Culture*

An analysis of the right of people with disabilities to participate in cultural life cannot but take into account the complex conceptual relationship between disability and culture. Foundational literature within disability studies, associated with the social model of disability, stressed the social and economic bases of disability (see, *inter alia*, Finkelstein, 1981; Oliver, 1990, 1996). However, in much scholarship that has followed, cultural re-evaluation has also come to be seen as central to the political struggles of people with disabilities (Riddell & Watson, 2003). These perspectives highlight the extent to which the socially dominant culture shapes how disability and impairment are viewed, and how this contributes to oppression (Riddell & Watson, 2003). As noted by Blanck (2023b, p. 178), 'disability language and identity are inescapably tied to history, culture, and political considerations at large'. Taking a feminist perspective, Garland-Thomson (2002, p. 5) famously argued that disability 'is not a natural state of corporeal inferiority, inadequacy, excess, or a stroke of misfortune. Rather, disability is a culturally fabricated narrative of the body'. Others, including Davis (2013, p. 12), challenged ideas of normalcy, identifying the 'problem' not in the disabled person but in how normalcy is constructed and suggesting the need to reverse the 'hegemony of the normal' and institute alternative ways of thinking about the 'abnormal'. Thus, in disability studies, critical and cultural disability studies have emerged in recent decades. They are open to 'a host of theoretical developments', each of which 'emphasizes the cultural, discursive and relational undergirdings of the disability experience' (Goodley, 2013, p. 634). In short, within these perspectives, disability is analysed as a social and cultural phenomenon, which says as much about normalising/non-disabled society as it does about the constitution of disability (Goodley & Bolt, 2010).

Simultaneously, people with disabilities have resisted socially dominant cultures by forging their own cultures, making culture a source both 'of oppression and of liberation' (Riddell & Watson, 2003, p. 1). Disability art, culture, and media studies engage with the stories told about what it means to be disabled in drama, dance, film, literature, media, and other art forms and also with how workers in these industries 'are developing new accounts of what it means to be disabled' (Hadley & McDonald, 2019, p. 2). Solvang (2018) outlines how disability arts emerged in association with the disability rights movement linked with expressions of disability experiences, often for audiences comprised of people with disabilities, but that, more recently, it is characterised by artists wanting to attract mainstream audiences and by a combination of disability issues and non-disability issues. Contributions from scholars and artists emphasise the potential for transformation of mainstream culture. Thus, instead of adapting to the way a mainstream art form has been created, disability art illuminates disability experiences and disabled bodies just as they are (Sandahl, 2018, p. 85).

### 4.2. *The Multifarious Concept of Culture*

The relationship between disability and culture is complex. Such complexity is also linked to the multifaceted concept of culture (Riddell & Watson, 2003), the definition of which depends on the context and the disciplinary perspective of the writer (Ferri, 2009; Johnson, 2020). Williams (1989, p. 4) highlights that the word 'culture' is broadly used to encompass a whole way of life but also to refer, more narrowly, to the arts and their learning, that is, 'the special processes of discovery and creative effort'. The first of these is the conception embraced by international human rights law (Chow, 2018; Jakubowski, 2020). The UN Committee on Economic, Social and Cultural Rights (CESCR, 2009) indicates that culture encompasses

> ways of life, language, oral and written literature, music and song, non-verbal communication, religion or belief systems, rites and ceremonies, sport and games, methods of production or technology, natural and man-made environments, food, clothing and shelter and the arts, customs and traditions through which individuals, groups of individuals and communities express their humanity and the meaning they give to their existence.

In a similar vein, the UN Educational, Scientific and Cultural Organization (UNESCO) has adopted a very extensive understanding of culture, as the 'set of distinctive spiritual, material, intellectual and emotional features of society or a social group, that encompasses, not only art and literature, but lifestyles, [and] ways of living together' (UNESCO, 1982, 2001).

The definition of culture encompasses that of cultural heritage. The UNESCO Convention concerning the Protection of the World Cultural and Natural Heritage, adopted in 1972 and which entered into force in 1977 (UNESCO, 1972), further defines 'cultural heritage' as encompassing 'monuments' – which include 'architectural works, works of monumental sculpture and painting, elements or structures of an archaeological nature, inscriptions, cave dwellings and combinations of features, which are of outstanding universal value from the point of view of history, art or science', 'groups of separate or connected buildings which, because of their architecture, their homogeneity or their place in the landscape, are of outstanding universal value from the point of view of history, art or science', and 'sites' – which refer to 'works of man or the combined works of nature and of man, and areas including archaeological sites which are of outstanding universal value from the historical, aesthetic, ethnological or anthropological points of view'. Another (similar and even wider) definition of cultural heritage is included in the Faro Convention on the Value of Cultural Heritage for Society, adopted within the remit of the Council of Europe (CoE) (Council of Europe, 2005). According to Article 2(a) of this Faro Convention 'cultural heritage is a group of resources inherited from the past which people identify, independently of ownership, as a reflection and expression of their constantly evolving values, beliefs, knowledge and traditions' and 'includes all aspects of the environment resulting from the interaction between people and places through time'.

The UNESCO Convention on the Protection and Promotion of the Diversity of Cultural Expressions (UNESCO, 2005) further defines concepts that are entrenched within the broader notion of culture. In particular, Article 4 states that cultural content 'refers to the symbolic meaning, artistic dimension and cultural values that originate from or express cultural identities'. It also defines cultural expressions as 'those expressions that result from the creativity of individuals, groups and societies, and that have cultural content', and cultural activities, goods and services as 'those activities, goods and services, which at the time they are considered as a specific attribute, use or purpose, embody or convey cultural expressions, irrespective of the commercial value they may have'.

In line with these definitions, the UNESCO Framework for Cultural Statistics (2009), which replaces an earlier framework from 1986 (UNESCO, 1986), defines culture 'through the identification and measurement of the behaviours and practices resulting from the beliefs and values of a society or a social group' (p. 9). In that regard, it adopts a broad concept of the cultural domain as encompassing a set of economic and social activities that traditionally have been regarded as being 'cultural' (UNESCO, 2009, p. 10).

This book acknowledges the current comprehensive definitions of culture and the cultural domain, but deliberately focuses on arts practices (including different art forms, including literature, dance, music, theatre, and visual arts) and heritage as forms of cultural expression (Caust, 2019). In this respect, considering the geographical scope of the book, it is worth noting that the Creative Europe Regulation (European Parliament and Council, 2021) articulates the cultural and creative sectors as including

> *inter alia*, architecture, archives, libraries and museums, artistic crafts, audio-visual (including film, television, video games and multimedia), tangible and intangible cultural heritage, design (including fashion design), festivals, music, literature, performing arts (including theatre and dance), books and publishing, radio, and visual arts.

When referring to museums, our analysis takes into account the broad (non-prescriptive) concept adopted in 2022 by the Extraordinary General Assembly of the International Council of Museums (ICOM, 2022), according to which

> [a] museum is a not-for-profit, permanent institution in the service of society that researches, collects, conserves, interprets and exhibits tangible and intangible heritage. Open to the public, accessible and inclusive, museums foster diversity and sustainability. They operate and communicate ethically, professionally and with the participation of communities, offering varied experiences for education, enjoyment, reflection and knowledge sharing.

On the whole, as will be further explored in Part II of the book, we consider arts practices and heritage visible and acknowledged forms of cultural expression which reflect a variety of voices and identities (Caust, 2019; European Commission, 2019).

### 4.3. *Cultural Participation as Human Right*

This book frames and investigates cultural participation as a human right, with a focus on Article 30 CRPD. Such choice tallies with the use of the human rights model of disability as a theoretical framework.

It has often been noted that cultural participation is difficult to define 'due to the variety of ways in which it can occur' (OECD, 2022, p. 44). Stevenson et al. (2017) regard cultural participation in a broad manner as engagement in cultural activities. A report produced in 2012 by a Working Group of EU experts through the Open Method of Coordination (OMC) – a voluntary cooperation amongst EU Member States – contextualises definitions of 'access to' and 'participation in' culture, and suggests that they are closely related. It further indicates that the concept of 'access' focuses on enabling new audiences to use the available culture on offer (EU Member States' Experts on Better Access to and Wider Participation in Culture, 2012; see also Tomka, 2013). That report also posits that participation in culture involves participation in relevant decision-making processes on cultural policies alongside creative processes. Most often, however, participation is considered as an umbrella term. In that regard, it is commonly acknowledged that cultural participation can take both active and passive forms. In particular, cultural participation can be active whereby the individual is 'creating meaning' and contributing directly and explicitly to the production of the cultural experience itself (OECD, 2022, p. 44). Passive participation is a synonym of 'access' or consumption of culture whereby 'individuals access and enjoy the experiences and contents created by someone else' (OECD, 2022, p. 44). This distinction between an active and a passive aspect of participation has become quite blurred in the digital era where social media and, more broadly, an array of digital tools allow for widespread co-production and co-creation (*inter alia* Gronemann et al., 2015). However, such a distinction remains useful and is referred to in this book as it somewhat matches the articulation of the right to participate in cultural life in international human rights law.

As will be explored in Part II of this book, the right to cultural participation is generally considered as encompassing a twofold individual dimension and a collective aspect (EPRS, 2017, pp. 10, 27; UNESCO, 2009). The twofold individual dimension entails, respectively, the right to access cultural activities, goods, services and heritage, and the right to active involvement in culture, which includes engagement in the creation of cultural activities, goods, and services (Romainville, 2015). The collective aspect refers to cultural communities being recognised and protected, as well as enabled to enjoy their cultural expressions (Jakubowski, 2016). These individual and collective facets do feature in Article 30 CRPD. As noted by Bantekas et al. (2018, p. 876) 'the emphasis on "participation" implies that the right to take part in cultural life is not confined to the freedom to enjoy (read: "consume") culture, but also the freedom to pursue and contribute to every aspect of cultural life'. Article 30(1) CRPD requires States Parties to take all appropriate measures to ensure that persons with disabilities have access to cultural materials, to be interpreted in a broad manner – television programmes, films, theatres, and other cultural activities, as well as to places where cultural performances are held or services are provided, and to monuments and sites. Article 30(2) CRPD obliges States Parties to take all appropriate measures to enable persons with disabilities to develop their creative, artistic, and intellectual potential. Article 30(4) CRPD provides for the recognition and support of the specific cultural and linguistic identity of people with disabilities, including sign languages and Deaf culture.

## 5. Socio-Legal Analysis as Methodological Approach

This book encompasses a socio-legal analysis of the right of people with disabilities to participate in cultural life, focusing on barriers to, and facilitators of, its realisation. In doing so, it embeds the examination of Article 30 CRPD within the social situations in which it applies.

This book conceives of socio-legal research as encompassing the examination of how law and legal phenomena and the legal system occur in the world and impact upon those who are touched by them (Hutchinson & Duncan, 2012). Consistent with this approach, the book is informed by the study of relevant multidisciplinary literature and combines traditional legal doctrinal methodology, which allows for an in-depth examination of legislative provisions, case law, and academic scholarship (Hutchinson, 2014, 2015), with qualitative methods. The latter entail document analysis and empirical research (mainly semi-structured interviews) with key informants. Document analysis is a type of qualitative research that uses a systematic procedure to analyse documentary evidence and answer specific research questions (Gross, 2018) or a method for reviewing or evaluating documents combining elements of content analysis and thematic analysis (Bowen, 2009, p. 27–32). Documents may be treated in a variety of ways, depending on the focus of the study, but a qualitative approach requires examination and interpretation to elicit meaning, gain understanding, and develop empirical knowledge (Bowen, 2009). Thus, qualitative document analysis seeks to make explicit the implications of various formulations and presentation strategies (Wolff, 2004, p. 289; Bowen, 2009; Coffey, 2013). In this book, document analysis of States Parties' reports and relevant documents of the CRPD Committee – Lists of Issues (LIs) and COs – is blended with traditional legal analysis to understand the normative facets and the implementation of Article 30 CRPD. This analysis relates to EU Member States plus the UK and the EU and focuses on the approach of each document to participation in culture with specific reference to arts practices and heritage. As will be further discussed in Chapter 4, our reference period is from January 2008, when the CRPD came into force, up until May 2024.

Semi-structured interviews aimed to identify the main barriers to cultural participation as perceived by key stakeholders of people with disabilities across Europe. As will be expounded in Part III, we pursued a purposeful sampling strategy and recruited representatives of 64 organisations drawn from 28 European countries (27 EU countries and the UK) involving at least two participating organisations from each country. Those invited to participate were drawn from three types of organisations: umbrella OPDs working at national level within their countries and representing a range of disability types (n = 28), national organisations of Deaf people (n = 11), and organisations that work in the cultural field, where we prioritised organisations that were disability-led (n = 25). In a few cases, where a national umbrella OPD did not agree to participate, we engaged with other organisations in that country, such as umbrella organisations of blind people or an organisation working on independent living. We prioritised organisations primarily governed by people with disabilities based on the definition in General Comment No. 7 of the CRPD Committee (CRPD Committee, 2018a, para. 11). According to this General Comment, organisations *of* persons with disabilities are 'those that are led, directed and governed by persons with disabilities' which entails that 'a clear majority of their membership should be recruited among persons with disabilities themselves' (CRPD Committee, 2018a, para. 11). We identified the target organisations through existing contacts, online searches, and, in some cases, snowball sampling (Taylor et al., 2015). We adopted a flexible approach which evolves in response to context (Taylor et al., 2015; Foley, 2021). Such flexibility was particularly necessary in this study, which involved participants using different languages or requiring a range of reasonable accommodations (such as sign-language interpretation). All participants received timely information on the study and gave written consent to participate.

The study received approval from the relevant Maynooth University ethics committee and took place from May 2021 to August 2023. The data were analysed using a reflexive approach to thematic analysis involving a series of steps that include systematic coding; generating initial themes; developing and reviewing themes; and refining, defining, and naming themes (Braun & Clarke, 2020). Thematic analysis is a flexible method for 'identifying and analysing patterns in qualitative data' and involves analytic processes common to most forms of qualitative research (Clarke & Braun, 2013, pp. 120–123, 2017). We expand more on the methods used in later chapters.

## 6. Structure of the Book

Further to this introduction, the book is structured into three main parts. Part I presents the context(s) in which our analysis is situated and includes two main chapters. Chapter 1 presents the scholarly context, locating our analysis within broader multidisciplinary debates about cultural participation of persons with disabilities. It refers to an array of literature in the field of contemporary critical and cultural disability studies, which currently foreground the role of culture in the production of disability, as well as to academic work in other fields which identifies and discusses barriers and facilitators to cultural participation for persons with disabilities. It also points at current gaps in data and scholarly analysis – gaps that the book attempts to address. As mentioned earlier, Chapter 2 introduces the overarching legal framework of the book, focusing on the CRPD as the global standard for the protection and promotion of disability rights. After a brief overview of the structure of the Convention, its general principles, and obligations, the chapter discusses the human rights model of disability and how that model and its vision of inclusive equality support the right to cultural participation.

Part II focuses on the right to cultural participation. Chapter 3 discusses the normative content of Article 30 CRPD and examines its key obligations. It critically engages with the relevant jurisprudence of the CRPD Committee, placing particular emphasis on how cultural rights have been dealt with in General Comments from the CRPD Committee so far. Chapter 4 examines the implementation of Article 30 CRPD in States Parties considered on foot of a comprehensive document analysis of the reports of States Parties, LIs and COs by the CRPD Committee. This chapter is based on a systematic document review, adopting a thematic qualitative approach to document analysis, but it links it back to the legal analysis conducted in Chapter 3 and to legal literature on the CRPD as well as to the CRPD Committee's jurisprudence.

Part III is dedicated to the empirical findings. Building on the context outlined in the first part of the book and on the analysis of Article 30 CRPD, Chapter 5 is the first of two chapters presenting and discussing the findings of the pan-European qualitative study that informs the book. It focuses on barriers which are identified in the areas of laws and policies, funding and access, as well as barriers constituted by negative attitudes, and lack of consultation and involvement or employment of people with disabilities in cultural sectors. In that regard, the chapter is underpinned by a reflection on environmental and attitudinal barriers to participation which is intrinsic to the human rights model of disability and the definition of disability contained in the CRPD examined in Chapter 2. Furthermore, the findings are discussed in light of the disability studies literature dealing with negative attitudes and prejudice introduced in Chapter 1. Chapter 6 critically examines the elements that study participants perceived as facilitating cultural participation. It highlights the growing interest amongst people working on culture in disability issues and recent improvements in access to, and participation in, culture by people with disabilities, especially as audiences. Facilitators discussed include funding mechanisms – ones that promote equality by mandating accessibility on the part of funded organisations and that promote knowledge and skills around anti-discrimination measures.

The concluding chapter presents critical reflections and conclusions. It draws together all the key arguments from the preceding chapters and bridges the legal analysis with the empirical findings, evidencing the essential steps to advance the implementation of Article 30 CRPD.

## References

Arbour, L. (2006). *Statement by Louise Arbour UN High Commissioner for Human Rights on the Ad Hoc Committee's adoption of the Convention on the Rights of Persons with Disabilities*. www.un.org/esa/socdev/enable/rights/ahc8hrcmsg.htm

Bantekas, I., Stephenson, C. P. Y., Karapapa, S., & Polymenopoulou, E. (2018). Participation in cultural life, recreation, leisure, and sport. In I. Bantekas, M. A. Stein, & D. Anastasiou (Eds.), *The UN Convention on the Rights of Persons with Disabilities: A Commentary* (pp. 863–923). Oxford University Press.

Barnes, C., & Mercer, G. (2010). *Exploring disability – a sociological introduction* (2nd ed.). Polity Press.

Bennoune, K. (2018). *Report of the Special Rapporteur in the field of cultural rights: Note by the Secretariat* (UN Doc. A/JRC/37/55). https://digitallibrary.un.org/record/1473375?ln=en

Best, K. L., Mortenson, B. W., Lauzière-Fitzgerald, Z., & Smith, E. (2022). Language matters: The long-standing debate between identity-first language and person-first language. *Assistive Technology*, *34*, 127–128.

Bickenbach, J. E., Chatterji, S., Badley, E. M., & Üstün, T. B. (1999). Models of disablement, universalism and the international classification of impairments, disabilities and handicaps. *Social Sciences and Medicine*, *48*, 1173–1187.

Bidault, B. (2009). *La protection internationale des droits culturels*. Bruylant.

Blanck, P. (2020). *Disability law and policy*. Foundation Press.

Blanck, P. (2023a). *Advanced introduction to U.S. disability law*. Edward Elgar.

Blanck, P. (2023b). On the importance of the Americans with Disabilities Act at 30. *Journal of Disability Policy Studies*, *34*(3), 176–198.

Bowen, G. A. (2009). Document analysis as a qualitative research method. *Qualitative Research Journal*, *9*(2), 27–40.

Braun, V., & Clarke, V. (2020). One size fits all? What counts as quality practice in (reflexive) thematic analysis? *Qualitative Research in Psychology*, *18*(3), 328–352.

Caust, J. (2019). Cultural rights as human rights and the impact on the expression of arts practices. *Journal of Citizenship and Globalisation Studies*, *3*(1), 17–30.

Chow, P. Y. S. (2018). *Cultural rights in international law and discourse: Contemporary challenges and interdisciplinary perspectives*. Brill Nijhoff.

Clarke, V., & Braun, V. (2013). Teaching thematic analysis: Overcoming challenges and developing strategies for effective learning. *The Psychologist*, *26*(2), 120–123.

Clarke, V., & Braun, V. (2017). Thematic analysis. *The Journal of Positive Psychology*, *12*(3), 297–298.

Coffey, A. (2013). Analysing documents. In U. Flick (Ed.), *The SAGE handbook of qualitative data analysis* (pp. 367–369). SAGE.

Council of Europe (CoE). (2005). *Council of Europe Framework Convention on the Value of Cultural Heritage for Society* (Faro, 27.X.2005 – Council of Europe Treaty Series, No. 199).

Davis, L. J. (2013). Introduction: Normality, power and culture. In L. J. Davis (Ed.), *The disability studies reader* (pp. 1–16). Routledge.

Degener, T. (2016a). A human rights model of disability. In P. Blanck & E. Flynn (Eds.), *Routledge handbook of disability law and human rights* (pp. 31–49). Routledge.

Degener, T. (2016b). Disability in a human rights context. *Laws*, *5*(3), 35.

Degener, T. (2017a). 10 years of the Convention on the Rights of Persons with Disabilities. *Netherlands Quarterly of Human Rights*, *35*(3), 152–157.

Degener, T. (2017b). A new human rights model of disability. In V. Della Fina, R. Cera, & G. Palmisano (Eds.), *The United Nations Convention on the Rights of Persons with Disabilities: A Commentary* (pp. 41–60). Springer.

Degener, T., & Begg, A. (2017). From invisible citizens to agents of change: A short history of the struggle for the recognition of the rights of persons with disabilities at the United Nations. In V. Della Fina, R. Cera, & G. Palmisano (Eds.), *The United Nations Convention on the Rights of Persons with Disabilities: A Commentary* (pp. 1–40). Springer.

Degener, T., & Gomez-Carrillo De Castro, T. (2022). Toward inclusive equality: Ten years of the human rights model of disability in the work of the UN Committee on the rights of persons with disabilities. In F. Felder, L. Davy, & R. Kayess (Eds.), *Disability law and human rights* (pp. 27–46). Springer.

European Commission – Directorate-General for Education, Youth, Sport and Culture. (2019). *From social inclusion to social cohesion – The role of culture policy*. Publications Office of the European Union.

European Parliament & Council of the EU. (2021). Regulation (EU) 2021/818 of the European Parliament and of the Council of 20 May 2021 establishing the Creative Europe Programme (2021 to 2027) and repealing Regulation (EU) No 1295/2013. *Official Journal of the European Union*, *189*, 34–60.

European Parliament Research Service (EPRS). (2017). *Access to culture in the European Union*. https://op.europa.eu/en/publication-detail/-/publication/66f298ec-6840-11e7-b2f2-01aa75ed71a1

Eurostat. (2024). *Eurostat Statistics Explained: Culture statistics – cultural participation*. [online] https://ec.europa.eu/eurostat/statistics-explained/index.php?title=Culture_statistics_-_cultural_participation#Cultural_participation_of_people_with_disabilities.

European Union Member States' Experts on Better Access to and Wider Participation in Culture – OMC. (2012). *Report on policies and good practices in the public arts and in cultural institutions to promote better access to and wider participation in culture*. https://ec.europa.eu/assets/eac/culture/policy/strategic-framework/documents/omc-report-access-to-culture_en.pdf

Felder, F. (2022). What does the CRPD tell us about being human? In F. Felder, L. Davy, & R. Kayess (Eds.), *Disability law and human rights. Palgrave studies in disability and international development* (pp. 47–66). Palgrave Macmillan.

Ferri, D. (2009). La dimensione prescrittiva della cultura. Un'analisi comparata tra significante e significato. *Diritto Pubblico Comparato ed Europeo*, 12–33.

Ferri, D., Broderick, A., & Leahy, A. (2025). The global governance of disability rights: Complexities, participatory trends and intersections. In A. O'Donoghue, R. Houghton, & S. Wheatle (Eds.), *Research handbook on global governance*. Edward Elgar.

Ferri, D., & Leahy, A. (2023). The right of people with disabilities to participate in cultural life: Is Cinderella going to the ball? In S. Robinson & K. R. Fisher (Eds.), *Research handbook on disability policy* (pp. 102–117). Edward Elgar.

Ferri, D., Palermo, F., & Martinico, G. (2023). Introduction. In D. Ferri, F. Palermo, & G. Martinico (Eds.), *Federalism and the rights of persons with disabilities. The implementation of the CRPD in federal systems and its implications* (pp. 1–21). Hart Publishing.

Finkelstein, V. (1981). Disability and the helper/helped relationship: An historical view. In A. Brechin, P. Liddiard, & J. Swain (Eds.), *Handicap in a social world* (pp. 12–22). Hodder & Stoughton.

Foley, G. (2021). Video-based online interviews for palliative care research: A new normal in COVID-19? *Palliative Medicine*, *35*(3), 625–626.

Garland-Thomson, R. (2002). Integrating disability, transforming feminist theory. *National Women's Studies Association Journal*, 1–32.

Goodley, D. (2013). Dis/entangling critical disability studies. *Disability & Society*, *28*(5), 631–644.

Goodley, D., & Bolt, D. (2010). Introduction. In D. Goodley & D. Bolt (Eds.), Special issue theorizing culture and disability: Interdisciplinary dialogues. *Review of Disability Studies: An International Journal*, *6*(3).

Gronemann, S. T., Kristiansen, E., & Drotner, K. (2015). Mediated co-construction of museums and audiences on Facebook. *Museum Management and Curatorship*, *30*(3), 174–190.

Gross, J. M. S. (2018). Document analysis. In B. Frey (Ed.), *The SAGE encyclopedia of educational research, measurement, and evaluation* (Vol. 4, pp. 545–548). SAGE.

Guibert, N. (2023). Legal framework: Is there a right to art? In F. Gantharet, N. Guilbert, & S. Stolk (Eds.), *Art and human rights. A multidisciplinary approach to contemporary issues* (pp. 20–38). Edward Elgar.

Hadley, B., & McDonald, D. (2019). Introduction: Disability arts, culture, and media studies – mapping a maturing field. In B. Hadley & D. McDonald (Eds.), *The Routledge handbook of disability arts, culture, and media* (pp. 1–18). Routledge.

Harpur, P. (2012). Embracing the new disability rights paradigm: The importance of the Convention on the Rights of Persons with Disabilities. *Disability & Society*, *27*(1), 1–14.

Hutchinson, T. (2014). Valé Bunny Watson? Law librarians, law libraries and legal research in the post-internet era. *Law Library Journal*, *106*(4), 579–592.

Hutchinson, T. (2015). The doctrinal method: Incorporating interdisciplinary methods in reforming the law. *Erasmus Law Review*, *3*, 130–138.

Hutchinson, T., & Duncan, D. J. (2012). Defining and describing what we do: Doctrinal legal research. *Deakin Law Review*, *17*(1), 83–119.

International Council of Museums (ICOM). (2022). *Museum definition*. https://icom.museum/en/resources/standards-guidelines/museum-definition/

Jakubowski, A. (Ed.). (2016). *Cultural rights as collective rights: An international law perspective*. Brill.

Jakubowski, A. (2020). Cultural rights and cultural heritage as a global concern. In M. C. Foblets, M. Goodale, M. Sapignoli, & O. Zenker (Eds.), *The Oxford handbook of law and anthropology* (pp. 475–492). Oxford University Press.

Johnson, K. (2020). Recognising cultural diversity: Implications for persons with disabilities. In E. J. Kakoullis & K. Johnson (Eds.), *Recognising human rights in different cultural contexts* (pp. 63–78). Palgrave Macmillan.

Laaksonen, A. (2010). *Making culture accessible: Access, participation and cultural provision in the context of cultural rights in Europe*. Council of Europe.

Lawson, A., & Beckett, A. E. (2020). The social and human rights models of disability: Towards a complementarity thesis. *International Journal of Human Rights*, *25*(2), 348–379.

Leahy, A., & Ferri, D. (2022). Barriers and facilitators to cultural participation by people with disabilities: A narrative literature review. *Scandinavian Journal of Disability Research*, *24*(1), 68–81.

Leahy, A., & Ferri, D. (2023). Barriers to cultural participation by people with disabilities in Europe: A study across 28 countries. *Disability & Society*, *39*(10), 2465–2487.

Manca, L. (2017). Article 30. In V. Della Fina, R. Cera, & G. Palmisano (Eds.), *The United Nations Convention on the Rights of Persons with Disabilities: A Commentary* (pp. 541–555). Springer.

Meekosha, H., & Soldatic, K. (2011). Human rights and the global south: The case of disability. *Third World Quarterly*, *32*(8), 1383–1397.

Office of the High Commissioner for Human Rights (OHCHR). (2020). *Data sources for outcome indicators on Article 30 CRPD*. Participation in cultural life, recreation, leisure and sport. www.ohchr.org/sites/default/files/data-sources-article-30.pdf

O'Keefe, R. (1998). The right to take part in cultural life under Article 15 of the ICESCR. *International and Comparative Law Quarterly*, *47*(4), 904–923.

Oliver, M. (1983). *Social work with disabled people*. Macmillan.

Oliver, M. (1990). *The politics of disablement*. Macmillan.

Oliver, M. (1996). *Understanding disability: From theory to practice*. Macmillan.

Oliver, M. (2013). The social model of disability: Thirty years on. *Disability & Society*, *28*(7), 1024–1026.
Organisation for Economic Co-operation and Development (OECD). (2022). *The culture fix: Creative people, places and industries*. OECD Publishing.
O'Toole, F. (2006). *Dismantling the barriers to participation in cultural life*. National Disability Authority, 5th National Research Conference, Dublin.
Quinn, G., & Degener, T. (2002). *Human rights and disability*. United Nations.
Riddell, S., & Watson, N. (2003). Disability, culture and identity: Introduction. In S. Riddell & N. Watson (Eds.), *Disability, culture and identity* (pp. 1–18). Pearson Education.
Romainville, C. (2015). On defining the right to participate in cultural life as a human right. *Netherlands Quarterly of Human Rights*, *33*(4), 405–436.
Sandahl, C. (2018). Disability art and culture: A model for imaginative ways to integrate the community. *Alter, European Journal of Disability Research/Revue européenne de recherche sur le handicap*, *12*(2), 79–93.
Schur, L., Kruse, D., & Blanck, P. D. (2013). *People with disabilities: Sidelined or mainstreamed?* Cambridge University Press.
Sépulchre, M. (2021). *Disability and citizenship studies*. Routledge.
Skarstad, K., & Stein, M. A. (2018). Mainstreaming disability in the United Nations treaty bodies. *Journal of Human Rights*, *17*(1), 1–24.
Solvang, P. K. (2018). Between art therapy and disability aesthetics: A sociological approach for understanding the intersection between art practice and disability discourse. *Disability & Society*, *33*(2), 238–253.
Stamatopoulou, E. (2007). *Cultural rights in international law: Article 27 of the Universal Declaration of Human Rights and beyond*. Brill.
Stamatopoulou, E. (2012). Monitoring cultural human rights: The claims of culture on human rights and the response of cultural rights. *Human Rights Quarterly*, *34*(4), 1170–1192.
Stevenson, D., Balling, G., & Kann-Rasmussen, N. (2017). Cultural participation in Europe: Shared problem or shared problematisation? *International Journal of Cultural Policy*, *23*(1), 89–106.
Symonides, J. (1998). Cultural rights: A neglected category of human rights. *International Social Science Journal*, *50*(158), 559–571.
Tatić, D. (2015). *Access for people with disabilities to culture, tourism, sports and leisure activities: Towards meaningful and enriching participation*. Council of Europe.
Taylor, S. J., Bogdan, R., & DeVault, M. (2015). *Introduction to qualitative research methods: A guidebook and resource* (4th ed.). John Wiley & Sons Incorporated.
Tennant, A. (1997). Models of disability: A critical perspective. *Disability and Rehabilitation*, *19*(11), 478–479.
Tomka, G. (2013). Reconceptualizing cultural participation in Europe: Grey literature review. *Cultural Trends*, *22*(3–4), 259–264.
UNESCO. (1972). *Convention concerning the protection of the world cultural and natural heritage*. www.unesco.org/en/legal-affairs/convention-concerning-protection-world-cultural-and-natural-heritage
UNESCO. (1982). *World conference on cultural policies* (UN Doc. CLT/MD/1).
UNESCO. (1986). *UNESCO framework for cultural statistics (FCS)*. https://uis.unesco.org/sites/default/files/documents/unesco-framework-for-cultural-statistics-1986-en_0.pdf
UNESCO. (2001). *Universal Declaration on Cultural Diversity*. https://unesdoc.unesco.org/ark:/48223/pf0000128347
UNESCO. (2005). *Convention on the protection and promotion of the diversity of cultural expressions* (UN Doc. CLT-2016/WS/7). https://unesdoc.unesco.org/ark:/48223/pf0000246264.page=13

UNESCO. (2009). *UNESCO framework for cultural statistics* (FCS). UNESCO Institute for Statistics. https://uis.unesco.org/sites/default/files/documents/unesco-framework-for-cultural-statistics-2009-en_0.pdf

United Nations. (1975). *Declaration on the rights of disabled persons*. UNGA Resolution 3447.

United Nations. (1993). *Standard rules on the equalization of opportunities for persons with disabilities*. UNGA Resolution 48/96.

United Nations. (2006). *Convention on the Rights of Persons with Disabilities* (UN Doc. A/RES/61/106, Annex I).

United Nations Committee on Economic, Social and Cultural Rights (CESCR). (2009). *General Comment No. 21, Right of everyone to take part in cultural life* (UN Doc. E/C.12/GC/21).

United Nations Committee on the Rights of Persons with Disabilities (CRPD Committee). (2018). *General Comment No. 6 (2018) on equality and non-discrimination*. (UN Doc. CRPD/C/GC/6).

United Nations Committee on the Rights of Persons with Disabilities (CRPD Committee). (2018a). *General Comment No. 7 (2018) on the participation of persons with disabilities, including children with disabilities, through their representative organizations, in the implementation and monitoring of the Convention*. (UN Doc. CRPD/C/GC/7).

Veal, A. J. (2022). Cultural participation as a human right: Holding nation states to account. *International Journal of Cultural Policy*, *29*(6), 686–700.

Williams, R. (1989). *Resources of hope*. Verso.

Williams, V., Tarleton, B., Heslop, P., Porter, S., Sass, B., Blue, S., Merchant, W., & Mason-Angelow, V. (2018). Understanding disabling barriers: A fruitful partnership between disability studies and social practices? *Disability & Society*, *33*(2), 157–174.

Wolff, S. (2004). Analysis of documents and records. In U. Flick, E. von Kardorff, & I. Steinke (Eds.), *A companion to qualitative research* (pp. 284–289). SAGE.

Xanthaki, A. (2015). Cultural rights. In *Oxford bibliographies*. www.oxfordbibliographies.com/view/document/obo-9780199796953/obo-9780199796953-0123.xml

# Part I

# The Context

# 1 The Scholarly Context

## Cultural Participation of People with Disabilities in Academic Scholarship and Grey Literature

*Ann Leahy and Delia Ferri*

### 1. Introduction

This chapter aims to situate the book within current multidisciplinary literature and to support the legal and empirical analysis conducted in Parts II and III. It presents a narrative review of relevant literature, with a focus on academic work and grey literature about what operates as barriers to cultural participation by people with disabilities and what facilitates participation.[1] This review takes into account the general distinction between active and passive aspects of participation and aligns with an understanding of the right to cultural participation as encompassing a twofold individual dimension and a collective aspect (EPRS, 2017, pp. 10, 27; UNESCO, 2009),[2] expounded earlier in the Introduction to this book. In doing so, it encompasses the participation of persons with disabilities as audiences and visitors to cultural venues, as artists and performers as well as employees within cultural industries, but also highlights issues related to the emergence and recognition of disability identities and the collective aspect of cultural participation. The literature review also presents an in-depth examination of barriers arising from the lack of, or limited, accessibility. The review is informed by a broad view of accessibility in line with Article 9 UN Convention on the Rights of Persons with Disabilities (CRPD or simply 'the Convention'). As will be discussed in Chapter 2, the CRPD 'enshrines accessibility as the precondition for persons with disabilities to live independently, participate fully

1 This chapter builds on our previous work and specifically on a literature review that was published in 2022 (Leahy & Ferri, 2022) as well as on subsequent articles which have been published within the remit of the project 'Protecting the Right to Culture of Persons with Disabilities and Enhancing Cultural Diversity through European Union Law: Exploring New Paths – DANCING', funded by the European Research Council.

2 As discussed in the introduction and as will be further examined in Part II of this book, the twofold individual dimension entails, respectively, the right to access cultural activities, goods, services, and heritage, and the right to active involvement in culture, which includes engagement in the creation of cultural activities, goods, and services. The collective aspect refers to cultural communities being recognised and protected, as well as enabled to enjoy their cultural expressions.

DOI: 10.4324/9781032619361-3

This chapter has been made available under a CC-BY-NC-ND 4.0 license.

and equally in society' (CRPD Committee, 2014) and embeds a capacious concept of accessibility, encompassing 'attitudinal accessibility, economic accessibility or affordability, physical accessibility, information accessibility and communication accessibility' (Charitakis, 2018).

After these brief introductory remarks, the chapter proceeds as follows. Section 2 presents contemporary debates within critical and cultural disability studies, which foreground the role of culture in the production of disability; it discusses disability arts and also engages with some broader areas of scholarship relevant to cultural participation. Section 3 outlines the methods used for our narrative review, within the broader remit of our socio-legal approach, already outlined in the introduction to the book. Section 4 presents our findings, placing an emphasis on the wide range of studies and disciplinary perspectives on cultural participation of persons with disabilities. In line with this, this section illustrates how barriers to, and facilitators of, participation in culture are currently apprehended in scholarly work. It also points to the challenges currently encountered in accessing cultural opportunities as well as some of the actions that can be facilitative of participation as identified in academic and grey literature. This literature review also expounds the potential of cultural participation to facilitate participation by people with disabilities in society, as well as to promote expressions of identity of people with disabilities and, more broadly, to offer opportunities for expressions of new ways of being in the world. The final section discusses the findings. While showing the mounting number of academic publications on the topic and the growing attention to the multifaceted ways in which disability and culture intersect, it also unveils significant gaps in current literature. It illustrates that existing work and literature reviews (Temple Jones et al., 2022) are narrow in their material or geographical scope, and often adopt a sectorial and fairly limited approach, and do not engage with the human rights framework or the CRPD. Further, it evidences that (unsurprisingly) existing work is often qualitative and, therefore, frequently based on limited sampling.

On the whole, the chapter highlights that the contribution of this book lies in departing from existing fragmentary approaches, trying to advance more comprehensive perspectives to cultural participation of persons with disabilities that align with the human rights model of disability and the CRPD.

## 2. Prolegomena on Disability and Culture

The scholarly exploration of the extent to which disability and culture intersect, and of disability art, is relatively recent. It is wide in its reach and rich but remains highly fragmentary as it stems from different disciplinary remits and from an array of works which have focused on diverse issues. The following subsections highlight the broader scholarly context of the narrative literature review presented in the remainder of the chapter, as well as foregrounding the important link between disability and culture which underpins the overall book.

### 2.1. *Multifaceted Approaches in Critical and Cultural Disability Studies . . .*

Critical and cultural disability studies are open to 'a host of theoretical developments', but they all emphasise cultural, discursive, and relational issues within disability experiences (Goodley, 2013, p. 634). Disablement, from within these perspectives, is experienced as the outcome of the withholding of social and cultural recognition (Watson, 2003). Furthermore, impairments, as well as disability, can be understood as a social construction, not an essential truth, rejecting a basis in nature or physiology (Titchkosky & Michalko, 2009). As mentioned in the introduction to this book, Garland-Thomson (2002, p. 5) argued that disability 'is not a natural state of corporeal inferiority, inadequacy, excess, or a stroke of misfortune. Rather, disability is a culturally fabricated narrative of the body' and Davis (2013, p. 12) challenged ideas of normalcy, identifying the 'problem', not in the disabled person but in how normalcy is constructed. Attention is, therefore, reorientated to ableism or to ideas about normativity constructed by those whose bodies and minds are deemed to constitute 'the normal' (Thomas & Milligan, 2018, p. 121). In this strand of academic work, what has come to be central to understanding disability is what dis/ability tells us about culture, with disability being understood as a social phenomenon that can illuminate culture (Titchkosky, 2003, p. 3). In other words, within these perspectives, disability is analysed as a social and cultural phenomenon (Goodley & Bolt, 2010). Simultaneously, people with disabilities have forged their own cultures (Stober & García Iriarte, 2023), making culture a source both 'of oppression and of liberation,' as mentioned already (Riddell & Watson, 2003, p. 1).

With regard to such views, the prevalence of merely therapeutic approaches to art and disability has been challenged by several scholars (*inter alia*, Darcy et al., 2022). As Solvang (2018, p. 241) argues, art therapy itself is not a problem, but for the 'artist struggling for recognition in the cultural field, being perceived as a patient seems like discrimination'. Nowadays, there are increasingly sophisticated ensemble groups of artists with disabilities and non-disabled artists engaged in high-production-value recreational arts, serious leisure, and semi-professional and professional performances and exhibitions (Darcy et al., 2022). The field of disability arts, which is acknowledged in Article 30 CRPD, particularly in its second paragraph, has become recognised as 'a powerful source of aesthetic innovation', although participation can require a number of different components of access, which are not always present (Hadley, Paterson et al., 2022, p. 74). 'Disability art', which pursues art as a form of visual expression created by people with disabilities, was originally associated with sharing experiences of living with disability (Solvang, 2012, 2018; Yoon et al., 2021). Solvang (2018) outlines two phases in the development of disability art – a first phase that emerged from the disability rights movement involving artwork informed by the disability experience and created by people with disabilities, and a second phase characterised by artists with disabilities wanting to perform and to exhibit for mainstream audiences, and by a combination of disability issues and non-disability issues. Nowadays, a key challenge for those involved is to try and move disability art 'out of the ghetto and into the mainstream, not leaving behind the spirit of anti-discrimination' (Solvang, 2018, p. 243). For Siebers (2006, p. 64), disability aesthetics seek to emphasise the presence of disability in the tradition of aesthetic representation and prizes difference as a value in itself, refusing to recognise 'the representation of the healthy body . . . as the sole determination of the aesthetic' (also Cameron, 2022). Thus, disability aesthetics seek to create a space for disability in the mainstream world of high art (Solvang, 2018). In relation to this, recent work contends that 'recognising and respecting disability culture, and what it takes to create culturally safe space for disabled artists, is a critical precursor to respectful artist – ally partnerships in disability arts' and that progress has been slow (Hadley, Rieger et al., 2022, p. 228).

Sandahl (2018, p. 84) argues that 'the break-through' work of artists with disabilities is that which 'tends to challenge, not replicate, mainstream traditions' and that without experiencing disabled artists' differences, the 'mainstream status quo may not be able to imagine the ways it could be transformed'. However, understandings of the creative potential of people with disabilities to reshape the mainstream 'remains largely untapped' (Sandahl, 2018, p. 85). This is also because, in spite of the entry into force of the CRPD, participation of people with disabilities in culture is still considered a minor issue or a luxury, both by states and by society more generally, as, for example, is argued in respect of Turkey where people with disabilities have limited access to basic human rights (Collins et al., 2023).

## 2.2. . . . *and Beyond Disability Studies*

There is a notable amount of literature on disability representation in the aesthetic realm (Fraser, 2018), and scholarship has increasingly engaged with disability art, culture, and media. Such multifaceted scholarly work encompasses analyses of mainstream representations of disability and of self-representation practices by artists with disabilities, as well as to some limited extent how spectators respond (Hadley & McDonald, 2019; Walters, 2023).

A discussion of disability in museums and heritage sites is relatively recent (Black, 2005). In particular, the enactment of national and supranational legislation relating to disability-discrimination in the last couple of decades, as well as the entry into force of the CRPD, has led to an increased awareness of access for people with disabilities to cultural sites (Argyropoulos & Kanari, 2015; Confino-Rehder, 2010). Debates are often about new audiences or equal access and focus on how to remove barriers hampering the participation of people with disabilities (Argyropoulos & Kanari, 2015; Rix et al., 2010). For Ott (2010, p. 271), museum visitors can learn to reframe what they know using a disability consciousness (see also Sandell & Dodd, 2010). Lid (2016, p. 87) suggests that cultural heritage often fails to represent people with disabilities as equal citizens, although visitors with disabilities can remind others 'of the plurality of humanity and equal status'.

Relatedly, literature focusing on cultural policy-making processes has articulated emancipatory and democratic approaches to cultural policy and supported processes that seek to extend the range and nature of relationships with the public, often embodied in audience development initiatives (Audience Agency, 2020, p. 33; Hadley, 2021). The need to diversify audiences and increase access is a priority in cultural policy internationally, and the goal of enhancing audience engagement is now a commonplace objective of arts organisations and projects (Glow et al., 2021). Traditionally, audience development initiatives focused on the removal of barriers to participation associated with an assumption that the people being targeted might be interested in the arts (Hadley, 2021; Kawashima, 2000). Noting some differences in understandings of 'audience development' in several European countries (with some emphasising cultural marketing aspects, others highlighting social aspects related to access to culture), Cuenca-Amigo and Makua (2017, p. 169) argue that audience development needs to be considered as a strategic process within cultural organisations. Democratisation processes and audience development initiatives are the subject of lively debate. Some scholarship, not specifically focused on disability issues, considers that audience development initiatives can perform a 'legitimating function' by discursively suggesting that an undemocratic cultural policy is in the process of being democratised in light of how people who attend the subsidised arts are predominantly from a particular demographic (Hadley, 2021, p. 233; Hadley, S. et al., 2022). Arguably, cultural organisations, while creating equity statements, often fail to engage in dismantling oppressive systems and practices. Further, evidence shows that the cultural sector is still not fully representative of their consumers and the wider society (Hadley, S. et al., 2022). While change may be happening, it is taking place in a slow and piecemeal fashion, largely due to the efforts of 'minoritized groups' (Hadley, S. et al., 2022, p. 16). Arguably, 'without transformational and structural changes, increased surface-level representation is meaningless' (Hill & Sobande, 2018, p. 109; see also Hadley, S. et al., 2022).

Veal (2022) argues that literature on cultural participation has generally neglected a human rights approach. However, most recent (yet scant) legal and socio-legal scholarship has discussed what hampers and facilitates cultural participation in light of the CRPD or national legal frameworks. From a human rights perspective, it has been highlighted that the right to participate in cultural life is key to realising the human rights model of disability envisaged by the CRPD (Ferri & Leahy, 2023). As highlighted earlier in the introduction to this book, scholars have emphasised how cultural participation (including in the arts) is one of a number of 'essential dimensions of life, both for persons with disabilities and for those without disabilities' (Tatić, 2015, p. 6), and how the implementation of Article 30

CRPD is essential in furthering 'the CRPD's transformative vision of persons with disabilities' full-fledged membership in an inclusive society' (Smith & Stein, 2020, p. 287). Despite the flourishing of commentaries on the CRPD (Bantekas et al., 2018; Della Fina, et al., 2017), the right to participate in culture remains 'one of the least studied human rights in the international literature' (Bantekas et al., 2018, p. 865).

Grey literature and policy analysis across a broad range of areas of life often address the concept of barriers. This is the case, for example, in the World Report on Disability (World Health Organization (WHO) & World Bank, 2011). This report contains no specific focus on barriers to participation in culture; however, it recognises that environments – physical, social, and attitudinal – can either disable people or foster their participation and inclusion in areas that include cultural life (WHO & World Bank, 2011, p. 193). It also reflects the emphasis on the concept of 'barriers' embedded within the CRPD and underpinning Article 30 CRPD. A report from the European Parliament (2018, p. 19) on access to culture refers to the existence of a series of structural and financial barriers to access and participation for people generally, as well as educational barriers, geographical barriers (referring to distance from cultural centres), and digital barriers and challenges. It calls on EU Member States and the European Commission to work towards the integration of people with disabilities through culture and to make efforts to remove existing barriers as a starting point for developing strategies to respond to the challenges involved in strengthening cultural access and participation (European Parliament, 2018, para. 53). Indeed, the European Commission (2023, p. 3–4) has recently stated that 'more efforts are needed to grasp the dimension of barrier that persons with disabilities continuously face'. Consistent with this, recent research conducted with artists and arts workers in Ireland found that 88% of disabled respondents reported that they faced barriers and 79% felt that they lost or missed opportunities due to disability, while specific challenges were identified for artists with intellectual disabilities, including barriers to training and development (Murphy et al., 2024).

## 3. A Narrative Literature Review: Rationale and Methodology

Section 2 has laid out the background to the narrative literature review presented, while this section aims to introduce its rationale and methods.

First, it is useful to recall that, generally, narrative reviews provide interpretation and critique intended to deepen understanding by selecting evidence judiciously and purposively, with an eye on what is relevant for key policy questions (Greenhalgh et al., 2018). By contrast, engaging in the explicit (though sometimes narrow) processes of systematic review would have emphasised technical, rather than interpretive, synthesis methods (Greenhalgh et al., 2018). In line with recommended practice for narrative reviews (Byrne, 2016), we first defined the review's scope, identifying the following review question: What do academic sources and grey literature identify as barriers to, or facilitators of, cultural participation by people with disabilities (as audiences and cultural creators)? The clarification and insight associated with the more interpretive and discursive synthesis characteristic of narrative reviews were essential to answer this question (Greenhalgh et al., 2018).

In narrative reviews, less explicit methods are the trade-off for broader coverage (Collins & Fauser, 2005). In that connection, the overarching aim of this review was to make a contribution by combining literature from different fields, with breadth and balance, and by citing studies that are representative of those available (Byrne, 2016). We drew on our prior knowledge of literature and included searches on websites of selected think-tanks and cultural actors for grey literature that identifies barriers or facilitators.

We conducted multiple searches on the databases Academic Search Complete, JSTOR Arts and Science, Heinoline as well as on Google and Google Scholar and our institutional library resources. Consistent with the conceptual framework discussed in the introduction to this book, the following keywords were used where appropriate 'disab*'/'special needs'/'access' plus 'barrier*' or 'facilitator*'; as well as any of the words: art, cultur*, museum, galler*, heritage, perform*, intellectual/learning, impairment. Furthermore, in line with the theoretical framework of this book and the relevance of the CRPD as the global standard on disability rights, we focused on literature which is more likely to embed the human rights model of disability enshrined in the CRPD by largely examining papers published later than 2006, when the CRPD was adopted by the UN General Assembly. We aimed at a multidisciplinary and cross-disciplinary publication search, albeit paying particular attention to disability studies, cultural studies (including museum studies), and socio-legal research. We also included grey literature in the form of policy reports. We sought to encompass different types of cultural participation: as audiences, as creators and/or professional artists, and as amateurs in the context of inclusive community practices.

Because of our conceptual focus on arts practices (encompassing different art forms, including literature, dance, music, theatre, and visual arts) and heritage as forms of cultural expression, we excluded scholarly work focusing on broader aspects, or tangential aspects, of cultural participation such as physical activity, sports or tourism, or articles that were primarily concerned with therapeutic or rehabilitative outcomes of cultural participation. Our searches were conducted in English, retrieving, for the most part, sources in the English language, while citing some reports published in other languages drawn especially from policy-making bodies. We did not assess the methodological quality of sources reviewed, but we excluded blogs or online contributions that were not peer reviewed.

While the DANCING project and the qualitative research conducted within it have a discrete geographical scope, which is reflected in this book, this narrative review is deliberately broader. It brings together works that relate to a range of countries from different parts of the world including countries in the Global North and South. This supports the identification of thematic axes that we also identified in our qualitative research. It also allows us to showcase general trends and the growing focus of scholarly work on cultural participation of persons with disabilities.

## 4. Literature on Barriers and Facilitators to Cultural Participation by People with Disabilities

As noted earlier, the reviewed sources approached cultural participation by people with disabilities from different disciplinary perspectives. The scholarship retrieved encompasses a variety of fields, including disability studies, cultural studies and museum studies, and other fields such as education, social exclusion, and employment, as well as leisure and management studies, and journals focused on specific art forms or impairment types. It often showcases findings from empirical research, or action research, with groups making art at different levels (amateur, professional or semi-professional, or in education), or within particular projects or settings (e.g. individual arts centres or museums).

Most of the reviewed sources involve small sample sizes. This clearly tallies with the lack of comparable data and large studies on the cultural participation of persons with disabilities. As mentioned in the introduction, the OHCHR (2020) report on 'Data sources for outcome indicators on Article 30 CRPD' indicates that most surveys that measure time spent on cultural activities do not assess disability status while national studies that address rates of participation in culture by people with disabilities are not always updated and not always comparable. The data available, however, seem to confirm persistent discrimination against people with disabilities and the existence of (and persistence of) barriers to accessing cultural events. Notably, results of the EU survey of income and living conditions (known as EU-SILC) for 2022 show a lower rate of cultural participation among people with disabilities compared with the overall population (aged 16 and over) across all EU countries (Eurostat, 2024). Persistent discrimination is also evident from a report published in 2024, which expounded the results of a survey commissioned by the Directorate-General for Justice and Consumers (DG JUST) and part of a series of Eurobarometer surveys examining discrimination across Europe (European Commission, 2024). This report indicated that half (49%) of the respondents in the EU say that discrimination on the basis of disability is widespread in their country. When it comes to barriers to accessing culture, the report is limited and does not present granular data on the issue of disability, although it highlights that over a quarter of respondents (26%) have faced barriers in trying to access cultural goods, events, places, and services (European Commission, 2024). The most mentioned form of barrier is 'the cost' that prevented respondents from attending (15%), but the report acknowledges that accessibility for persons with disabilities is also a barrier (European Commission, 2024).

In general, the discussion of barriers and facilitators tends to focus on audiences and visitors to cultural venues. Further, scholarship is generally art form specific or tends to relate to a specific type of disability. In a similar vein, a report from a government ministry in the Netherlands suggests that many studies on increasing the accessibility of cultural institutions for people with disabilities are case studies that do not always address accessibility comprehensively (Jongerius et al., 2020). Although some barriers identified in the context of a particular art form (such as aesthetic barriers in dance) or sector (such as specific accommodations needed within museums) do not always emerge in other contexts, there are similarities in barriers and facilitators identified across diverse studies. Relatedly, barriers faced in fulfilling one type of task are likely to exist for others (Wilkinson-Meyers et al., 2014). As Rix et al. (2010) state, in the context of cultural venues and heritage sites, developments intended to improve access for people with physical or sensory disabilities also facilitate access for people with intellectual disabilities. This confirms the findings of the empirical research discussed in Part III of the book that many barriers and facilitators operate across sectors and disability types.

Our narrative review is presented in the subsequent sections under three main headings or themes. The first heading addresses studies focusing on attendance as audience of artistic performances or visitors of cultural venues, including museums, galleries, or heritage sites. This heading relates to the first individual dimension of the right to cultural participation (i.e. the right to access cultural activities, goods, services, and heritage), which is encompassed by Article 30(1) CRPD. The second discusses professional engagement, and the third engages with amateur creation or community arts. The second and third themes partially overlap, as amateur creation could also involve a professional or semi-professional approach to the work involved, and some studies included a focus on training or education towards such a professional engagement. They both relate to the second individual dimension of the right to cultural participation (i.e. right to active involvement in culture), which is protected and promoted in Article 30(2) CRPD. Interestingly, issues of disability culture and cultural identity of people with disabilities were not always foregrounded in the literature reviewed.

## 4.1. *Barriers and Facilitators to Access: Audiences in Arts Venues, Museums, and Heritage Sites*

### 4.1.1. *Barriers*

The literature reviewed identifies physical accessibility barriers and inaccessible content, often within research concerned with particular venues or disability types. Most attention focuses on physical access (Argyropoulos & Kanari, 2015; Cho & Jolley, 2016). Relatedly, and consistent with this, a review of the implementation of Australia's Disability Discrimination Act, 1992, in respect of the cultural life of people with disabilities (including arts participation but also sports, leisure, and tourism) found that many complaint cases involved direct exclusion from premises due to lack of basic physical access (e.g. pathways, kerb cuts, ramps, lifts, handrails and the like) with issues relative to access to parking and toilets featuring also (Darcy & Taylor, 2009; see also Collins et al., 2022). While improving access for disabled visitors to historic buildings can conflict with conservation aims (Goodall et al., 2004; Pretto, 2020), Guffey (2015) also highlights how the lack of seating in modernist museums is a barrier for some people. Heritage sites are experienced as being amid rough terrain, with uneven surfaces, steps, narrow doorways, and lacking disabled parking, toilets, and lifts (Rahim & Mavra, 2009). In addition, scholarship reports less-than-optimum experiences available, such as limited options for accessible seating for wheelchair users in concert and other cultural venues (Ma, 2022) and long waits for accessible parking (Cerdan Chiscano & Jiménez-Zarco, 2021). These issues could also require ongoing negotiations on access (Ma, 2022). Ma's (2022, p. 16) self-reflection illustrates that this can operate as a constant reminder of the social exclusion of people with disabilities and 'itself becomes a chronic stressor'.

Problems with physical access are not confined to wheelchair users or to people with mobility impairments, although guidelines for institutions sometimes focus only on people with physical or sensory disabilities (Jongerius et al., 2020), and cultural heritage projects that address only physical barriers are often, nonetheless, considered to be accessible (Muscarà & Sani, 2019). Within museums, it is highlighted how adopting solely visual cues for navigation may exclude people with visual disabilities; auditory-only cues may exclude Deaf people or people with hearing impairments, while people with intellectual disabilities may be excluded when wayfinding cues are complicated (Renel, 2019, p. 383; Mastrogiuseppe et al., 2020; National Education Centre Slovak Republic, 2020). For blind or visually impaired museum visitors, inaccessible signage and lack of multisensory information are identified as barriers, and frequent changes in flooring materials and tall doorway thresholds could also be challenging (Fortuna et al., 2023). A study involving 28 museums across Europe suggests that accessibility for people with visual disabilities was limited, even in museums that had implemented accessibility strategies, and that research assessing accessibility across museums is lacking (Mesquita & Carneiro, 2016). Thus, dismantling physical barriers is prioritised, and a broader understanding of accessibility is still lacking (Swedish Authority for Participation, 2016). At the same time, it is argued that more attention has been paid to people with sensory disabilities than to people with intellectual disabilities (Seale et al., 2021). Thus, some groups, such as people with neurodivergent conditions such as dementia and a broad range of cognitive disabilities, are underrepresented in terms of navigational information design (Renel, 2019).

A lack of access to cultural content is another issue discussed by an array of scholarly work. For example, the limited availability of tools that allow access to content (such as hearing loops) and a lack of interpretation in sign language are identified as key barriers in Sweden across a range of cultural settings (Swedish Authority for Participation, 2016). Martínez Amador (2016) highlights the lack of accessibility of Spanish cinemas for Deaf people. Watlington (2019) posits that despite video art being intended to be 'radically accessible', a reticence to 'alter' works of art means that it remains inaccessible to Deaf users due to a lack of closed captioning in the presentation of videos. Museum exhibitions, being mainly visual, pose a problem for blind and visually impaired people, and, even in attempts to make exhibitions accessible, many things can continue to operate as barriers, such as content explanations using visual descriptive terminology with which those experiencing lifelong blindness are not familiar (Vas, 2020). Access to technologies, and familiarity with them, cannot be assumed for all groups, including people with disabilities on low incomes, but Constantinou et al. (2016) suggest that barriers to a more widespread use of technology for access to cultural content and exhibitions in museums are not always the cost but often a lack of awareness and willingness. Similarly, Weisen (2012, p. 163) contends that 'little thought goes into designing inclusive experiences', despite how technology can enhance museum experiences and widen access for people with disabilities. Furthermore, technologies are more typically explored relative to sensory disabilities than other forms of disability, such as intellectual disabilities (Seale et al., 2021). Indeed, cultural venues and heritage sites are said to have few resources to assist in developing provision for people with intellectual disabilities and in attracting this audience, something that is also affected by the range of individuals who can fall within this label (Rix et al., 2010).

A lack of accessible information, transport, and support to reach cultural venues represents further barriers. For example, some reports contend that ongoing barriers include transportation issues, the price of tickets, and a lack of information and support at venues (Gratton, 2020; Shape, 2013). Another report suggests that the costs involved and difficulties with travel are obstacles when it comes to attending arts events, museums, or libraries and that people with disabilities are more likely than others to consider that the types of activities available are not of interest or relevant (Arts Council England, 2018). A study from the Swedish Authority for Participation (2016) includes similar findings and posits that lower levels of education amongst people with disabilities were linked to lower levels of participation. This is consistent with scholarship arguing that the type of education available to people with disabilities does not always inculcate an interest in the arts, and that poverty in combination with disability could prevent families – even those with a level of social and cultural capital – from investing in arts education in after-school programmes (Leahy & Ferri, 2023). Lack of accessible websites and information about cultural venues, goods, and services is also identified as a barrier (Argyropoulos & Kanari, 2015; Primorac et al., 2017; Dubiel,

2020) as is an inability to access useful information in advance of a visit to a heritage site (Rahim & Mavra, 2009). For example, based on a review of websites of professional theatres, a UK report found that, despite overall improvements, some 15% of the venues' websites did not provide any access information – 21% provided no information about accessible toilets and nine venues did not have any (VocalEyes et al., 2023).

The lack of a comprehensive approach to accessibility and, instead, access facilitated only in limited ways or to limited shows or exhibitions are consistently highlighted in studies addressing different disability types and settings (Argyropoulos & Kanari, 2015; Eardley et al., 2016; Mesquita & Carneiro, 2016; Rix et al., 2010). For example, Renel (2019, p. 378) suggests that people with disabilities are still positioned as 'special' patrons, invited only to engage with specific parts of a museum collection or with certain events. For Rappolt-Schlichtmann and Daley (2013), things have improved in terms of accessibility, particularly with regard to physical access, at exhibitions in the United States, but participation in learning and engagement lags behind.

Other barriers identified by an array of scholarly and policy work include attitudinal barriers, financial ones, and knowledge gaps. A survey of people with disabilities and arts organisations in the United States found that nearly half of respondents with disabilities felt that attending arts opportunities was difficult, with stigma perceived as sometimes harder to overcome than physical or programme-related barriers (Ludwig, 2012). Similarly, Renel (2019) suggests that a range of people with disabilities and Deaf people can experience negative museum interactions. Blind people and people with visual impairments experience constraints due to unavailability of staff or negative attitudes and a lack of specific knowledge of staff (Fortuna et al., 2023; Mesquita & Carneiro, 2016; National Education Centre Slovak Republic, 2020). Argyropoulos and Kanari (2015) found that participants with visual impairments could have positive experiences of museums (including feeling included through accessible exhibits and positive staff interactions) or negative ones linked to inaccessible content or a lack of understanding on the part of staff. Lack of knowledge on the part of staff is also a barrier for people with a range of disabilities (Cerdan Chiscano & Jiménez-Zarco, 2021). Dubiel (2020, p. 140) contends that, in the context of Poland, the lack of official guidance from government means that cultural accessibility 'has been created through trial and error'. The limited awareness of staff of cultural institutions constrains participation by children with disabilities which is compounded by low budgets and inadequate time devoted to access issues (Cho & Jolley, 2016). Lack of funding for implementing accessibility is also identified as a barrierin the museum sector (Chenu, 2018). Cost of access to heritage sites as well as the lack of clarity around charging for people with disabilities and/or their companions are other identified barriers (Rahim & Mavra, 2009).

#### *4.1.2. Facilitators*

While some of the factors enhancing access to culture are implicit in the discussion of barriers, a broad range of facilitative practices are evident from the studies reviewed. A UK report relating to professional theatres suggests that there has been an increase in the availability of access information online between 2019 and 2023 and that the number of accessible productions reported in 2023 has steadily increased to 85% (VocalEyes et al., 2023). These were typically measures providing access to performances using sign language, audio description, and/or a relaxed, or relaxed environment, or performances with captioning. Some 85% of the websites offered additional access information, including how to get to the venue and the venue layout, and 61% of venues provided some kind of discount for access users (although the information could be unclear or inconsistent from one venue to another) (VocalEyes et al., 2023).

To create spaces that are socially inclusive and equitable to a wide range of people, Renel (2019) highlights providing diverse sonic environments that support different cognitive needs. For people with intellectual disabilities, to feel safe and welcome in mainstream cultural activities was an important facilitator, and social interaction was central to participants' understanding of culture (Gratton, 2020). Jongerius et al. (2020) posit that existing regulation does not always lead to creating an inclusive and equally accessible environment for everyone, but they mention examples of accessible festivals, cinemas, theatres, and museums in the Netherlands, including the use of an app enabling audio-descriptions of Dutch-language films. Other examples designed to remove barriers to museum learning include taped guides, touch tours, handling sessions, tactile plans, large-print and Braille information, clear labels and signs, sign-language interpreted tours, and lip speaking and reading (Seale et al., 2021). Facilitators for people with visual impairments include both good physical design of buildings (e.g. avoiding glass doors, steps, and steep slopes) and accessible supports for way-finding, appropriate lighting and sound systems, good visibility of text and figures, accessibility of publications (e.g. leaflets/guides, interpretative panels, and identification labels), magnification of objects (e.g. traditional magnifying glasses or more advanced equipment), and ability to explore based on senses other than sight (such as audio explanations), tactile experiences (including the use of replicas or the use of gloves when touching objects) (Argyropoulos & Kanari, 2015, p. 132; Mesquita & Carneiro, 2016), as well as dialogical approaches to verbal descriptions with visitors (Hoyt O'Brien, 2013). Use of a range of technologies, and offering possibilities of interacting with touchable representations of exhibits, can also provide additional information about them, broadening the sensory experiences of blind and visually impaired visitors (Vas, 2020). Technology and digitalisation are also considered important facilitators within archaeological/heritage sites and museums (Agostiano, 2016; Renel, 2019, p. 379; Seale et al., 2021).

Digital advancements, especially in the Covid-19 period, have made virtual museum tours more common. Relatedly, scholarship from disability studies engages with opportunities for unconventional gallery settings such as virtual platforms to 'crip' art history and contemporary arts practice (Cachia, 2013). Nevertheless, as already mentioned, familiarity with technologies and with using the internet is not a given for all groups of people with disabilities (Dubiel, 2020). In fact, the greater digitisation of culture, which received an impetus during the Covid-19 pandemic, was found to be both a promising alternative for blind and visually impaired persons and a poorer version of accessibility of live events due largely to its lack of a social dimension, as well as other issues such as technical barriers (Dubiel, 2020).

Other facilitative factors include better communication with potential audiences (VocalEyes et al., 2023) as well as input from stakeholder groups, particularly input from persons with disabilities themselves. This is considered central to addressing barriers within cultural heritage (Lid, 2016). Levent and Pursley (2013) stress the importance of outreach as well as programme development with input from a variety of people who are blind or have low vision. Thus, following universal design principles of involving users from an early stage of design, as well as carrying out assessments with them, is considered essential for improving experiences of visually impaired people in museums (Vas, 2020; see also Lazar & Briggs, 2015; Levent et al., 2013). However, museum collaborations to co-produce exhibitions with blind or visually disabled visitors are more common than those involving people with intellectual disabilities, according to Seale et al. (2021, p. 24). Arising from research with arts organisations and people with different disabilities, Ludwig (2012) argues for a range of organisational facilitators, including creating an advisory council of staff and people with disabilities; internal evaluation assessing accessibility on physical and perceptual levels (management practices, employment, grievance procedures, communications); staff training that focuses on accessibility issues; and marketing communication to promote accessible, welcoming environments.

It is also notable that all museum visitors are considered to benefit when exhibitions and programmes provide access to people with disabilities (Eardley et al., 2016; Levent et al., 2013; Rappolt-Schlichtmann & Daley, 2013; Weisen, 2012), and multisensory information can enhance learning for all (Eardley et al., 2016). Similar arguments are made in respect of heritage sites (Muscarà & Sani, 2019). Indeed, as Flys and Amidei (2021) highlight, accessibility improvements lead to benefits across many demographic groups, instancing how, in the context of arts education, adding captioning helps not only Deaf students but also second-language learners. Finally, factors designed to engage visitors, not just to provide technological solutions, can be facilitative of building a sense of community (Hoyt O'Brien, 2013).

### 4.2. *Barriers and Facilitators for People with Disabilities in Cultural Organisations as Artists or Creators and in Other Roles*

A review of disability strategies across Europe found that greater attention is given to the consumption side of cultural participation (that is, as audiences) than to the production of culture by people with disabilities (Šubic & Ferri, 2022). As will be discussed in Part II, the analysis of reports of States Parties to the CRPD suggests that there is a rather limited understanding of people with disabilities as makers and shapers of culture in their own right, and that references to professional employment of people with disabilities within cultural organisations are very rare. Our literature review uncovered some research focused on experiences of people with disabilities as creators and makers of culture and, to a lesser extent, on people with disabilities as arts workers and professionals within cultural industries. This literature often considers engagement by different groups in professional or semi-professional capacities, or examines the development of skills or education in specific art forms towards professional engagement. It frequently identifies barriers and facilitators to participation, even if this is not always the stated aim or research question. Sometimes it incorporates discussion of expressions of identity and of the potential to transform the societal mainstream.

#### 4.2.1. *Barriers*

It almost goes without saying that physical barriers are found to impact on experiences of people with disabilities who were artists, performers, and employees, as well as within professional training opportunities (*inter alia*, Collins et al., 2023; Flys & Amidei, 2021; Randle & Hardy, 2017). For example, musicians and aspirant musicians with physical disabilities experienced barriers constituted by inaccessible music venues as well as, sometimes, being challenged to find ways to play their preferred musical instruments (Low, 2018; Skinner et al., 2022). Amongst others, Low (2018) refers to physical barriers and goes on to emphasise attitudinal barriers, suggesting that the way in which musicians with physical impairments are regarded by other musicians can be off-putting or actively impede their ability to engage in music making.

Literature evidences that arts engagement by people with disabilities not being taken seriously or being treated merely as social, recreational, therapeutic or educational endeavour could hamper access to cultural opportunities and funding (Collins et al., 2022). In a similar vein, a lack of knowledge on the part of professionals in the performing arts about the work of artists with disabilities may hamper cultural participation (British Council, 2021). A study with professionals working in culture across Europe indicates that a lack of knowledge and experience in relation to disability on the part of people working in the arts hampered equal access to the cultural sector not only for audiences but also for artists and arts professionals with disabilities (British Council, 2021). Notably, such lack of knowledge is evident across a range of cultural organisations and amongst funders. There are also financial barriers – including lack of funding to sustain inclusive art programmes (Yoon et al., 2021). Scholarly work also contends that other barriers faced by artists with disabilities participating in a range of art forms (literature, fine arts, music, and performing arts) are underpinned by negative attitudes related to assumptions that disability art is merely a hobby or form of therapy, not a professional endeavour (Bang & Kim, 2015, p. 543–4). Further, scholars posit that stigma and prejudice can be linked to an extent with a lack of adequate education and a lack of empowerment. Focusing on experiences within a theatre involving actors with intellectual disabilities, Saur and Johansen (2013, p. 258) highlight how the theatre is considered as educative, not professional, something they link to the actors not having a formal education (see also Nijkamp & Cardol, 2020). In response, Saur and Johansen (2013) argue for recognition that people with intellectual disabilities can develop their own mode of expression, which should be treated on equal terms. Similarly, Yoon et al. (2021) suggest that stereotypical perspectives limit the development of professional careers, beyond therapy and recreation, for artists living with cognitive disability. Also, relevant to seeking work in the arts, such as acting, is that opportunities can be intermittent, something compounded for actors with disabilities, who are rarely considered for roles where disability is not the focus (Band et al., 2011). In addition, welfare policies that can create 'welfare traps'[3] by involving risk of loss of benefits (despite income from artistic work often being intermittent) and discourage entrance into the labour market were also identified as barriers, along with a challenging working culture (involving unpredictability and long hours) (Arts Council England, 2017; Finn, 2023; Yoon et al., 2021). Finn's study (2023) carried out with artists with disabilities in receipt of disability supports in Ireland found that there is an intersection between disability-related barriers, low pay, and the sporadic nature of work in the arts, as well as welfare regulations, all of which undermine the working ability of artists with disabilities.

As emerges implicitly from the discussion conducted thus far, a lack of educational opportunities could hamper development or progression, as, for example, accessing professional performance training can be challenging (Band et al., 2011; Collins et al., 2023). A literature review on barriers to dance training for young people noted that most relevant dance provision is recreational, focusing on creativity and fun, instead of technical development (Aujla & Redding, 2013). Examining participation in contemporary dance, Marsh (2016) argues that attitudinal and perceptual barriers limit progression

3 'Welfare traps' are identified in contexts other than cultural employment. Bonfils et al. (2017), for example, reference how benefit traps (that is, risk of loss of social benefits) operate as barriers to the implementation of individual placements and employment supports.

for artists with disabilities, who may be discounted as potential leaders because their bodies are not perceived to signify key physical markers of leadership. She argues that we lack role models to counter negative perceptions. Again, in the context of dance training, Aujla & Redding (2013) identify four main barriers to engagement, which resonate with findings in several other studies. These were aesthetic barriers (related to ideas of ideal body types for dancers), attitudinal barriers (which can be internalised or come from others including parents, teachers, and companies), training-related barriers (including a lack of technical training and teachers' lack of knowledge or confidence), and logistical barriers (e.g. a lack of transport, support needs, and financial costs). Additional barriers identified by these scholars related to physical accessibility (including the fact that venues are sometimes accessible for audiences but not performers) and a lack of knowledge or a lack of information about opportunities (Aujla & Redding, 2013). Amongst the recommendations for facilitating access are help in identifying role models and the development of dance and disability networks (Aujla & Redding, 2013, pp. 83–84).

Interestingly, some studies focus on workers in cultural sectors (British Council, 2021; Kuna, 2023; Randle & Hardy, 2017, p. 459; Yeshanew, 2022). A study with workers in the TV and film industries in a range of roles (including researchers, producers, filmmakers, directors, and actors) suggests that workers with disabilities face multiple barriers to entry and subsequently experience both 'glass ceilings and glass partitions', often finding themselves ghettoised in specialist programming or expelled from the labour market (Randle & Hardy, 2017, pp. 452–454). Barriers discussed in scholarly works are echoed in grey literature and policy analysis. For example, a study by Arts Council England (2017) with people with disabilities working in the cultural sector, as well as people aspiring to enter the workforce, identified similar barriers (including attitudinal barriers and a lack of networks and of showcasing work by people with disabilities).

If we turn to disability representation in decision-making bodies of cultural organisations, there is some evidence that similar barriers to those identified operate, although as yet this has not been as significant a focus of scholarship. A review of disability strategies across Europe found that measures relating to participation by people with disabilities in policy decision-making and in management within cultural life are rare (Šubic & Ferri, 2022). A study from Australia suggests that there were a range of challenges to participation in governance by people with disabilities, which include frustration with organisations satisfying quotas ('ticking boxes') as well as the lack of a 'culture' of dealing with disability-related issues (Grant, 2014).

#### 4.2.2. *Facilitators*

There are many facilitative factors identified in the literature. As Flys and Amidei (2021, p. 16) contend, in the context of the performing arts, change must start in training programmes within higher education, 'the pipeline for future creators', utilising principles of universal design for learning. Similarly, for Skinner et al. (2022), providing music teachers with a grounding in the needs of students with disabilities is necessary as is self-advocacy in the face of systemic barriers. A study with young people with a range of disability types engaged in visual art within pre-degree and higher education detailed facilitative factors within education, including disability awareness in the delivery of the arts curriculum; highly developed support systems in terms of practical assistance and IT; employment of teachers who are art specialists; an accessible arts curriculum delivered innovatively; constructive criticism; an accessible environment; and, critically, disabled artists as role models (Taylor, 2005, p. 777).

Similar facilitators were identified in a study concerning artists with cognitive disabilities, including individualised support strategies to improve artistic capacity and mentorship programmes with professional artists as well as appropriate environmental settings, which included having relaxed studio atmospheres, giving artists the freedom to make choices and ensuring that all staff are respectful of the artists, as well as public exhibition opportunities (Yoon et al., 2021). Consistent with this, performance professionals experiencing autism suggested that having the support of a mentor was helpful, and this was echoed by employers of autistic performers, some of whom wished for consultants who could support them in making disability accommodations within their company (Buckley et al., 2021). There is also scholarship focusing on techniques, strategies, and accommodations to work with actors with intellectual disabilities used by directors and arts educators (Kundin, 2022). Arising from a case study of inclusive theatre practices, in which actors with and without intellectual disabilities collaborated, Nijkamp and Cardol (2020) conclude that all participants together need to develop new ways of working and co-creating, and different modes of expression resulting in new skills and views.

Curricular changes within education, as well as organisational and attitudinal changes within arts companies and cultural institutions, are identified as needed to facilitate entry and progression. This includes not only changes to curricula and teaching practices but building supportive teams and mentorship; access to advice for employers (including on making reasonable accommodations); mentoring and peer support; inclusive board recruitment and working practices; and employers supporting employees through welfare claims (Arts Council England, 2017). Young disabled artists, in particular, need professional networking opportunities, as they may not be well connected with stakeholders in the arts community (Boeltzig et al., 2009).

Bang and Kim (2015) focused on a broad range of art forms and made a number of policy recommendations for change in Korea. They highlighted the role of effective law and policies to advance disability art, the importance of government bureaux focused on disability art, and the role of disability arts centres as a hub for development. Other recommendations included (the rather debated) use of quota systems to ensure opportunities to practice arts, personal assistance services to support artistic work, and measures to solve financial problems experienced by artists (Bang & Kim, 2015, pp. 553–554).

These authors also cite a survey with artists with disabilities suggesting that the best way for disability arts to be promoted would be financial support by government (35.1%), legislation that promotes artists with disabilities (33.4%), and expansion of arts education for persons with disabilities (9.6%) (Bang & Kim, 2015, p. 545).

As mentioned earlier, literature often discusses the role of artistic expression in representation, in self-expression, in expressions of identity, and in relation to the control of those expressions. For example, young people could find art engagement as empowering (Taylor, 2005) or use art to cope with the negative aspects of living with disability, including stigma, with some young visual artists perceiving that impairment could enhance their artistic ability (Boeltzig et al., 2009). Yoon et al. (2021) cite literature on the role played by art in the lives of artists living with cognitive disability who are non-verbal in terms of self-expression and in connecting with the world, such as exhibiting their artwork in public. Further, in a discussion of the performing arts, Collins et al. (2022, p. 322) suggest that if more people with disabilities are empowered to engage, whether as staff, performers, or audience members, 'it increases their representation, and a form of representation is self-generated'.

### 4.3. *Barriers and Facilitators for People with Disabilities as Amateur Creators: Community Arts*

The last sub-heading under which we present the findings of our review relates to studies on participation in community arts and the role of persons with disabilities as non-professional creators, which, as will be mentioned in Chapter 3, is also covered by Article 30 CRPD and by the active dimension of the right to participate in cultural life.

The disability arts movement in the UK has a long history of community-based collaborative arts practice (Levy & Young, 2020; Penketh et al., 2019). This literature often takes the issue of inclusion as its focus, or its impact on people with disabilities (Levy et al., 2017, p. 257) and participation in community arts can have a range of benefits that include enabling people, regardless of disability, to develop skills relating to confidence, self-esteem, and communication (Richards et al., 2019). However, while the identification of barriers and facilitators or challenges to participation is not always the stated objective or central research question, it is dealt with to varying degrees. In addition, some studies engage with disability identity, or focus on the impact of participation on perceptions of disability within society.

#### 4.3.1. *Barriers*

Barriers identified in this area are broadly consistent with those already discussed. For example, medicalised or paternalistic attitudes to disability and to arts engagement by people with disabilities are often mentioned by scholars. Considering initiatives focused on younger people, Penketh et al. (2019) suggest that funding streams in community arts can be closely aligned with medical and charity models, where children with disabilities and young people are 'defined by dependence and need' and arts-based initiatives may involve arts therapy and rehabilitation, not creative practice. A report focusing on access by young Deaf people and young people with a range of disabilities to arts in Scotland (Lawrence & Birds of Paradise Theatre Company, 2016) shows that challenges remain in finding accessible arts provision. In that regard, the report also evidences difficulties with travel and transport, as well as a lack of information on access, contributing to difficulty gauging whether one would be welcome and encouraged to engage (Lawrence & Birds of Paradise Theatre Company, 2016).

#### *4.3.2. Facilitators*

Facilitative factors to community-based arts practice included access provision, 'Front Door to Stage Door' (referring to all elements and stages of how young people gain access), centralised information about arts opportunities, connections built with communities of people with disabilities and Deaf people, and education and awareness for arts providers (Lawrence & Birds of Paradise Theatre Company, 2016). Amongst other factors identified as facilitators were training and access to IT. For example, in relation to visual art, adult learners with disabilities could benefit from computer technology, which provided greater autonomy in creating art (Young, 2008). A qualitative study with people experiencing disability who are musicians (the Drake Music Project) found that specialised equipment and training operate as facilitators that 'enhance[s] the substantive freedoms of the musicians to choose and lead the good life' and 'to appear in public without shame' (Watts & Ridley, 2012, pp. 367–368). These authors suggest that music-making became a means of articulating identities that might otherwise be muted by dis/ability, while simultaneously musical performance can shape how dis/ability is perceived more generally, allowing others to recognise the fundamental humanity of the musicians (Watts & Ridley, 2012, p. 367). Similar points are made in the context musical performances by disabled students of music, which reinforce positive identity and collaboration (Honisch, 2009).

On the whole, while the meanings attaching to barriers to participation tend to be related to the inhibition of expressions of self-hood, facilitating participation is understood as having the potential to support development of a positive sense of identity, promote diversity, and transform how disability is conceived of (Richards et al., 2019).

## 5. Concluding Remarks

The literature discussed in this chapter is intended to provide context for subsequent analysis, including the presentation of empirical findings in Part III.

The literature review showcases that cultural participation has been rarely looked at through a human rights lens and that it has been dealt with in disciplinary silos and from relatively narrow perspectives. Indeed, this literature review unveils that, on issues related to cultural participation of persons with disabilities, there is still very limited interdisciplinarity and an even more limited interaction amongst disciplines such as international human rights law, disability studies, cultural studies, and cultural policy. The right to culture of people with disabilities has been discussed only within the remit of commentaries to the CRPD, and other disciplines rarely engage with a human rights perspective and the human rights model of disability. Further, although interest in cultural participation of persons with disabilities has grown significantly (mirroring a burgeoning general interest in disability and disability rights across various fields as a result of the CRPD), especially in recent years, current literature tends to approach cultural participation from discrete and narrow perspectives. The scholarly work reviewed often adopts a focus on case studies, a particular group of persons with disabilities, or specific cultural experiences. In fact, many of the articles reviewed concern a single organisation or a single venue type. The mostly qualitative approach to research on cultural participation is also consistent with the lack of comparable data and the absence of larger quantitative studies.

With regard to barriers and facilitators, the literature review highlights the complexity of accessibility, and the particular challenges in facilitating access to culture, that is, in realising the 'passive' individual dimension of the right to culture. Accessibility of culture depends on the complex interplay between a specific person's individual characteristics and the environment (Mastrogiuseppe et al., 2020) and is dynamic and inter-relational (Lid, 2016). This also mirrors the CRPD understanding of accessibility, as discussed by Charitakis (2018), which will be examined in Chapter 2. In this context, our review, focusing on attendance at cultural venues and heritage as audiences, details factors operating as barriers and facilitators for particular groups that connect to the various dimensions of accessibility: attitudinal accessibility, economic accessibility or affordability, physical accessibility, information accessibility, and communication accessibility (Charitakis, 2018). It also evidences that facilitating access for people with disabilities may ultimately benefit all people in their engagement with cultural venues, heritage, and cultural content. Furthermore, our review suggests that the 'hierarchy of impairments' that is identified in general approaches to societal participation (Waltz & Schippers, 2020, p. 9) also operates in the cultural sector, with least attention having been paid to date to people with intellectual disabilities or cognitive disabilities. There is also a tendency to provide access by way of 'special' or occasional events or exhibitions, rather than to incorporate them in the mainstream.

Second, the literature examined does point to the adoption of binding accessibility norms as an important tool. However, this is unlikely to be sufficient. As we will discuss further in Part III, there is a need to combine legal provisions with effective guidelines for various stakeholders. Current scholarship shows that existing guidelines often focus on particular disability types, or on facilitating physical access, and that many barriers occur in the realm of attitudes and the lack of knowledge of a range of actors. In fact, while there are checklists and toolkits available to guide cultural professionals in providing greater access, these are not widely circulated and are often focused on a single country or available in only one language (British Council, 2021). In that connection, the importance of awareness raising on accessibility, of fostering transfer of knowledge, and of dissemination of best practices and mutual learning as facilitative elements emerges strongly. This is clearly in line with the emphasis placed by the CRPD on awareness-raising in general and on the need to 'educate' different stakeholders on accessibility needs. Article 8 CRPD *inter alia* requires States Parties to 'raise awareness throughout society, including at the family level, regarding persons with disabilities, and to foster respect for the rights and dignity of persons with disabilities', and 'to combat stereotypes'. Focusing on accessibility, Article 9 CRPD requires States Parties to provide training for stakeholders on accessibility issues facing persons with disabilities.

Third, the literature reviewed also shows that there is a tendency to treat arts initiatives involving people with disabilities as education or therapy failing to recognise or develop more artistic or professional approaches. This is in contrast with Article 30(2) CRPD, which instead obliges States Parties to take all appropriate measures to enable persons with disabilities to develop their creative, artistic, and intellectual potential.

Further, besides ensuring development of greater knowledge about disability and wider accessibility, amongst key facilitators identified in the literature are consultations with people with disabilities and organisational changes that support the employment of people with disabilities within the cultural sector. While the literature reviewed was not focused on the CRPD for the most part, it is evident that participatory practices in policy-making and organisational structures do align with the ethos of the CRPD as well as with the principle of participation laid out in Article 3 CRPD and further expressed in other provisions of the Convention.

On the whole, this literature review shows that there is a growing body of literature focusing on identifying barriers to, and facilitators of, cultural participation by people with disabilities across different academic fields. However, as noted earlier, it shows a marked disciplinary fragmentation, which hampers the transfer of knowledge and mutual learning.

This chapter, therefore, has not only identified key barriers and facilitators discussed in scholarship but attempted to address disciplinary silos which have, thus far, caused conceptual fragmentation and epistemic gaps. In this respect the book as a whole, and this chapter in particular (in line with the broader project 'DANCING') tries to break that fragmentation by bringing together different strands of literature to advance the state of knowledge and to contribute to cross-fertilisation between different areas of scholarship. Further, while the focus on barriers and facilitators in the works retrieved remains for the most part disjointed from the human rights model of disability, this chapter has endeavoured to link the findings of our literature review with the CRPD.

## References


Agostiano, M. (2016). The 'compensatory solutions' for an alternative accessibility of cultural heritage sites. In A. Arenghi, I. Garofolo, & O. Sørmoen (Eds.), *Accessibility as a key enabling knowledge for enhancement of cultural heritage* (pp. 131–147). Franco Angeli.

Argyropoulos, V. S., & Kanari, C. (2015). Re-imagining the museum through 'touch': Reflections of individuals with visual disability on their experience of museum-visiting in Greece. *Alter, European Journal of Disability Research/Revue européenne de recherche sur le handicap*, *9*(2), 130–143.

Arts Council England. (2017). *Making a shift report: Disabled people and the arts and cultural sector workforce in England: Understanding trends, barriers and opportunities*. Arts Council England. https://www.artscouncil.org.uk/making-shift

Arts Council England. (2018). *The conversation. A report by Britain Thinks*. www.artscouncil.org.uk/sites/default/files/download-file/ACE_10YSConversation%20Findings%20Report_19July18_0.pdf

Audience Agency. (2020). *Creating an effective audience development plan: An introductory guide to audience development planning*. www.theaudienceagency.org/resources/guide-to-audience-development-planning

Aujla, I. J., & Redding, E. (2013). Barriers to dance training for young people with disabilities. *British Journal of Special Education*, *40*(2), 80–85.

Band, S. A., Lindsay, G., Neelands, J., & Freakley, V. (2011). Disabled students in the performing arts – are we setting them up to succeed? *International Journal of Inclusive Education*, *15*(9), 891–908.

Bang, G. H., & Kim, K. M. (2015). Korean disabled artists' experiences of creativity and the environmental barriers they face. *Disability & Society*, *30*(4), 543–555.

Bantekas, I., Stephenson, C. P. Y., Karapapa, S., & Polymenopoulou, E. (2018). Article 30: participation in cultural life, recreation, leisure, and sport. In I. Bantekas, M. A. Stein, & D. Anastasiou (Eds.), *The UN Convention on the Rights of Persons with Disabilities: A Commentary* (pp. 863–923). Oxford University Press.

Black, G. (2005). *The engaging museum. Developing museums for visitor involvement*. Routledge.

Boeltzig, H., Sulewski, J. S., & Hasnain, R. (2009). Career development among young disabled artists. *Disability & Society*, *24*(6), 753–769.

Bonfils, I. S., Hansen, H., Dalum, H. S., & Falgaard Eplov, L. (2017). Implementation of the individual placement and support approach – facilitators and barriers. *Scandinavian Journal of Disability Research*, *19*(4), 318–333.

British Council. (2021). *Time to act: How lack of knowledge in the cultural sector creates barriers for disabled artists and audiences* (Final report November 2021. A research report authored by On the Move, commissioned by the British Council). https://www.disabilityartsinternational.org/wp-content/uploads/2022/01/TIMETO2.pdf

Buckley, E., Pellicano, E., & Remington, A. (2021). The real thing I struggle with is other people's perceptions: The experiences of autistic performing arts professionals and attitudes of performing arts employers in the UK. *Journal of Autism and Developmental Disorders*, *51*(1), 45–59.

Byrne, J. A. (2016). Improving the peer review of narrative literature reviews. *Research Integrity and Peer Review*, *1*(1), 1–4.

Cachia, A. (2013). Disabling the museum: Curator as infrastructural activist. *Canadian Journal of Disability Studies*, *2*(4), 257–289.
Cameron, C. (2022). Disability, normality and absurdity: A reflection on stuckist disability art. *Disability & Society*, *37*(2), 338–344.
Cerdan Chiscano, M., & Jiménez-Zarco, A. I. (2021). Towards an inclusive museum management strategy. An exploratory study of consumption experience in visitors with disabilities. The Case of the CosmoCaixa Science Museum. *Sustainability*, *13*(2), 660.
Charitakis, S. (2018). *Access denied: The role of the European Union in ensuring accessibility under the United Nations Convention on the Rights of Persons with Disabilities*. Intersentia.
Chenu, R. (2018). Museums and disability: The obstacles to accessibility. A survey of 127 museums. *Culture & Musées*, *31*, 207–209.
Cho, H., & Jolley, A. (2016). Museum education for children with disabilities: Development of the nature senses traveling trunk. *Journal of Museum Education*, *41*(3), 220–229.
Collins, A., Fillis, I., & Goknil Sanal, Z. (2023). Social inclusion of disabled performers in the performing arts: A case from Turkiye. *Equality, Diversity and Inclusion: An International Journal*, *42*(8), 968–985.
Collins, A., Rentschler, R., Williams, R., & Azmat, F. (2022). Exploring barriers to social inclusion for disabled people: Perspectives from the performing arts. *Journal of Management & Organization*, *28*(2), 308–328.
Collins, J. A., & Fauser, B. C. J. M. (2005). Editorial: Balancing the strengths of systematic and narrative reviews. *Human Reproduction Update*, *11*(2), 103–104.
Confino-Rehder, S. (2010). Art experiences for everyone: Opening the doors to the blind and people with low vision. *The International Journal of the Inclusive Museum*, *3*(2), 27–38.
Constantinou, V., Loizides, F., & Ioannou, A. (2016). *A personal tour of cultural heritage for deaf museum visitors*. Euro-Mediterranean Conference.
Cuenca-Amigo, M., & Makua, A. (2017). Audience development: A cross-national comparison. *Academia Revista Latinoamericana de Administración*, *30*(2), 156–172.
Darcy, S., Maxwell, H., Grabowski, S., & Onyx, J. (2022). Artistic impact: From casual and serious leisure to professional career development in disability arts. *Leisure Sciences*, *44*(4), 514–533.
Darcy, S., & Taylor, T. (2009). Disability citizenship: An Australian human rights analysis of the cultural industries. *Leisure Studies*, *28*(4), 419–441.
Davis, L. J. (2013). Introduction: Normality, power and culture. In L. J. Davis (Ed.), *The disability studies reader* (pp. 1–16). Routledge.
Della Fina, V., Cera, R., & Palmisano, G. (Eds.). (2017). *The United Nations Convention on the Rights of Persons with Disabilities: A Commentary*. Springer.
Dubiel, M. N. (2020). Together or separated? The segregative and integrative model of cultural accessibility for persons with disabilities. *Studia Humanistyczne AGH*, *19*(3), 139–156.
Eardley, A. F., Mineiro, C., Neves, J., & Ride, P. (2016). Redefining access: Embracing multimodality, memorability and shared experience in museums. *Curator: The Museum Journal*, *59*(3), 263–286.
European Commission. (2023). *Replies of the European commission to the European court of auditors' special report: Supporting persons with disabilities* (Practical impact of EU action is limited). www.eca.europa.eu/en/publications/SR-2023-20
European Commission. (2024). *Special Eurobarometer 535 – Discrimination in the European Union*. https://op.europa.eu/en/publication-detail/-/publication/e29733eb-b4ee-11ee-b164-01aa75ed71a1?pk_campaign=OPNewsletter_May2024&pk_source=EUP
European Parliament. (2018). *Report on structural and financial barriers in the access to culture A8–0169/2018*. https://www.europarl.europa.eu/doceo/document/A-8-2018-0169_EN.html

European Parliament Research Service (EPRS). (2017). *Access to culture in the European Union*. https://op.europa.eu/en/publication-detail/-/publication/66f298ec-6840-11e7-b2f2-01aa75ed71a1

Eurostat. (2024). *Eurostat Statistics Explained: Culture statistics – cultural participation*. [online] https://ec.europa.eu/eurostat/statistics-explained/index.php?title=Culture_statistics_-_cultural_participation#Cultural_participation_of_people_with_disabilities

Ferri, D., & Leahy, A. (2023). The right of people with disabilities to participate in cultural life: Is Cinderella going to the ball? In S. Robinson & K. R. Fisher (Eds.), *Research handbook on disability policy* (pp. 102–117). Edward Elgar.

Finn, P. (2023). *Artists at intersection of work and welfare: Disabled artists navigation of welfare – short interim report*. ALL Institute and School of Law and Criminology, Maynooth University.

Flys, E. S. V., & Amidei, A. (2021). Access and inclusion for students with disabilities in performing arts higher education. *Acotaciones. Investigación y Creación Teatral*, *2*(47), 15–44.

Fortuna, J., Harrison, C., Eekhoff, A., Marthaler, C., Seromik, M., Ogren, S., & VanderMolen, J. (2023). Identifying barriers to accessibility for museum visitors who are blind and visually impaired. *Visitor Studies*, *26*(2), 103–124.

Fraser, B. (2018). *Cognitive disability aesthetics: Visual culture, disability representations, and the (In)visibility of cognitive difference*. University of Toronto Press.

Garland-Thomson, R. (2002). Integrating disability, transforming feminist theory. *National Women's Studies Association Journal*, *14*(3), 1–32.

Glow, H., Kershaw, A., & Reason, M. (2021). Leading or avoiding change: The problem of audience diversification for arts organisations. *International Journal of Cultural Policy*, *27*(1), 130–148.

Goodall, B., Pottinger, G., Dixon, T., & Russell, H. (2004). Heritage property, tourism and the UK Disability Discrimination Act. *Property Management*, *22*(5), 345–357.

Goodley, D. (2013). Dis/entangling critical disability studies. *Disability & Society*, *28*(5), 631–644.

Goodley, D., & Bolt, D. (2010). Introduction. In D. Goodley & D. Bolt (Eds.), Special issue theorizing culture and disability: Interdisciplinary dialogues. *Review of Disability Studies: An International Journal*, *6*(3).

Grant, C. (2014). Participating in arts- and cultural-sector governance in Australia: Experiences and views of people with disability. *Arts & Health*, *6*(1), 75–89.

Gratton, N. (2020). People with learning disabilities and access to mainstream arts and culture: A participatory action research approach. *British Journal of Learning Disabilities*, *48*(2), 106–114.

Greenhalgh, T., Thorne, S., & Malterud, K. (2018). Time to challenge the spurious hierarchy of systematic over narrative reviews? *European Journal of Clinical Investigation*, *48*(6), e12931.

Guffey, E. (2015). The disabling art museum. *Journal of Visual Culture*, *14*(1), 61–73.

Hadley, B., & McDonald, D. (2019). Introduction: Disability arts, culture, and media studies – mapping a maturing field. In B. Hadley & D. McDonald (Eds.), *The Routledge handbook of disability arts, culture, and media* (pp. 1–18). Routledge.

Hadley, B., Paterson, E., & Little, M. (2022). Quick trust and slow time: Relational innovations in disability performing arts practice. *International Journal of Disability and Social Justice*, *2*(1), 74–94.

Hadley, B., Rieger, J., Ellis, K., & Paterson, E. (2022). Cultural safety as a foundation for allyship in disability arts. *Disability & Society*, *39*(1), 213–233.

Hadley, S. (2021). *Audience development and cultural policy*. Palgrave Macmillan.

Hadley, S., Heidelberg, B., & Belfiore, E. (2022). Reflexivity and the perpetuation of inequality in the cultural sector: Half awake in a fake empire? *Journal for Cultural Research*, *26*(3–4), 244–265.

Hill, L. R., & Sobande, F. (2018). In our own words: Organising and experiencing exhibitions as Black women and women of colour in Scotland. In R. Finkel, B. Sharp, & M. Sweeney (Eds.), *Accessibility, inclusion and diversity in critical event studies* (pp. 107–121). Routledge.

Honisch, S. H. (2009). 'Re-narrating disability' through musical performance. *Music Theory Online*, *15*(3).

Hoyt O'Brien, B. (2013). Emphasizing observation in a gallery program for blind and low-vision visitors: Art beyond sight at the museum of fine arts, Houston. *Disability Studies Quarterly*, *33*(3).

Jongerius, M., Bilo, N., Gielen, M., & Scholten, N. (2020). *Onbeperkt Cultuur Beleven. Eindrapport.* https://open.overheid.nl/documenten/ronl-0f8d5c5f-7a21-4546-8bc0-7b60a56d306f/pdf

Kawashima, N. (2000). *Beyond the division of attenders vs. non-attenders: A study into audience development in policy and practice.* University of Warwick, Centre for Cultural Policy Studies. http://wrap.warwick.ac.uk/35926/1/WRAP_Kawashima_ccps_paper_6.pdf

Kuna, S. (2023). Far from Fauda: Creators with disabilities in an established-outsider figuration in the Israeli film and television industries. *Employee Relations*, *45*(1), 69–89.

Kundin, C. (2022). Directing actors with learning disabilities: A meta-analysis of past and current practices. *Youth Theatre Journal*, *36*(1–2), 41–60.

Lawrence, M., & Birds of Paradise Theatre Company. (2016). *Barriers to access. Report on the barriers faced by young disabled and D/deaf people in accessing youth arts provision in Scotland.* https://strathprints.strath.ac.uk/62143/

Lazar, J., & Briggs, I. (2015). Improving services for patrons with print disabilities at public libraries: Moving forward to become more inclusive. *Library Quarterly: Information, Community, Policy*, *85*(2), 172–184.

Leahy, A., & Ferri, D. (2022). Barriers and facilitators to cultural participation by people with disabilities: A narrative literature review. *Scandinavian Journal of Disability Research*, *24*(1), 68–81.

Leahy, A., & Ferri, D. (2023). Cultivating cultural capital and transforming cultural fields: A study with arts and disability organisations in Europe. *The Sociological Review*, *72*(6), 1–19.

Levent, N., Kleege, G., & Pursley, J. M. (2013). Museum experience and blindness. *Disability Studies Quarterly*, *33*(3).

Levent, N., & Pursley, J. M. (2013). Sustainable museum access: A two-way street. *Disability Studies Quarterly*, *33*(3).

Levy, S., & Young, H. (2020). Arts, disability and crip theory: Temporal re-imagining in social care for people with profound and multiple learning disabilities. *Scandinavian Journal of Disability Research*, *22*(1), 68–79.

Levy, S. A., Robb, A. J., & Jindal-Snape, D. (2017). Disability, personalisation and community arts: Exploring the spatial dynamics of children with disabilities participating in inclusive music classes. *Disability & Society*, *32*(2), 254–268.

Lid, I. M. (2016). Access to cultural heritage: A multiscaled approach. In A. Arenghi, I. Garofolo, & O. Sørmoen (Eds.), *Accessibility as a key enabling knowledge for enhancement of cultural heritage* (pp. 77–89). Franco Angeli.

Low, G. A. (2018). *Where are all the disabled musicians? An exploration of the attitudinal and physical barriers that impact on the identities and lived experiences of musicians with a physical impairment* [PhD thesis, University of Edinburgh].

Ludwig, E. (2012). Stigma in the arts: How perceptual barriers influence individuals' with disabilities participation in arts organizations. *The Journal of Arts Management, Law, and Society*, *42*(3), 141–151.

Ma, G. Y. K. (2022). An ecological approach to self-reflections on the inaccessibility of arts and cultural activities to wheelchair users. *Disability & Society*, *39*(5), 1276–1296.

Marsh, K. (2016). *Taking charge – dance, disability and leadership: Exploring the shifting role of the disabled dance artist* [PhD thesis, Arts and Humanities, Coventry University].

Martínez Amador, E. (2016). Deaf people do not go to the movies: Accessibility for people with hearing disabilities in the Spanish cinema. *Fonesca: Journal of Communication*, *12*(12), 133–147.

Mastrogiuseppe, M., Span, S., & Bortolotti, E. (2020). Improving accessibility to cultural heritage for people with intellectual disabilities: A tool for observing the obstacles and facilitators for the access to knowledge. *Alter, European Journal of Disability Research*, *15*(2), 113–123.

Mesquita, S., & Carneiro, M. J. (2016). Accessibility of European museums to visitors with visual impairments. *Disability & Society*, *31*(3), 373–388.

Murphy, C., Parry, R., Hoover, S., Ó Duibhir, C., & Lydon, M. (2024). *Amplify: A call for transformative action*. Irish Theatre Institute. www.safetocreate.ie/

Muscarà, M., & Sani, C. (2019). Accessibility to cultural heritage, some project outcomes. *Education Sciences & Society-Open Access*, *10*(1), 244–280.

National Education Centre Slovak Republic. (2020). *A culture without barriers/ Kultúra bez bariér*. National Outreach Center.

Nijkamp, J., & Cardol, M. (2020). Diversity, opportunities, and challenges of inclusive theatre. *Journal of Social Inclusion*, *11*(2).

Office of the High Commissioner for Human Rights (OHCHR). (2020). *Data sources for outcome indicators on Article 30 CRPD: Participation in cultural life, recreation, leisure and sport*. www.ohchr.org/sites/default/files/data-sources-article-30.pdf

Ott, K. (2010). Collective bodies: What museums do for disability studies. In R. Sandell, J. Dodds, & R. Garland-Thomson (Eds.), *Re-presenting disability: Activism and agency in the museum* (pp. 289–299). Routledge.

Penketh, C., James, A., Wade, S., & Nutter, R. (2019). DaDaFest ensemble: Leadership, voice, and collaboration in the arts. In A. Wexler & J. Derby (Eds.), *Contemporary art and disability studies* (pp. 76–86). Routledge.

Pretto, A. (2020). A study on accessibility in an Old Italian City: When the past is worth more than the present. *Disability & Society*, *37*(3), 496–521.

Primorac, J., Obuljen Koržinek, N., & Uzelac, A. (2017). Access to culture in Croatian cultural policy: Moving towards explicit policies. *International Journal of Cultural Policy*, *23*(5), 562–580.

Rahim, N., & Mavra, L. (2009). *Barriers to engagement in heritage by currently under-represented groups. An Inclusion Report to the National Audit Office*. www.nao.org.uk/wp-content/uploads/2009/07/0809881_barriers.pdf

Randle, K., & Hardy, K. (2017). Macho, mobile and resilient? How workers with impairments are doubly disabled in project-based film and television work. *Work, Employment and Society*, *31*(3), 447–464.

Rappolt-Schlichtmann, G., & Daley, S. G. (2013). Providing access to engagement in learning: The potential of universal design for learning in museum design. *Curator: The Museum Journal*, *56*(3), 307–321.

Renel, W. (2019). Sonic accessibility: Increasing social equity through the inclusive design of sound in museums and heritage sites. *Curator: The Museum Journal*, *62*(3), 377–402.

Richards, M., Lawthom, R., & Runswick-Cole, K. (2019). Community-based arts research for people with learning disabilities: Challenging misconceptions about learning disabilities. *Disability & Society*, *34*(2), 204–227.

Riddell, S., & Watson, N. (2003). Disability, culture and identity: Introduction. In S. Riddell & N. Watson (Eds.), *Disability, culture and identity* (pp. 1–18). Pearson Education Limited.

Rix, J., Lowe, T., & The Heritage Forum. (2010). Including people with learning difficulties in cultural and heritage sites. *International Journal of Heritage Studies*, *16*(3), 207–224.

Sandahl, C. (2018). Disability art and culture: A model for imaginative ways to integrate the community. *Alter, European Journal of Disability Research/Revue européenne de recherche sur le handicap*, 12(2), 79–93.
Sandell, R., & Dodd, J. (2010). Activist practice. In R. Sandell, J. Dodd, & R. Garland-Thomson (Eds.), *Re-presenting disability: Activism and agency in the museum* (pp. 3–22). Routledge.
Saur, E., & Johansen, O. (2013). Stepping into the unknown – welfare, disability, culture and theatre as an opportunity for equality? *Research in Drama Education: The Journal of Applied Theatre and Performance*, *18*(3), 246–260.
Seale, J., Garcia Carrizosa, H., Rix, J., Sheehy, K., & Hayhoe, S. (2021). A participatory approach to the evaluation of participatory museum research projects. *International Journal of Research & Method in Education*, *44*(1), 20–40.
Shape. (2013). *Understanding disabled people as audiences 2012–13*. Shape, Supported by Arts Council England.
Siebers, T. (2006). Disability aesthetics. *Journal for Cultural and Religious Theory*, *7*(2), 63–73.
Skinner, A., Thompson, G., & Skewes McFerran, K. (2022). Professional pathways for musicians with disability in Victoria, Australia. *Musicology Australia*, *44*(1), 21–42.
Smith, M. S., & Stein, M. A. (2020). Article 30 of the CRPD as a vehicle for social transformation: Harnessing the CRPD's potential for persons with intellectual disabilities. In E. J. Kakoullis & K. Johnson (Eds.), *Recognising human rights in different cultural contexts* (pp. 269–294). Palgrave Macmillan.
Solvang, P. K. (2012). From identity politics to dismodernism? Changes in the social meaning of disability art. *Alter, European Journal of Disability Research/Revue Europeen De Recherche Sur Le Handicap*, *6*(3), 178–187.
Solvang, P. K. (2018). Between art therapy and disability aesthetics: A sociological approach for understanding the intersection between art practice and disability discourse. *Disability & Society*, *33*(2), 238–253.
Stober, K., & García Iriarte, E. (2023). Intellectual disability, art and identity: A qualitative exploration of the experiences of professional artists with intellectual disabilities. *Disability & Society*, *38*(10), 1871–1894.
Šubic, N., & Ferri, D. (2022). National disability strategies as rights-based cultural policy tools. *International Journal of Cultural Policy*, *29*(4), 467–483.
Swedish Authority for Participation. (2016). *Utvärdering och analys av funktionshinderspolitiken 2011–2016 Redovisning av regeringsuppdrag om ett samlat uppföljningssystem för funktionshinderspolitiken*. Myndigheten för delaktighet serie A, 14 (Diarienummer 2015/0228).
Tatić, D. (2015). *Access for people with disabilities to culture, tourism, sports and leisure activities: Towards meaningful and enriching participation*. Council of Europe.
Taylor, M. (2005). Self-identity and the arts education of disabled young people. *Disability & Society*, *20*, 763–778.
Temple Jones, C., Johner, R., Lozhkina, A., & Walliser, R. (2022). Voice, communication technology, disability, and art: An interdisciplinary scoping review and reflection. *Disability & Society*, *39*(5), 1297–1316.
Thomas, C., & Milligan, C. (2018). Dementia, disability rights and disablism: Understanding the social position of people living with dementia. *Disability & Society*, *33*(1), 115–131.
Titchkosky, T. (2003). *Disability, self, and society*. University of Toronto Press.
Titchkosky, T., & Michalko, R. (2009). Introduction. In T. Titchkosky & R. Michalko (Eds.), *Rethinking normalcy: A disability studies reader* (pp. 1–14). Canadian Scholars' Press.

UNESCO. (2009). *UNESCO framework for cultural statistics* (FCS). UNESCO Institute for Statistics. https://uis.unesco.org/sites/default/files/documents/unesco-framework-for-cultural-statistics-2009-en_0.pdf

United Nations Committee on the Rights of Persons with Disabilities (CRPD Committee). (2014). *General Comment No. 2 on Article 9: Accessibility* (UN Doc. CRPD/C/GC/2).

Vas, R. (2020). Blind and visually impaired visitors' experiences in museums: Increasing accessibility through assistive technologies. *The International Journal of the Inclusive Museum*, *13*(2), 57–80.

Veal, A. J. (2022). Cultural participation as a human right: Holding nation states to account. *International Journal of Cultural Policy*, *29*(6), 686–700.

VocalEyes, Stagetext & Centre for Accessible Environments. (2023). *State of theatre access*. https://vocaleyes.co.uk/research/state-of-theatre-access-2023/

Walters, T. (2023). The InterACT disability arts festival: Creating revolutionary futures? *International Journal of Event and Festival Management*, *14*(2), 205–220.

Waltz, M., & Schippers, A. (2020). Politically disabled: Barriers and facilitating factors affecting people with disabilities in political life within the European Union. *Disability & Society*, *36*(4), 517–540.

Watlington, E. (2019). The radical accessibility of video art (for hearing people) author(s): Source: Future Anterior: *Journal of Historic Preservation, History, Theory, and Criticism*, *16*(1), 111–121.

Watson, N. (2003). Daily denials: The routinisation of oppression and resistance. In S. Riddell & N. Watson (Eds.), *Disability, culture and identity* (pp. 34–51). Pearson Education.

Watts, M., & Ridley, B. (2012). Identities of dis/ability and music. *British Educational Research Journal*, *38*(3), 353–372.

Weisen, M. (2012). Digital access to culture. *Journal of Assistive Technologies*, *6*(2), 163–166.

Wilkinson-Meyers, L., Brown, P., Reeve, J., McNeill, R., Patston, P., Dylan, S., Baker, R., Ryan, B., & McEldowney, J. (2014). Reducing disablement with adequate and appropriate resources: A New Zealand perspective. *Disability & Society*, *29*(10), 1540–1553.

World Health Organization & The World Bank. (2011). *World report on disability*. World Health Organization.

Yeshanew, Y. T. (2022). Barriers to employment of young cultural practitioners with visual impairments in the cultural industries of Ethiopia. *Journal of Visual Impairment & Blindness*, *116*(5), 678–688.

Yoon, J. H., Ellison, C., & Essl, P. (2021). Shifting the perspective from 'incapable' to 'capable' for artists with cognitive disability; case studies in Australia and South Korea. *Disability & Society*, *36*(3), 443–467.

Young, G. C. (2008). Autonomy of artistic expression for adult learners with disabilities. *International Journal of Art & Design Education*, *27*(2), 116–123.

# 2 The Legal Context

## The CRPD as Human Rights Framework

*Delia Ferri*

### 1. Introduction

After having examined the scholarly context in which the book is located, this chapter outlines the broader legal context. It focuses on the UN Convention on the Rights of Persons with Disabilities (CRPD) as the key legal framework for the socio-legal analysis propounded in this book (United Nations, 2006). Purposely, this chapter does not discuss the long trajectory that led to the CRPD, nor what was the main forerunner of the CRPD, the non-binding Standard Rules on the Equalization of Opportunities for Persons with Disabilities, which have been dealt with by an array of scholarly work (Degener & Begg, 2017; Ferri & Broderick, 2019) and recalled already in the introduction to this book. The emphasis on the CRPD is underpinned by an understanding that this Convention currently represents the global standard for disability rights (Broderick & Ferri, 2019; Felder et al., 2022; Kakoullis & Kelley, 2020), including the right to cultural participation of persons with disabilities which is at the core of this book. It is also premised on the idea that the CRPD can act 'as a tool for the transformation of how cultures think about disabled people' (Scully, 2012, p. 73), and it is thus vital to grasp barriers faced by persons with disabilities and dismantle them.

The CRPD epitomises the culmination of a long process of the emergence of disability rights (Stein, 2007), which occurred at the global level (Degener & Begg, 2017), as well in regional and national systems. As cursorily highlighted in the introduction to this book, such a process of development has been influenced by the wide academic debate on the social model of disability (Oliver, 1983, 1990, 1996, 2013; Dewsbury et al., 2004; Riddle, 2020; Shakespeare, 2013), which is rooted in the UK disability movement. In fact, the social model originated in the mid-1970s, being embedded in the manifesto of the British Union of the Physically Impaired Against Segregation (UPIAS), which put forward the idea that society disables people with impairments and distinguished the 'impairment' itself from the 'situation' of people with impairments, which entails a 'disability' (Finkelstein, 1980). Particularly influential has also been the US civil rights movement (Blanck, 2020; Charlton, 1998), which began to impact on US policy in the same

DOI: 10.4324/9781032619361-4

This chapter has been made available under a CC-BY-NC-ND 4.0 license.

period (around the 1970s) and led to the enactment of the Americans with Disabilities Act (ADA) in 1990 (Blanck, 2023a). The ADA, in turn, has been considered a significant advancement and, for some scholars, has represented the vanguard of EU equality law (Quinn & Flynn, 2012) and a trailblazer for the CRPD itself (Blanck, 2023b).

Degener and Begg (2017), in their chronological appraisal of the development of disability rights, suggest that persons with disabilities began to be recognised as 'subjects of human rights' only around the 2000s and were fully acknowledged as holders of rights with the approval of the CRPD by the UN General Assembly on 13 December 2006. With a somewhat similar trajectory, disability rights have also emerged at the national level (Kanter, 2003). While disability featured in several constitutional documents approved in the aftermath of the Second World War (Bianchi, 2013; Vadalà, 2009; WORLD Policy Analysis Center (WORLD), 2020), most of these constitutional provisions embedded the medical model of disability, whereby the focus was on the individual deficit (Barnes & Mercer, 2010). They were mainly geared towards 'curing' or 'protecting' persons with disabilities, rather than ensuring equal rights. According to the WORLD Policy Analysis Center (WORLD, 2020), only '12% of current constitutions adopted before 1970 prohibit discrimination against people with disabilities, compared to 71% of those adopted in 2010–2017', that is, after the entry into force of the CRPD.[1] Most recent constitutional texts or amendments have outlawed or revised outdated medicalised approaches and embraced the language of the CRPD and its human rights model. A notable example is the recent amendment to Article 49 of the Spanish Constitution that replaces the term 'diminished' ('*disminuidos físicos, sensoriales y psíquicos*') with 'people with disabilities' ('*personas con discapacidad*') and fully recognises that people with disabilities enjoy equal rights (BOE, 2024).

Against this background, and following these initial remarks, this chapter is divided into a further four sections. Section 2 presents the key features of the CRPD. It builds on the wealth of literature on the Convention and recalls the scholarly debate on the innovative aspects of the CRPD (amongst many others, Kakoullis & Kelley, 2020; Kayess & French, 2008; Mégret, 2008a, 2008b; Mégret & Msipa, 2014; Stein & Lord, 2009). This section does not aim to replicate existing work. Rather, it seeks to give the reader a broad overview of the CRPD and the scholarly debate surrounding its text. Section 3 focuses on the Convention's general principles, placing particular emphasis on accessibility and participation, and general obligations. Section 4 moves on to explore the human rights model of disability, stemming from the CRPD, which constitutes the theoretical framework of this book, and the

1 WORLD has also calculated that a significant number of national constitutions still contain restrictions on rights for people with disabilities or use outdated language that fails to acknowledge the role of social, legal, and environmental factors in causing disability.

intertwined conception of inclusive equality put forward by the UN Committee on the Rights of Persons with Disabilities (CRPD Committee). In that regard, building on the initial appraisal conducted in the introduction to the book and on our previous work (Ferri & Leahy, 2023), it highlights the way in which Article 30 CRPD is related to the human rights model of disability. Section 5 discusses the role of the CRPD Committee as a monitoring body and as a quasi-judicial body to support the analysis that will be set out in Part II of the book. Section 6 presents some concluding remarks. On the whole, this chapter, being inherently reconstructive, aims to locate discussions about cultural participation of persons with disabilities within contemporary debates on disability rights and to link to the CRPD.

## 2. The CRPD at a Glance

The CRPD is the first binding international human rights treaty that specifically addresses disability. Widely celebrated by disability advocates and equally praised by academics, it has been defined as 'revolutionary' (Perlin, 2009, 2014) because it 'sets out explicitly the many steps that States must take to create an enabling environment so that persons with disabilities can enjoy authentic equality in society' (Perlin, 2014, p. 538). It is considered a pioneering treaty, which, as Lawson (2007) puts it, 'require[s] the reshaping of societies in a way required by no other human rights treaty'. Much ink has been spilled on the CRPD and, as noted earlier, there is a wealth of scholarship on various facets of the CRPD. Building on this scholarship, the following subsections present the key features of the Convention but do not endeavour to offer a comprehensive discussion of its complexities.

### 2.1. *The Purpose of the CRPD*

The overt aim of the CRPD is to 'promote, protect and ensure the full and equal enjoyment of all human rights and fundamental freedoms by all persons with disabilities, and to promote respect for their inherent dignity'. It aims to ensure that all human rights already recognised and protected in existing human rights treaties are enjoyed by persons with disabilities on an equal basis with others (Della Fina, 2017; Kakoullis & Ikehara, 2018). It has also been suggested that the purpose of the CRPD is that of empowering 'disabled people by offering them entitlements in order to do so' (de Beco, 2021, p. 37). Dhanda (2008) argues that the CRPD

> has signalled the change from welfare to rights; introduced the equality idiom to grant both same and different to persons with disabilities; recognized autonomy with support for persons with disabilities and most importantly made disability a part of the human experience.

The CRPD re-reads and re-writes existing rights through the lens of disability. It is, however, well accepted that, while the rights per se articulated in the CRPD might not be new and are rooted in human rights law (this is certainly true for the right to cultural participation, as noted in the introduction of the book), yet the CRPD is greatly innovative. The way in which the rights are spelled out is novel, and some provisions are in fact quite new. This is the case in relation to the principle of accessibility and of 'reasonable accommodation'. In that regard, in one of the earliest and most cited commentaries on the CRPD, Kayess and French (2008) contend that

> [d]espite what might be characterised as the 'official fiction' that the CRPD does not set down any new human rights, it would seem clear that it has, in fact, modified, transformed and added to traditional human rights concepts in key respects. The CRPD does contain entirely new or amplified formulations of human rights, including a number of collective or social group rights.

In a similar fashion, Mégret (2008a, p. 510) asserts that the CRPD 'comes very close to either creating new rights or formulating rights in the context of disability that have never been framed as such'. In that regard, for example, de Beco (2022) posits that the right to *inclusive* education is a new right, that is differentiated from original articulations of the right to education. The originality of the CRPD is also linked to the level of detail included in its text. As Mégret (2008a, p. 504) puts it, 'the Convention makes a very significant effort to highlight, sometimes with considerable detail, how the rights it proposes to protect are to be implemented and guaranteed'. According to Perlin (2014, p. 538), the CRPD 'sets out explicitly the many steps that States must take to create an enabling environment so that persons with disabilities can enjoy authentic equality in society'. This is very true for Article 30 CRPD, which lays out a set of comprehensive obligations to ensure that people with disabilities can enjoy their right to culture on an equal basis with others. With such a detailed articulation of rights, the CRPD deeply challenges the traditional gap between (immediately attainable) civil and political rights and (progressively realised) socio-economic rights (Dhanda, 2008; Stein, 2007). In a similar way, de Beco (2019, 2021) posits that the CRPD blurs the distinction between these two traditional categories of rights.

On the whole, as MacKay, Chairman of the committee that negotiated the Convention, states, the CRPD endeavours 'to elaborate in detail the rights of persons with disabilities and set out a code of implementation' (United Nations, n.d.). In a similar vein, Quinn (2009b) highlights that the CRPD provides a 'moral compass' for change.

### 2.2. *The Personal Scope of the CRPD*

The personal scope of the CRPD extends to persons with disabilities, who include, according to Article 1, 'those who have long-term physical, mental, intellectual or sensory impairments which in interaction with various barriers may hinder their full and effective participation in society on an equal basis with others'. The non-binding Preamble, at recital (e), also affirms that 'disability is an evolving concept' and that disability 'results from the interaction between persons with impairments and attitudinal and environmental barriers'. In *S.C. v. Brazil* (CRPD Committee, 2014a), the CRPD Committee emphasised that 'the difference between illness and disability is a difference of degree and not a difference of kind' and that a 'health impairment which initially is conceived of as illness can develop into an impairment in the context of disability as a consequence of its duration or its chronicity'. In several cases against Tanzania, the CRPD Committee (2017, 2018a, 2019) argued that albinism falls within the personal scope of the Convention, which focuses on the barriers faced by people with impairments.

Having regard to the Preamble and Article 1(2) CRPD, some scholars contend that the CRPD embraces the social model of disability (Arstein-Kerslake, 2017). Kakoullis and Ikehara (2018) argue that Article 1(2) CRPD provides 'a description, rather than a definition, of the persons whose human rights the CRPD aims to protect' which is 'underpinned by a social model of disability'. In a similar vein, de Beco (2021, p. 37) argues that, even though the CRPD 'has not wholly adopted the social model of disability, it has in fact legally anchored this model in international human rights law'. Kayess and French (2008), while mentioning the social model as an 'intellectual antecedent' for Article 1(2) CRPD, contend that the Convention cannot be construed strictly in accordance with the social model. In a similar vein, Broderick (2015) and Broderick and Ferri (2019) refer to the CRPD as embracing a social-contextual model of disability. In fact, the Convention builds on the social model and takes into account cultural, discursive, and relational issues within disability experiences outlined by disability studies, discussed earlier in Chapter 1, but puts forward a refined version of the social model that focuses on the interaction between the impairment and external barriers, rather than solely on external barriers (Ferri, 2024).

## 2.3. *The Structure of the CRPD*

The CRPD consists of a preamble and 50 articles. It is complemented by an Optional Protocol (OP-CRPD), which enables individuals in a State Party to the Convention to bring a claim in respect of an alleged violation of his/her rights through submitting an individual communication to the CRPD Committee.

Articles 1 and 2 CRPD have an interpretive and explanatory character. Article 1 outlines the purpose of the Convention, while Article 2 contains definitions which are relevant to the CRPD. Articles 3–9 CRPD can be considered as cross-cutting provisions. Article 3 enunciates the CRPD's general principles, while Article 4 includes general obligations. Article 5 CRPD requires States Parties to 'prohibit all discrimination on the basis of disability'. Article 6 CRPD strives to ensure that States Parties recognise the multiple and intersectional nature of discrimination that women with disabilities face, while Article 7 CRPD aims to protect the rights of children with disabilities. By including these provisions, the CRPD recognises 'different layers of identity' of persons with disabilities (CRPD Committee, 2018c, para. 9). As noted earlier in Chapter 1, Article 8 recognises that awareness-raising is necessary to remove attitudinal barriers faced by people with disabilities and to allow for the full realisation of the paradigm shift intended by the CRPD. It requires States Parties to combat stereotypes 'through immediate, effective and appropriate measures' and to promote positive perceptions of persons with disabilities. Article 9 explicates the general principle of accessibility, which is enunciated in Article 3 CRPD.

Articles 10 to 30 provide for the substantive rights and obligations of the Convention. These encompass the broad spectrum of both civil and political rights as well as economic, social, and cultural rights. Those rights must be afforded to persons with disabilities on an equal basis with others, and States Parties must address environmental and socio-economic barriers, and combat stigma, all of which hamper the participation of people with disabilities in society. With regard to social rights, Kayess and French (2008, p. 31) contend that these provisions oblige States Parties to incorporate 'disability sensitive measures into mainstream service delivery' and to ensure 'the provision of necessary specialist services and special measures in a manner that facilitates the inclusion and participation of persons with disability within the general community'. None of these provisions can be read in isolation, and they must be interpreted in light of the general principles enunciated in Article 3. The violation of disability rights should be actionable and, according to Article 13 CRPD, States Parties shall *inter alia* 'ensure effective access to justice for persons with disabilities on an equal basis with others, including through the provision of procedural and age-appropriate accommodations'. Quinn (2009a) argues that Article 13 CRPD rounds out access rights in the context of justice and enables persons with disabilities to vindicate their rights.

Articles 31 to 40 broadly concern the implementation and monitoring of the CRPD. Article 31 has an instrumental nature, obliging States Parties to carry out extensive data collection in order to support the enactment of effective policy and to enhance the efficient implementation of the CRPD. Article 32 focuses on international cooperation as a tool to facilitate the realisation of the rights in the CRPD through, for example, the transfer of knowledge on key issues. Articles 33 to 40 set out the monitoring system of the CRPD. Notably, Article 33 requires the establishment of focal points, coordination mechanisms, and independent monitoring mechanisms at the national level (de Beco, 2013). Further, as will be discussed later, Article 34 provides for the establishment of a treaty body, the CRPD Committee, to monitor the implementation of the Convention at the international level.

The final ten provisions of the CRPD address the accession processes to, and the entry into force of, the Convention. Article 44 CRPD permits the accession of 'regional integration organizations', which are defined as organisations 'constituted by sovereign States of a given region, to which its member

States have transferred competence in respect of matters governed by the present Convention'. This provision was included specifically to allow for the accession of the European Union (EU) to the CRPD.

## 3. The General Principles and General Obligations of the CRPD

The CRPD revolves around the key principles of dignity, autonomy, non-discrimination, equality, accessibility, and participation, which are outlined in Article 3 and further elaborated on in several other provisions of the Convention (Kayess & French, 2008). General principles are complemented by general obligations laid out in Article 4 CRPD (Broderick, 2018). Both general principles and obligations guide States Parties in the implementation of the Convention and represent a benchmark against which States Parties can assess the conformity of domestic laws with the Convention (Broderick & Ferri, 2019).

### 3.1. *The General Principles of the CRPD*

The CRPD connects the principle of respect for human dignity with that of individual autonomy and freedom to make one's own choices. The latter principle has significant relevance for people with disabilities, who have experienced, and continue to face, deprivations of their legal capacity. In fact, this principle directly links to Article 12 on legal capacity (Series & Nilsson, 2018). Notably, Article 12 CRPD, which is one of the most debated provisions of the Convention, indicates that States Parties 'shall recognise that persons with disabilities enjoy legal capacity on an equal basis with others in all aspects of life'. Article 12(3) requires that States Parties 'shall take appropriate measures to provide access to persons with disabilities to the support they may require in exercising their legal capacity'. The CRPD Committee deliberately chose Article 12 as the topic of its first General Comment considering that there had been 'a general failure to understand that the human-rights-based model of disability implies a shift from the substitute decision-making paradigm to one that is based on supported decision-making' (CRPD Committee, 2014d). The principle of dignity and autonomy also links to Article 19 CRPD on independent living.

Non-discrimination is another general principle of the Convention. In that regard, Article 2 CRPD provides a broad definition of 'discrimination on the basis of disability', highlighting that such discrimination includes the denial of reasonable accommodation. The CRPD Committee (2022a), in *M.R. i V. v Spain*, has clarified that 'all forms of discrimination are equally contrary to the Convention'. It has also highlighted that it is 'inappropriate to differentiate among contraventions of the right to equality and non-discrimination in terms of their so called degree of seriousness' (CRPD Committee, 2022a). The duty to reasonably accommodate is defined in Article 2 CRPD as 'necessary and appropriate modification and adjustments', 'where needed in a particular case, to ensure to persons with disabilities the enjoyment or exercise on an equal basis with others of all human rights and fundamental freedoms'. Reasonable accommodation is individualised and entails an *ex nunc* duty, which is enforceable 'from the moment an individual with an impairment needs it in a given situation, for example, workplace or school, in order to enjoy her or his rights on an equal basis in a particular context' (CRPD Committee 2014b, para. 26, 2020). The denial of reasonable accommodation may be justified only if it constitutes a 'disproportionate' or 'undue burden'. By contrast, accessibility obligations are generalised and group-based and are unconditional. As affirmed by the CRPD Committee (2014c) in *Jungelin v. Sweden*, States Parties enjoy a margin of discretion when ascertaining if a burden can be regarded as 'undue' or 'disproportionate'.

The principle of non-discrimination enunciated in Article 3(b) CRPD is intertwined with that of equality of opportunity set out in Article 3(e), with gender equality mentioned in Article 3(f), and also with the principle of respect for difference contained in Article 3(d). In addition, it is connected to the principle of respect for the evolving capacities of children with disabilities in Article 3(h) CRPD. These general principles hint to a multidimensional approach to equality, which is the model of inclusive equality which will be discussed later. Further, equality and non-discrimination are articulated in Article 5 CRPD.

Article 3(f) CRPD characterises accessibility as a general principle. As noted already in Chapter 1, accessibility occupies a key position in the Convention, and references to this principle, further clarified in Article 9 CRPD, can be found in several other provisions such as Article 21 CRPD on accessibility of information and communication. Accessibility is conceived of as 'the precondition for persons with disabilities to live independently, participate fully and equally in society' (CRPD Committee 2014b, para. 14), but its nature of mere principle or enforceable individual right remains contested in scholarship (Broderick, 2020; Lawson, 2018). Article 9(1) CRPD requires States Parties to the Convention to

> take appropriate measures to ensure to persons with disabilities access, on an equal basis with others, to the physical environment, to transportation, to information and communications, including information and communications technologies and systems, and to other facilities and services open or provided to the public, both in urban and in rural areas.

Article 9(2) lays out the specific measures to be undertaken by States Parties, highlighting a range of access needs of different people with disabilities in different social contexts. Charitakis (2018, 2020) identifies several dimensions of accessibility as emerging from Article 9 CRPD: 'attitudinal accessibility, economic accessibility or affordability, physical accessibility, information accessibility and communication accessibility'. The first feature of accessibility 'refers to the removal of stigma and other negative behaviour that people with disabilities, their families and their caretakers experience throughout their lives' (Charitakis, 2018, p. 25). The second 'economic' dimension attaches to 'the idea that facilities, goods and services must be affordable to people with disabilities' (Charitakis, 2018, p. 26). The physical aspect of accessibility entails that all spaces, facilities, goods, and services must 'be adjusted so that they are accessible to persons with disabilities, with or without assistance' (Charitakis, 2018, p. 28). Charitakis (2018) also distinguishes information accessibility – which requires that general information about facilities, goods, and services as well about accessibility is to be made available to all – from communication accessibility – which directly concerns making available information in alternative modes and means of communication (e.g. Braille, large print, audio formats, and so on).

The CRPD Committee has discussed in some detail States Parties' obligations under Article 9 both in General Comment No. 2 (2014b) and in its jurisprudence. For example, in *Nyusti and Takàcs v Hungary* it posited that, while the CRPD does not impose obligations on private entities, States Parties must guarantee that such private entities offer accessible services and do not discriminate against persons with disabilities (CRPD Committee, 2013; see also 2018d). Further, the CRPD Committee (2014b, para. 24) has identified accessibility as an obligation subject to progressive realisation: albeit States Parties can implement it gradually, they 'should establish definite time frames and allocate adequate resources for the removal of existing barriers'.

Finally, the principle of full and effective participation and inclusion of people with disabilities in society features amongst the core objectives of the CRPD, and it is closely linked to the full enjoyment of both civil and political rights as well as economic, social, and cultural rights. The CRPD Committee (2018b, paras 27, 33) posits that full and effective participation necessitates 'engaging with all persons, including persons with disabilities, to provide for a sense of belonging to and being part of society' and can also represent a 'transformative tool for social change, and promote agency and empowerment of individuals'.

### 3.2. *The General Obligations of the CRPD*

Article 4 CRPD lists general obligations and requires States Parties to 'ensure and promote' the full realisation of the rights of persons with disabilities under the Convention by adopting legislative, administrative, financial, judicial, and all other necessary measures to ensure the achievement of the overarching purpose of the CRPD as laid out in Article 1. In addition, States Parties must review and amend national laws and policies to guarantee compliance with the CRPD, as well as mainstream disability in all their policies. In that regard, Article 4(1) hints at an inherent obligation for States Parties to carry out periodic screening to assess the compliance of policies and programmes with the CRPD. Besides, Article 4(1)(d) requires States Parties to maintain that public authorities and institutions act in compliance with the

Convention. This provision can be read in conjunction with Article 4(5), which affirms that the obligations laid out in the Convention 'extend to all parts of federal States without any limitations or exceptions' (Ferri et al., 2023). Article 4(1)(e) CRPD obliges States Parties to take all necessary measures to ban discrimination on the grounds of disability by persons, organisations, or private enterprises. Further, Article 4(1) CRPD includes an array of specific obligations that link to the principle of accessibility. These include the obligation to engage in or promote the research and development of new technologies and the obligation to provide accessible information about assistive technology to persons with disabilities.

Article 4(1)(i) CRPD requires States Parties to promote training on the rights provided for in the CRPD to those working with persons with disabilities. This tallies with awareness-raising obligations laid out in Article 8 CRPD. In particular, Article 8(2)(d) compels States Parties to promote training programmes on the rights of persons with disabilities. Training is also essential when it comes to the implementation of Article 9 CRPD. In its General Comment No. 2 on accessibility, the CRPD Committee (2014b, para. 19) affirms that 'since a lack of accessibility is often the result of insufficient awareness and technical know-how, Article 9 requires that States Parties provide training to all stakeholders on accessibility for persons with disabilities'. This affirmation of the CRPD Committee mirrors some of the findings of the literature examined in Chapter 1 in relation to accessibility in the cultural sector and resonates with the findings of the empirical research expounded in Part III, where OPDs placed great emphasis on the need to 'educate' cultural operators and make them knowledgeable about accessibility requirements.

Even though, as noted earlier, the CRPD blurs the distinction between civil and political rights, on the one hand, and social, economic, and cultural rights, on the other (de Beco, 2019), Article 4(2) CRPD recalls the traditional distinction between these rights. Namely, it differentiates between rights subject to immediate implementation (i.e. civil and political rights) and those that are to be realised progressively (i.e. economic, social, and cultural rights). It allows States Parties to realise socio-economic rights progressively, with a view to achieving their full protection and promotion over time because the realisation of these rights is often heavily dependent on the availability of resources. However, as highlighted by the UN Committee on Economic, Social and Cultural Rights (CESCR, 1990), progressive realisation should not be used a shield to refrain from implementing obligations but instead requires states to move 'as expeditiously and effectively as possible' and devote the maximum available resources towards the full realisation of rights. In its General Comment No. 4 on the right to education, the CRPD Committee commented on progressive realisation, reiterating that 'Article 4(2) requires that States parties take measures to the maximum of their available resources' and should act, 'where needed, within a framework of international cooperation, with a view to achieving progressively the full realization of those rights' (CRPD Committee, 2016a, para. 40). However, as noted by Broderick (2018), in spite of existing guidance on the concept of allocating the maximum available resources, the obligation remains unclear in its contours and in terms of priority-setting. The Committee has also recalled in line with the jurisprudence of other treaty bodies that progressive realization 'means that States parties have a specific and continuing obligation to move as expeditiously and effectively as possible towards the full realization of' the right (CRPD Committee, 2016a, para. 40). Furthermore, the CRPD Committee has stated that non-discrimination encompassing all internationally prohibited grounds of discrimination should also be implemented immediately in relation to the enjoyment of economic, social, and cultural rights (CRPD Committee, 2016a, para. 41). In connection with the right to education, the CRPD Committee also reiterated the transversal and immediate application of reasonable accommodations duties which are intrinsic to non-discrimination (CRPD Committee, 2016a, para. 41). This, as will be further explored in Part III, is relevant with regard to Article 30 CRPD which is not subject to immediate realisation.

Article 4(3) CRPD requires close consultation with, and the active involvement of, people with disabilities, through their representative organisations, in the development and implementation of legislation and policies and in all decision-making processes concerning issues relating to persons with disabilities. This provision embeds the slogan that was adopted by the disability rights movement during the negotiation process: 'Nothing About Us Without Us'. This provision is of key importance as the successful implementation of all provisions of the CRPD can only be achieved through the involvement of people with disabilities to identify challenges, concerns, gaps, and adequate policy solutions.

## 4. The CRPD Model of Disability

### 4.1. *The Human Rights Model of Disability*

Retief and Letšosa (2018) assert that, often, variants of the social model and the human rights model have been considered as synonymous. Degener and Gomez-Carrillo de Castro (2022, p. 43) have also highlighted that the CRPD Committee initially used the terms 'human rights model of disability' interchangeably with 'social model of disability', but currently it refers exclusively to the human rights model of disability.

In spite of such inconsistent terminological use, Degener (2017) authoritatively argues that the human rights model does not focus merely on social barriers but revolves around the human dignity of persons with disabilities, valuing impairments as part of human diversity (Degener, 2017). Further, this model 'encompasses both sets of human rights, civil and political as well as economic, social and cultural rights' and offers 'room for minority and cultural identification', unveiling the occurrence of intersectional discrimination (Degener, 2017). According to Degener (2017), the human rights model acknowledges the importance of public health policies that aim to prevent impairments. Finally, Degener (2017) posits that the human rights model is a tool to implement the CRPD and to achieve social justice. In that regard, in line with Lawson and Beckett (2020), Degener and Gomez-Carrillo de Castro (2022, p. 35) suggest that the human rights model 'provides a framework to conceptualize agency, rights and the content of rights' and recognises different experiences of impairment and disability. In its General Comment No. 8, the CRPD Committee (2022b, para. 7) reiterates the concerns expressed in its Concluding Observations (COs), which are transmitted to States Parties to the CRPD Committee within the remit of the reporting procedure which will be discussed later 'that the legislation and policies of States parties still reflect an ableist approach to disability, through charity and/or medical models, despite the incompatibility of those models with the Convention'.

As discussed in the introduction of this book, the CRPD Committee, in its General Comment No. 6 (2018c, para. 11), articulates the human rights model of disability around two intertwined conceptual axes: dignity and inclusive equality. First, in the acceptance of impairments as part of human diversity, the human rights model recognises the inherent dignity of people with disabilities and their self-worth (Ferri & Broderick, 2019). The CRPD Committee (2022b, para. 8) has recalled, most recently in General Comment No. 8, that

> [d]isability is acknowledged as one of many multidimensional layers of identity, meaning that laws and policies must take the diversity of persons with disabilities into account. Human rights are recognized as being interdependent, interrelated and indivisible.

### 4.2. *Inclusive Equality*

According to the CRPD Committee (2018c), the CRPD embraces a capacious view of equality that goes even further than substantive equality. It has hence articulated the model of inclusive equality, which embraces four dimensions:

1 a fair redistributive dimension: to address socio-economic disadvantages;
2 a recognition dimension: to combat stigma, stereotyping, prejudice, and violence and to recognise the dignity of human beings and their intersectionality;
3 a participative dimension: to reaffirm the social nature of people as members of social groups and the full recognition of humanity through inclusion in society; and
4 an accommodating dimension: to make space for difference as a matter of human dignity.

As noted by Ferri and Broderick (2019), the first dimension of this model of equality supports the adoption of widespread positive measures in the form of awareness-raising, accessibility measures, and general positive action measures (such as quotas and preferential treatment for persons with disabilities in certain circumstances). In that regard, de Beco (2023) suggests that the removal of barriers in society through the input of resources is an inherent part of the rights of people with disabilities and that the CRPD calls for the elaboration of a range of redistributive mechanisms, either in cash or in kind. The fourth accommodating dimension is underpinned by the idea put forward by the same CRPD Committee of the diversity of individuals with disabilities from one another (CRPD Committee, 2014a). It also makes reference to reasonable accommodation as provided for in Article 2 CRPD. This fourth dimension may also be linked with accessibility as a pre-condition for the effective implementation and the full enjoyment of all the rights set out in the CRPD. In fact, the acknowledgement of conceptual differences between accessibility and reasonable accommodation traced by the CRPD Committee (CRPD Committee, 2014b, 2018c) should go hand in hand with the search for 'practical synergies' (Lawson, 2017) in accommodating diversity.

### 4.3. *The Right to Participate in Cultural Life and Its Role in Realising the Human Rights Model of Disability and Inclusive Equality*

This book (and the analysis conducted in Parts II and III) is premised on the idea that the human rights model represents an important tool 'to challenge statements and practices which run in a contrary direction' (Lawson & Beckett, 2020, p. 21) in the cultural field. Further, as noted elsewhere (Ferri & Leahy, 2023) and recalled in the introduction to the book, the right to participate in cultural life is encompassed by, and essential for, the realisation of the human rights model. As will be further discussed in Chapter 3, culture is the expression of human nature. Hence, the right to participate in cultural life links to the acknowledgement of the inherent dignity of persons with disabilities. It is also indispensable to realise all four dimensions of inclusive equality. Enjoying culture is a vital part of personhood, of being a citizen and of being a fully-fledged member of society.

## 5. The CRPD Committee

### 5.1. *The CRPD Committee as a Monitoring Body*

As mentioned earlier, Article 34 CRPD provides for the establishment of the CRPD Committee, whose task is to examine States Parties' reports on the implementation of the Convention. The CRPD Committee is composed of 18 independent experts of high moral standing, who are elected from a list of persons nominated by States Parties for a four-year term, with the possibility of being re-elected once. These experts are elected taking into consideration the need for an equitable geographical distribution and gender balance.

The CRPD Committee gives an authoritative interpretation of the CRPD through General Comments, which include recommendations on how to implement specific provisions of the Convention. Legal scholarship affirms that General Comments have come to have 'quasi-legislative character' (Ando, 2012). Most recently, it has also been argued that General Comments 'can become influential instruments for norm development, and informal and formal decisions in human rights' (Lesch & Reiners, 2023, p. 379; see also McCall-Smith, 2016).

The CRPD Committee is also in charge of monitoring the implementation of the Convention. In that regard, Article 35 CRPD requires States Parties to submit regular reports to the Committee regarding the implementation of the Convention. The first report was to be submitted within two years after the entry into force of the Convention for the State Party concerned, and subsequent reports are due at least every four years thereafter. The Committee on Economic Social and Cultural Rights (CESCR) in its General Comment No. 1 (1981) has indicated the purposes of a reporting process. While the CESCR focused in particular on the process laid out in the International Covenant on Economic Social and Cultural Rights (ICESCR), such purposes are relevant generally in relation to reporting procedures of UN treaty bodies, including the CRPD Committee. The CESCR (1981) specifically indicated that the reporting procedure is intended to

1 review the State Party legislation, administrative rules and procedures, and practices which are in relevant areas;
2 to ensure that the State Party provides a realistic assessment of the actual human rights situation;
3 to enable State Parties to highlight the progress achieved in the realisation of human rights;
4 to facilitate public scrutiny of the State Party actions;
5 to establish a basis on which the State Party itself, as well as the UN treaty body, can effectively evaluate the extent to which progress has been made in the realisation of the rights provided in the treaty;
6 to enable the State Party to develop a better understanding of the problems and shortcomings encountered in efforts to realise the rights provided in the treaty;
7 to facilitate the exchange of information amongst State Parties with a view of developing a better understanding of the common problems they face and the measures needed to fully realise human rights.

In order to advise States Parties on the structure and content of their reports and to simplify the preparation of these reports, with a view to making the procedure more efficient and effective, the CRPD Committee has released Reporting Guidelines (CRPD Committee, 2009, 2016b). These guidelines also aim to ensure that States Parties' reports are comprehensive and presented in a uniform manner. For the purpose of this book, it is worth recalling that, under Article 30 CRPD, the CRPD Committee (2016b, para. 32) requires States Parties to specifically report *inter alia* on the following:

(a) Measures adopted to ensure that cultural, leisure, tourism and sporting facilities and services in the public and private sector are accessible to persons with disabilities, taking into account children with disabilities, including through the conditional use of public procurement and public funding;
(b) Measures adopted to ensure that cultural materials and contents are accessible to persons with disabilities, including through the use of information and communications technology;
(c) Measures to ensure that persons with disabilities enjoy access to television programmes, films, theatre and other cultural activities, in accessible formats;
(d) Measures adopted to recognise and promote the right of persons with disabilities to take part on an equal basis with others in cultural life, including opportunities to enable persons with disabilities to develop and utilize their creative, artistic and intellectual potential;
(e) Measures adopted, including participation in relevant international efforts such as the Marrakesh Treaty to Facilitate Access to Published Works for Persons Who Are Blind, Visually Impaired or Otherwise Print Disabled, to ensure that intellectual property laws do not become a barrier for persons with disabilities in accessing cultural materials;
(f) Measures adopted to recognize and support the specific cultural and linguistic deaf identity, including sign languages and deaf culture of persons with disabilities.

Article 36 CRPD enables the Committee to consider States Parties' reports and give recommendations. In particular, following a dialogue with the reporting state, and further to an initial List of Issues (LIs) to which states shall respond, the CRPD Committee adopts COs, which are transmitted to the state concerned and which are also made public. In critically examining the effectiveness of the reporting process in UN treaty bodies generally, Yoshida espouses that COs allow treaty bodies to raise concerns but also to indicate corrective measures that States Parties should take, providing them 'with clear understanding of the actions they need to take to advance human rights' (Yoshida, 2023, p. 169). This requires, however, COs to be clear and detailed if they are expected to change states' behaviours. This holds particularly true for the CRPD Committee, especially considering that the disability rights articulated in the CRPD present different layers of complexity and require States Parties to engage with an array of actions. Yoshida (2023) further argues that the role of treaty bodies is not punitive but must be apt to encourage States Parties to change their behaviour and must engage in dialogue with States and NGOs on controversial practices. Such dialogue does not stop with the COs. In the case of the CRPD, under the follow-up procedure, the CRPD Committee can require States Parties to focus on specific issues of concern that it has identified in its COs and provide written information on the adoption of the measures recommended by the Committee.

This reporting procedure, which is mandatory for all States Parties, allows the CRPD Committee not only to assess states' reports but also to consider shadow reports submitted by NGOs and OPDs in order to thoroughly evaluate the performance of states. Scholarship has investigated in a general fashion the role and effects of reporting procedures in international law, with a focus on UN Treaty bodies (including the CRPD Committee), and there is growing evidence that self-reporting to treaty bodies improves states compliance (*inter alia*, Creamer & Simmons, 2020).

States began the first cycle of reporting to the CRPD Committee in May 2010, two years after the treaty entered into force. As will be discussed in Chapter 4, at the time of writing, all Member States of the EU and the EU itself have submitted at least the initial report, with many of them having fully completed one cycle and having submitted a combined second and third report.

### 5.2. *The CRPD as a Quasi-Judicial Body in the Optional Protocol*

The OP-CRPD, which has not been ratified by all States Parties to the CRPD, provides for para-judicial enforcement mechanisms. First, it allows the CRPD Committee to receive and consider complaints – referred to as individual communications – 'from or on behalf of individuals or groups of individuals subject to its jurisdiction, who claim to be victims of a violation' of their rights recognised in the CRPD. As for all UN treaty bodies, the individual communications procedure empowers the CRPD Committee to adopt findings in disputes between an individual and a respondent State Party. However, as highlighted by Ulfstein (2012, p. 74),

> while the function of the treaty bodies in deciding individual complaints is comparable to that of courts, they are formally designated 'Committees', not courts; they receive 'Communications' rather than cases; they are composed of experts and not judges; their procedure is confidential and the proceedings are written, with no oral elements; and their decisions are termed 'Views' (or comparable denominations) rather than judgments. Thus their decisions in such cases are not 'judicial decisions' under article 38(1)(d) of the ICJ Statute.

Without engaging with admissibility issues and procedural requirements of individual communications, which are elucidated in other works (Broderick & Ferri, 2019), it suffices here to point out that, in line with general trends of UN Treaty bodies (Çalı & Galand, 2020), the CRPD Committee has adopted a rather broad approach to its jurisdiction as well as to the definition of victim status. Still, victimhood is a condition *sine qua non* for the CRPD Committee to hear the individual communication. In *A.M. v. Australia*, the CRPD Committee (2015) clarified that

> for a person to claim to be the victim of a violation of a right protected by the Convention, he or she must show either that an act or an omission of the State party concerned has already adversely affected his or her enjoyment of that right, or that such an effect is imminent, for example on the basis of existing law and/or judicial or administrative decision or practice.

Within the individual communication process, the CRPD Committee ascertains whether a violation of the CRPD has occurred. If so, in line with general UN treaty bodies practice, it can demand specific individual remedies on a case-by-case basis (Çalı & Galand, 2020). The individual complaints procedure, hence, allows for a detailed legal analysis of violations of individual disability rights, in some way unveiling the existence of systemic failures. It can also provide relief to victims. More broadly, however, such process can also contribute to the interpretation of CRPD norms and to carve out various facets of States Parties' obligations.

Notably, the OP-CRPD also empowers the CRPD Committee to conduct *ex officio* enquiries if it receives reliable information indicating grave or systemic violations of disability rights provided for in the CRPD.

## 6. Concluding Remarks

The CRPD has spurred change and evolution in international human rights law (Celik, 2017; de Beco, 2021). Thus far, it has had important spillover effects, emboldening disability policies elaborated by the UN and regional organisations. The CRPD has further propelled the development of supranational, particularly EU, disability law (Ferri, 2023, 2024; Ferri & Broderick, 2020; Ferri & Šubic, 2023), and has supported cross-fertilisation trends across regional human rights systems (Appiagyei-Atua, 2017; Cogburn & Kempin Reuter, 2017; Ferri & Broderick, 2019). Notably, the Convention has also prompted States Parties to adopt an array of national disability legislation and policies to implement CRPD provisions. In that regard, Stein and Bantekas (2021) contend that 'the CRPD's passage – and near-universal ratification – has engendered substantial law and policy reform, in part because states have been forced to consider for the first time, how to treat their largest minority group equally'. More generally, the CRPD has triggered a renewed attention to disability in society as well as in academic literature. Thus, the CRPD is the most relevant legal framework when discussing disability rights.

Embedding the key principles of dignity, autonomy, non-discrimination, equality, accessibility, and participation, the CRPD values disability as part of human diversity. It enshrines the human rights model of disability and adopts the multidimensional concept of inclusive equality. The latter concept as well as the interdependency and indivisibility of the rights provided for in the CRPD require that Article 30 be read taking into account the overall texture and fabric of the Convention. In fact, the shortcomings in the implementation of the right to participate in cultural life and the barriers that will be examined in Parts II and III do link to the failure to realise the general principles of the CRPD and other provisions. Conversely, the realisation of Article 30 CRPD can only be achieved in line with a general effort to promote CRPD compliance.

## References

Ando, N. (2012). General comments/recommendations. In R. Wolfrum (Ed.), *The Max Planck encyclopedia of public international law*. Oxford University Press.

Appiagyei-Atua, K. (2017). A comparative analysis of the United Nations Convention on the Rights of Persons with Disability and the African draft protocol on the rights of persons with disabilities. *Law, Democracy & Development*, *21*(1), 153–175.

Arstein-Kerslake, A. (2017). *Restoring voice to people with cognitive disabilities: Realizing the right to equal recognition before the law*. Cambridge University Press.

Barnes, C., & Mercer, G. (2010). *Exploring disability* (2nd ed.). Polity Press.

Bianchi, P. (2013). La tutela delle persone con disabilità nella prospettiva comparata. In C. Colapietro & A. Salvia (Eds.), *Assistenza inclusione sociale e diritti delle persone con disabilità* (pp. 364–382). Editoriale Scientifica.

Blanck, P. (2020). *Disability law and policy*. Foundation Press.

Blanck, P. (2023a). *Advanced introduction to U.S. disability law*. Edward Elgar.

Blanck, P. (2023b). On the importance of the Americans with Disabilities Act at 30. *Journal of Disability Policy Studies*, *34*(3), 176–198.

BOE (Boletín Oficial Del Estado). (2024, February 15). *Reforma del artículo 49 de la Constitución Española*. www.boe.es/boe/dias/2024/02/17/pdfs/BOE-A-2024-3099.pdf

Broderick, A. (2015). *The long and winding road to equality and inclusion for persons with disabilities*. Intersentia.

Broderick, A. (2018). Article 4. In I. Bantekas, M. A. Stein, & D. Anastasiou (Eds.), *The UN Convention on the Rights of Persons with Disabilities: A Commentary* (pp. 106–139). Oxford University Press.

Broderick, A. (2020). Of rights and obligations: The birth of accessibility. *The International Journal of Human Rights*, *24*(4), 393–413.

Broderick, A., & Ferri, D. (2019). *International and European disability law and policy. Text, cases and materials*. Cambridge University Press.

Çalı, B., & Galand, A. S. (2020). Towards a common institutional trajectory? Individual complaints before UN treaty bodies during their 'booming' years. *The International Journal of Human Rights*, *24*(8), 1103–1126.

Celik, E. (2017). The role of CRPD in rethinking the subject of human rights. *The International Journal of Human Rights*, *21*(7), 933–955.

Charitakis, S. (2018). *Access denied: The role of the European Union in ensuring accessibility under the United Nations Convention on the Rights of Persons with Disabilities*. Intersentia.

Charitakis, S. (2020). Accessibility of goods and services. In D. Ferri & A. Broderick (Eds.), *Research handbook on EU disability law* (pp. 221–242). Edward Elgar.

Charlton, J. I. (1998). *Nothing about us without us: Disability oppression and empowerment*. University of California Press.

Cogburn, D. L., & Kempin Reuter, T. (Eds.). (2017). *Making disability rights real in Southeast Asia: Implementing the UN Convention on the Rights of Persons with Disabilities in ASEAN*. Lexington Books.

Creamer, C. D., & Simmons, B. A. (2020). The proof is in the process: Self-reporting under international human rights treaties. *American Journal of International Law*, *114*(1), 1–50.

de Beco, G. (2013). *Article 33 of the UN Convention on the Rights of Persons with Disabilities. National structures for the implementation and monitoring of the convention*. Martinus Nijhoff Publishers.

de Beco, G. (2019). The indivisibility of human rights in light of the Convention on the Rights of Persons with Disabilities. *International and Comparative Law Quarterly*, *68*(1), 141–160.

de Beco, G. (2021). *Disability in international human rights law* (1st ed.). Oxford University Press.

de Beco, G. (2022). The right to 'inclusive' education. *Modern Law Review*, *85*(6), 1329–1356.

de Beco, G. (2023). The revival of human rights: A new perspective on human rights through the lens of disability. *Human Rights Quarterly*, *45*(4), 665–694.

Degener, T. (2017). *A new human rights model of disability*. In V. Della Fina, R. Cera, & G. Palmisano (Eds.), *The United Nations Convention on the Rights of Persons with Disabilities: A Commentary* (pp. 41–60). Springer.

Degener, T., & Begg, A. (2017). From invisible citizens to agents of change: A short history of the struggle for the recognition of the rights of persons with disabilities at the United Nations. In V. Della Fina, R. Cera, & G. Palmisano (Eds.), *The United Nations Convention on the Rights of Persons with Disabilities: A Commentary* (pp. 1–40). Springer.

Degener, T., & Gomez-Carrillo De Castro, T. (2022). Toward inclusive equality: Ten years of the human rights model of disability in the work of the UN Committee on the rights of persons with disabilities. In F. Felder, L. Davy, & R. Kayess (Eds.), *Disability law and human rights* (pp. 27–46). Springer.

Della Fina, V. (2017). Article 1: Purpose. In V. Della Fina, R. Cera, & G. Palmisano (Eds.), *The United Nations Convention on the Rights of Persons with Disabilities: A Commentary* (pp. 89–104). Springer.

Dewsbury, G., Clarke, K., Randall, D., Rouncefield, M., & Sommerville, I. (2004). The anti-social model of disability. *Disability & Society*, *19*(2), 145–158.

Dhanda, A. (2008). Constructing a new human rights Lexicon: Convention on the Rights of Persons with Disabilities. *SUR International Journal on Human Rights*, *5*(8), 43–59.

Felder, F., Davy, L., & Kayess, R. (2022). *Disability law and human rights*. Springer.

Ferri, D. (2023). The role of soft law in advancing the rights of persons with disabilities in the EU: A 'hybridity' approach to EU disability law. *European Law Journal*, *28*(4–6), 134–153.

Ferri, D. (2024). The role of disability studies in the advancement of EU law scholarship. In R. Deplano, G. Gentile, L. Lonardo, & T. Nowak (Eds.), *Interdisciplinary research methods in EU law: A handbook* (pp. 39–58). Edward Elgar.

Ferri, D., & Broderick, A. (2019). The European Court of human rights and the human rights model of disability convergence, fragmentation and future perspectives. In P. Czech, L. Heschl, K. Lukas, M. Nowak, & G. Oberleitner (Eds.), *European Yearbook on Human Rights 2019* (pp. 261–294). Intersentia.

Ferri, D., & Broderick, A. (2020). Introduction. In D. Ferri & A. Broderick (Eds.), *Research handbook on EU disability law* (pp. 1–10). Edward Elgar.

Ferri, D., & Leahy, A. (2023). The right of people with disabilities to participate in cultural life: Is Cinderella going to the ball? In S. Robinson & K. R. Fisher (Eds.), *Research handbook on disability policy* (pp. 102–117). Edward Elgar.

Ferri, D., Palermo, F., & Martinico, G. (Eds.). (2023). *Federalism and the rights of persons with disabilities. The implementation of the CRPD in federal systems and its implications*. Hart Publishing.

Ferri, D., & Šubic, N. (2023). The European Union: Federal trends in disability rights. In D. Ferri, F. Palermo, & G. Martinico (Eds.), *Federalism and the rights of persons with disabilities. The implementation of the CRPD in federal systems and its implications* (pp. 23–42). Hart Publishing.

Finkelstein, V. (1980). Attitudes and disabled people: Issues for discussion. *World Rehabilitation Fund*, *47*.

Kakoullis, E., & Ikehara, Y. (2018). Article 1: Purpose. In I. Bantekas, M. A. Stein, & D. Anastasiou (Eds.), *The UN Convention on the Rights of Persons with Disabilities: A Commentary* (pp. 35–62). Oxford University Press.

Kakoullis, E. J., & Kelley, J. (2020). *Recognising human rights in different cultural contexts: The United Nations Convention on the Rights of Persons with Disabilities (CRPD)*. Palgrave Macmillan.

Kanter, A. S. (2003). The globalization of disability rights law. *Syracuse Journal of International Law and Commerce*, *30*(2), 241.

Kayess, R., & French, P. (2008). Out of darkness into light? Introducing the Convention on the Rights of Persons with Disabilities. *Human Rights Law Review*, *8*(1), 26.

Lawson, A. (2007). The United Nations Convention on the Rights of Persons with Disabilities: New era or false dawn? *Syracuse Journal of International Law and Commerce*, *34*, 563–618.

Lawson, A. (2017). *Accessibility of information, technologies and communication for persons with disabilities. Contribution to the Council of Europe Strategy on the Rights of Persons with Disabilities*. Council of Europe. https://rm.coe.int/final-study-accessibility-of-information/168072b420

Lawson, A. (2018). Article 9: Accessibility. In I. Bantekas, M. A. Stein, & D. Anastasiou (Eds.), *The UN Convention on the Rights of Persons with Disabilities: A Commentary* (pp. 258–285). Oxford University Press.

Lawson, A., & Beckett, A. E. (2020). The social and human rights models of disability: Towards a complementarity thesis. *International Journal of Human Rights*, *25*(2), 348–379.

Lesch, M., & Reiners, N. (2023). Informal human rights law-making: How treaty bodies use 'general comments' to develop international law. *Global Constitutionalism*, *12*(2), 378–401.

McCall-Smith, K. L. (2016). Interpreting international human rights standards: Treaty body general comments as a chisel or a hammer. In S. Lagoutte, T. Gammeltoft-Hansen, & J. Cerone (Eds.), *Tracing the roles of soft law in human rights* (pp. 27–46). Oxford University Press.

Mégret, F. (2008a). The disabilities convention: Human rights of persons with disabilities or disability rights? *Human Rights Quarterly*, *30*(2), 494–516.

Mégret, F. (2008b). The disabilities convention: Towards a holistic concept of rights. *The International Journal of Human Rights*, *12*(2), 261–278.

Mégret, F., & Msipa, D. (2014). Global reasonable accommodation: How the Convention on the Rights of Persons with Disabilities changes the way we think about equality. *South African Journal on Human Rights*, *30*(2), 252–274.

Oliver, M. (1983). *Social work with disabled people*. Macmillan.

Oliver, M. (1990). *The politics of disablement*. Macmillan.

Oliver, M. (1996). *Understanding disability: From theory to practice*. Macmillan.

Oliver, M. (2013). The social model of disability: Thirty years on. *Disability & Society*, *28*(7), 1024–1026.

Perlin, M. L. (2009). A change is gonna come: The implications of the United Nations Convention on the Rights of Persons with Disabilities for the domestic practice of constitutional mental disability law. *Northern Illinois University Law Review*, *29*, 483.

Perlin, M. L. (2014). The ladder of the law has no top and no bottom: How therapeutic jurisprudence can give life to international human rights. *International Journal of Law and Psychiatry*, *37*(6), 535–542.

Quinn, G. (2009a). Short guide to the United Nations Convention on the Rights of Persons with Disabilities. *European Yearbook of Disability Law*, *1*, 89–114.

Quinn, G. (2009b). Resisting the 'temptation of elegance': Can the Convention on the Rights of Persons with Disabilities socialise states to right behaviour? In O. M. Arnardóttir & G. Quinn (Eds.), *The UN Convention on the Rights of Persons with Disabilities: European and Scandinavian perspectives* (pp. 215–256). Brill.

Quinn, G., & Flynn, E. (2012). Transatlantic borrowings: The past and future of EU non-discrimination law and policy on the ground of disability. *The American Journal of Comparative Law*, *60*, 23–48.

Retief, M., & Letšosa, R. (2018). Models of disability: A brief overview. *HTS Teologiese Studies/Theological Studies*, *74*(1).

Riddle, C. A. (2020). Why we do not need a 'stronger' social model of disability. *Disability & Society*, *35*(9), 1509–1513.

Scully, J. L. (2012). The Convention on the Rights of Persons with Disabilities and cultural understandings of disability. In J. Anderson & J. Philips (Eds.), *Disability and universal human rights: Legal, ethical, and conceptual implications of the Convention on the Rights of Persons with Disabilities* (pp. 71–84). Utrecht University.

Series, L., & Nilsson, A. (2018). Article 12 CRPD: Equal recognition before the law. In I. Bantekas, M. A. Stein, & D. Anastasiou (Eds.), *The UN Convention on the Rights of Persons with Disabilities: A Commentary* (pp. 339–380). Oxford University Press.

Shakespeare, T. (2013). The social model of disability. In L. J. Davis (Ed.), *The disability studies reader* (pp. 214–221). Routledge.

Stein, M. (2007). Disability human rights. *California Law Review*, *95*, 75.

Stein, M., & Lord, J. (2009). Future prospects for the United Nations Convention on disability. In G. Quinn & O. M. Arnardóttir (Eds.), *The UN Convention on the Rights of Persons with Disabilities: European and Scandinavian perspectives* (pp. 17–64). Brill.

Stein, M. A., & Bantekas, I. (2021). Including disability in business and human rights discourse and corporate practice. *Business and Human Rights Journal*, *6*(3), 490–513.

Ulfstein, G. (2012). Individual complaints. In H. Keller & G. Ulfstein (Eds.), *UN human rights treaty bodies: Law and legitimacy* (pp. 73–115). Cambridge University Press.

United Nations. (2006). *Convention on the Rights of Persons with Disabilities* (UN Doc. A/RES/61/106, Annex I).

United Nations. (n.d.). Department of Economic and Social Affairs – Social Inclusion. *The Convention in Brief*. www.un.org/development/desa/disabilities/convention-on-the-rights-of-persons-with-disabilities/the-convention-in-brief.html

United Nations Committee on Economic, Social and Cultural Rights (CESCR). (1981). *General Comment No. 1: Reporting by States Parties* (UN Doc. E/1989/22).

United Nations Committee on Economic, Social and Cultural Rights (CESCR). (1990). *General Comment No. 3: The nature of states parties' obligations* (UN Doc. E/1991/23).

United Nations Committee on the Rights of Persons with Disabilities (CRPD Committee). (2009). *Guidelines on treaty-specific document to be submitted by States Parties under article 35, paragraph 1, of the Convention on the Rights of Persons with Disabilities* (UN Doc. CRPD/C/2/3).

United Nations Committee on the Rights of Persons with Disabilities (CRPD Committee). (2013). *Nyusti and Takàcs v. Hungary* (Communication No. 1/2010, UN Doc. CRPD/C/9/D/1/2010).

United Nations Committee on the Rights of Persons with Disabilities (CRPD Committee). (2014a). *S.C. v. Brazil* (Communication No. 10/2013, UN Doc. CRPD/C/12/D/10/2013).

United Nations Committee on the Rights of Persons with Disabilities (CRPD Committee). (2014b). *General Comment No. 2 on Article 9: Accessibility* (UN Doc. CRPD/C/GC/2).

United Nations Committee on the Rights of Persons with Disabilities (CRPD Committee). (2014c). *Jungelin v. Sweden* (Communication No. 5/2011, UN Doc. CRPD/C/12/D/5/2011).

United Nations Committee on the Rights of Persons with Disabilities (CRPD Committee). (2014d). *General Comment No 1, Article 12: Equal recognition before the law* (UN Doc. CRPD/C/GC/1).

United Nations Committee on the Rights of Persons with Disabilities (CRPD Committee). (2015). *A.M. v. Australia* (Communication No. 12/2013, UN Doc. CRPD/C/13/D/12/2013).

United Nations Committee on the Rights of Persons with Disabilities (CRPD Committee). (2016a). *General Comment No. 4 (2016) on the right to inclusive education* (UN Doc. CRPD/C/GC/4).

United Nations Committee on the Rights of Persons with Disabilities (CRPD Committee). (2016b). *Guidelines on periodic reporting to the CRPD, including under the simplified reporting procedures adopted by the Committee at its 16th session* (UN Doc. CRPD/C/3).

United Nations Committee on the Rights of Persons with Disabilities (CRPD Committee). (2017). *X v. Tanzania* (Communication No. 22/2014, UN Doc. CRPD/C/18/D/22/2014).

United Nations Committee on the Rights of Persons with Disabilities (CRPD Committee). (2018a). *Y v. Tanzania* (Communication No. 23/2014, UN Doc. CRPD/C/20/D/23/2014).

United Nations Committee on the Rights of Persons with Disabilities (CRPD Committee). (2018b). *General Comment No. 7 on the participation of persons with disabilities, including children with disabilities, through their representative organizations, in the implementation and monitoring of the Convention* (UN Doc. CRPD/C/GC/7).

United Nations Committee on the Rights of Persons with Disabilities (CRPD Committee). (2018c). *General Comment No. 6 on equality and non-discrimination* (UN Doc. CRPD/C/GC/6).

United Nations Committee on the Rights of Persons with Disabilities (CRPD Committee). (2018d). *Bacher v. Austria* (Communication No. 26/2014, UN Doc. CRPD/C/19/D/26/2014).

United Nations Committee on the Rights of Persons with Disabilities (CRPD Committee). (2019). *Z. v. Tanzania* (Communication No. 24/2014, UN Doc. CRPD/C/22/D/24/2014).

United Nations Committee on the Rights of Persons with Disabilities (CRPD Committee). (2020). *JM v. Spain* (Communication No. 37/2016, UN Doc. CRPD/C/23/D/37/2016).

United Nations Committee on the Rights of Persons with Disabilities (CRPD Committee). (2022a). *M.R. i V. v. Spain* (Communication No. 48/2018, UN Doc. CRPD/C/26/D/48/2018).

United Nations Committee on the Rights of Persons with Disabilities (CRPD Committee). (2022b). *General Comment No. 8 on the right of persons with disabilities to work and employment* (UN Doc. CRPD/C/GC/8).

Vadalà, V. (2009). *La tutela delle disabilità*. Giuffrè.

WORLD Policy Analysis Center (WORLD). (2020). *Constitutional equal rights of people with disabilities*. www.worldpolicycenter.org/constitutional-equal-rights-of-people-with-disabilities

Yoshida, A. (2023). Beyond non-bindingness: States' implementation of UN human rights treaties bodies' concluding observations. *Nordic Journal of Human Rights*, *42*(2), 158–176.

# Part II

# The Right of Persons with Disabilities to Participate in Cultural Life

# 3 The Right of Persons with Disabilities to Participate in Cultural Life

*Delia Ferri*

## 1. Introduction

On foot of the multidimensional context expounded in Part I, this chapter discusses the normative content of Article 30 of the UN Convention on the Rights of Persons with Disabilities (CRPD), with a focus on participation in cultural life, critically engaging with the relevant jurisprudence of the UN Committee on the Rights of Persons with Disabilities (CRPD Committee). While building on existing commentaries and previous work, this chapter endeavours to carve out a novel perspective on Article 30 CRPD and to disentangle the obligations arising from this provision, with a view to supporting the analysis conducted in the following chapters. In line with the goal and scope of this book, this chapter does not engage with CRPD obligations relating to sport and leisure.

As highlighted in the introduction to this book, the right to participate in cultural life was first enshrined in Article 27 of the Universal Declaration of Human Rights (UDHR) (Stamatopoulou, 2007, 2012). Reference to cultural rights is also included in Article 22 UDHR, which, besides providing for the right to social security, states that everyone 'is entitled to realization, through national effort and international co-operation and in accordance with the organization and resources of each State, of the economic, social and *cultural* rights indispensable for his dignity and the free development of his personality'. Article 10 of the International Covenant on Civil and Political Rights (ICCPR) protects the right to freedom of expression in line with Article 19 UDHR, while Article 27 protects ethnic, religious, or linguistic minorities. However, Article 15(1)(a) of the International Covenant on Economic Social and Cultural Rights ICESCR explicitly recognises 'the right of everyone to take part in cultural life' (O'Keefe, 1998). Furthermore, other international provisions guarantee, to various extents, the right to participate in culture, to enjoy cultural heritage, and to articulate the collective cultural rights of minorities and indigenous peoples, which are also enshrined in soft law documents (Chow, 2022). In that regard, Chow (2018, p. 89) contends that 'the right to take part in cultural life is generally considered the broadest of all cultural rights' but highlights that 'references to cultural rights can be found

DOI: 10.4324/9781032619361-6
This chapter has been made available under a CC-BY-NC-ND 4.0 license.

scattered across various treaties', mentioning, for example, Article 29(1)(c) of the Convention on the Rights of the Child (CRC), which requires the education of the child to be directed to 'respect for the child's parents, his or her own cultural identity, language and values, for the national values of the country in which the child is living' and Article 31 of the Convention on Migrant Workers which refers to the 'cultural identity of migrant workers and members of their families'.

All European States within the scope of this book are signatories to, or have ratified, both the ICCPR and ICESCR. Further, they must implement a range of regional instruments. Within the remit of the Council of Europe (CoE), culture is considered a 'significant factor in the effective delivery of its core mission: to promote human rights, the practice of democracy and the rule of law among its member states' (Whyatt, 2023). The European Convention on Human Rights (ECHR) protects freedom of expression, which encompasses artistic and creative expression, but does not articulate cultural rights specifically. One of the earliest cases in which the European Court of Human Rights (ECtHR) established that Article 10 covered freedom of artistic expression under the freedom to receive and impart ideas was *Müller and Others v. Switzerland* in 1988 (ECtHR, 1988). Further, the ECtHR did engage with cultural rights to varying degrees in its decisions under other provisions of the ECHR (ECtHR, 2011). It has also considered the protection of heritage. Most recently in the case of *The J. Paul Getty Trust and Others v. Italy* (ECtHR, 2024, para. 340), the ECtHR stressed that

> the conservation of cultural heritage and, where appropriate, its sustainable use, have as their aim, in addition to the maintenance of a certain quality of life, the preservation of the historical, cultural and artistic roots of a region and its inhabitants.

Besides the ECHR, the CoE, through a range of bespoke hard and soft law instruments, has promoted culture as the 'soul of democracy' and supported 'access, participation and creativity, respect for identity and diversity, intercultural dialogue and cultural rights'.[1] In the European Union (EU), the Charter of Fundamental Rights (CFR) of the EU proclaims the freedom of the arts and sciences in Article 13 and establishes that the EU must 'respect cultural, religious and linguistic diversity' (Article 22 CFR).

While all these international and regional (i.e. European) provisions either are relevant to or apply to persons with disabilities, they do not address their specific needs. This gap has been filled by Article 30 CRPD. As noted earlier, this provision sheds light on the need for appropriate policies that enhance the cultural participation of persons with disabilities, and it is the focus of this chapter, in line with the overall approach adopted by the book.

1 See at www.coe.int/en/web/culture-and-heritage/culture.

Further to these brief remarks, this chapter first introduces the right to participate in cultural life and its multidimensional content and complexities (Section 2). This foregrounds the analysis of the obligations laid out in Article 30 CRPD (Section 3). Section 4 closes the chapter by recalling the key innovative dimensions of Article 30 CRPD, its role as the normative standard within the book, and reiterates its value within the human rights model of disability, which constitutes the theoretical framework of the book (as already mentioned in the introduction and in Chapter 2).

## 2. The Right to Participate in Cultural Life in International Law: Dimensions, Scope, and Complexities

The most prominent amongst cultural rights in international human rights law is considered the right to take part in cultural life (amongst other rights, such as the right of members of minorities to enjoy their own culture, practise their own religion, and speak their own language) (Donders, 2019, p. 62). However, the extent to which this right coexists and overlaps with other cultural rights is still subject to discussion. Donders (2019, p. 65) suggests that the very notion of 'cultural rights' is the 'first aspect of the complexity of these rights' and that it 'is remarkable that the category or group of cultural rights is often referred to as one single unit' instead of focusing on one or more substantive provisions. Without engaging with scholarly debates on cultural rights, which remain outside the scope of this book, this section briefly addresses the nuanced conceptual relationship between the right to culture and cultural rights and, building on existing scholarship and international jurisprudence, moves on to trace the boundaries of this right and highlight its complexities.

### 2.1. *Cultural Rights: Nuances and Blurred Lines*

Some scholars interpret cultural rights as 'legal entitlements to the protection and promotion of a given culture by the state' (de Vries, 2022) or connect cultural rights to the idea of cultural diversity which can challenge the very idea of universal human rights (*inter alia*, Logan, 2012). According to Donders (2019, p. 16), cultural rights 'can be broadly defined as those human rights that directly promote and protect the cultural interests of individuals and communities, and that are meant to advance their capacity to preserve, develop and change their cultural identity'. According to this author, cultural rights 'is an umbrella notion that covers provisions containing rights that explicitly refer to culture and rights that have a direct link with culture' (Donders, 2019, p. 65). However, those rights are often investigated as – and somewhat identified with – the core yet multilayered right to partake in culture provided in Articles 27 UDHR and Article 15 ICESCR (Chow, 2018, p. 89). This is linked to the fact that, as McGoldrick (2007) notes, international instruments embed a limited notion of cultural rights, 'both quantitatively and qualitatively', which mostly do connect to the right to participate in cultural life. In this regard, Donders (2012) states that many UNESCO instruments do focus on culture and reaffirm the importance of cultural rights, but 'only seldom do these instruments include cultural rights to be invoked by individuals or communities and those that do are not legally binding', such as the UNESCO Declaration on Cultural Diversity (UNESCO, 2001). Article 5 of this Declaration confirms a clustered approach to cultural rights but also somewhat confirms a focus on cultural participation, albeit broadly conceived of, by stating:

> Cultural rights are an integral part of human rights, which are universal, indivisible and interdependent. [. . .] All persons have therefore the *right to express themselves and to create and disseminate their work in the language of their choice, and particularly in their mother tongue*; all persons are entitled to quality education and training that fully respect their cultural identity; and all persons have the right to *participate in the cultural life* of their choice and *conduct their own cultural practices*, subject to respect for human rights and fundamental freedoms.
>
> (emphasis added)

### 2.2. *A Layered Right*

As noted earlier and in the introductory chapter to this book, Article 27 UDHR is the first formulation of the right to participate in cultural life (Cerqueira, 2023). Mirroring Article 27 UDHR, Article 15 ICESCR remains the most important articulation of this right in international human rights law, although this right, as mentioned earlier, has been further enshrined in other instruments, and protected in regional systems. It provides for the right to take part in cultural life (Article 15(1)(a)); the right to enjoy the benefits of scientific progress and its applications (Article 15(1)(b)); and the right to benefit from the protection of the moral and material interests resulting from any scientific, literary, or artistic production of which an individual is the author (Article 15(1)(c)) (Saul et al., 2014; Chow, 2018). As noted by the UN Committee on Economic Social and Cultural rights (CESCR) (CESCR, 2009, para. 2) in its General Comment No. 21:

> [T]he right of everyone to take part in cultural life is [. . .] intrinsically linked to the right to education (Arts. 13 and 14), through which individuals and communities pass on their values, religion, customs, language and other cultural references, and which helps to foster an atmosphere of mutual understanding and respect for cultural values. The right to take part in cultural life is also interdependent on other rights enshrined in the Covenant, including the right of all peoples to self-determination (Art. 1) and the right to an adequate standard of living (Art. 11).

The CESCR (2009, para. 6) has further highlighted that the right to take part in cultural life requires

> from the State party both abstention (i.e. non-interference with the exercise of cultural practices and with access to cultural goods and services) and positive action (ensuring preconditions for participation, facilitation and promotion of cultural life, and access to and preservation of cultural goods).

Notably, the CESCR (2009, paras. 14–15) further identifies 'three interrelated main components of the right to participate or take part in cultural life: (a) participation in, (b) access to, and (c) contribution to cultural life' and defines these three dimensions by stating:

> (a) *Participation* covers in particular the right of everyone – alone, or in association with others or as a community – to act freely, to choose his or her own identity, to identify or not with one or several communities or to change that choice, to take part in the political life of society, to engage in one's own cultural practices and to express oneself in the language of one's choice. Everyone also has the right to seek and develop cultural knowledge and expressions and to share them with others, as well as to act creatively and take part in creative activity;
> (b) *Access* covers in particular the right of everyone – alone, in association with others or a community – to know and understand his or her own culture and that of others through education and information, and to receive quality education and training with due regard for cultural identity. Everyone has also the right to learn about forms of expression and dissemination through any technical medium of information or communication, to follow a way of life associated with the use of cultural goods and resources such as land, water, biodiversity, language or specific institutions, and to benefit from the cultural heritage and the creation of other individuals and communities;
> (c) *Contribution to cultural life* refers to the right of everyone to be involved in creating the spiritual, material, intellectual and emotional expressions of the community. This is supported by the right to take part in the development of the community to which a person belongs, and in the definition, elaboration and implementation of policies and decisions that have an impact on the exercise of a person's cultural rights.
>
> (CESCR, 2009, para. 15)

The terminology used in General Comment No. 21 (CESCR, 2009), in subsequent soft law and in scholarly work, remains somewhat blurred. Chow (2018, p. 105) suggests that 'as culture encompasses a vast range of human activities, the right to take part in cultural life may embody a wide array of rights'. In that regard, Chow (2018, p. 105) highlights that the right to culture:

> entails, *inter alia*, the right to popular participation in cultural life (including access to cultural institutions and participation in creative activities), the right to intellectual property, the right to education, the right of minorities to preserve and maintain their cultural distinctiveness (such as the right to use their own language, to practise their religion, to preserve their heritage and to use, develop and conserve their land) and the right to cultural identity.

In fact, the majoritarian approach is that of considering 'participation' as an umbrella term that covers active and passive forms of participation (Chow, 2018, p. 111; Donders, 2019, p. 71). As mentioned earlier in the introduction, the former occur where the individual is contributing to cultural life, 'creating meaning' and contributing directly and explicitly to the production of the cultural experience itself (CESCR, 2009; OECD, 2022, p. 44), but also encompass the right of everyone to choose their own identity (CESCR, 2009). Passive participation hints at 'access' or consumption of culture (OECD, 2022, p. 44). Laaksonen (2010, p. 18) suggests that participation in cultural life can be understood as access but also as 'being able to have a say in decision-making processes, expressing an opinion, using creative self-expression or enjoying diverse cultural experiences'. She also maintains it 'enables people to associate with a particular community and to contribute to the design and formulation of policies for it' (Laaksonen, 2010, p. 18).

The right to participate in cultural life can be considered to encompass (or tally with) what have been defined as 'cultural heritage rights', articulated overtly in several international and regional instruments (*inter alia*, Donders, 2020; Francioni, 2011; Vícha, 2014; Francioni & Vrdoljak, 2020; Guangyu, 2023). Such rights, as Guangyu (2023) notes, have been subject to an evolving and broadening interpretation and have attracted a wealth of scholarly attention. The CESCR General Comment No. 21 mentions heritage at various junctures but engages with it in a somewhat limited way. Other documents, such as the 2011 report of the independent expert in the field of cultural rights, Farida Shaheed (Human Rights Council, 2011), have elaborated a capacious interpretation of the 'the right of access to and enjoyment of cultural heritage' as encompassing the right of individuals and communities

> to, *inter alia*, know, understand, enter, visit, make use of, maintain, exchange and develop cultural heritage, as well as to benefit from the cultural heritage and creations of others, without political, religious, economic or physical encumbrances. Individuals and communities cannot be seen as mere beneficiaries or users of cultural heritage.

> Access and enjoyment also imply contributing to the identification, interpretation and development of cultural heritage, as well as to the design and implementation of preservation/safeguard policies and programmes.
>
> (Human Rights Council, 2011, para. 58)

The CESCR General Comment No. 21 focuses on individual prerogatives within the layered right to participate in cultural life. However, this General Comment also alludes to a collective dimension of the right when speaking of the duty of States Parties to 'respect and protect cultural heritage of all groups and communities, in particular the most disadvantaged and marginalized individuals and groups, in economic development and environmental policies and programmes' (CESCR, 2009, para. 50(b)). It is questioned nevertheless whether Article 15 ICESCR does articulate a collective right (Leckie & Gallagher, 2006). While it is generally accepted that culture requires the recognition of collective rights of those communities that share common cultural values (Donders, 2016), Article 15 ICESCR does not take a clear-cut approach in this respect. A similar suggestion has been made in relation to Article 27 ICCPR. This provision does protect 'cultural rights exercised jointly in communities with others', but such rights 'despite their quasi-collective form remain of an individual nature' (Sikora, 2021).

Thus far, legal scholarship tends to interpret Article 15 ICESCR and, more generally, the right to participate in cultural life, as encompassing the *individual* right to access cultural activities, goods and services, and heritage and be actively involved in culture, and the right of cultural *communities* to be recognised, protected, and enabled to enjoy their cultural expressions (EPRS, 2017, pp. 10 and 27; UNESCO, 2009). This entails a collective dimension of individual rights pertaining to those belonging to cultural communities but also collective rights of communities as such. In a similar fashion, Article 27 ICCPR is recognised as having both individual and collective dimensions, based on the fact that 'all cultural rights are two-dimensional, regardless of how the norms are constructed' (Sikora, 2021, p. 157).

Besides appraising its layered content and multiple dimensions, the right to participate in cultural life must be interpreted in light of the general principle of non-discrimination (Chow, 2018, p. 101). In that regard, as will be further discussed, it must be afforded to persons with disabilities.

### 2.3. *Material Scope*

The right to participate in cultural life is often perceived to be ambivalent and 'remains contested' (Bantekas et al., 2018, p. 865), not only because of the dimensions of participation that it encompasses but also because the interpretation of culture varies widely and tends to be broad.

As recalled earlier, the CESCR (2009), in General Comment No. 21, has adopted a concept of culture which encompasses 'all manifestations of human existence'. The CESCR (2009) also states that the 'expression "cultural life" is an explicit reference to culture as a living process, historical, dynamic and evolving, with a past, a present and a future'. In that regard, the definition of culture provided by the CESCR embraces cultural practices in the traditional 'highbrow' sense (e.g. art, literature, classical music, theatre and architecture, and so on), 'popular culture', meaning the 'creative expressions of the general public – such as popular, folk and contemporary music, films, commercial radio and television and other leisure-related activities including organised sports and social events' (Chow, 2018, p. 106; O'Keefe, 1998), as well as culture in the 'anthropological sense' as a 'way of life', encompassing values, beliefs, and ways of doing things (Ferri, 2008, 2009). The notion of culture also subsumes that of tangible and intangible cultural heritage. Further, as recalled by Donders (2019, p. 69), 'while culture as a concept may be referred to in the singular, it should actually be understood as being plural' as cultures. This author also maintains that 'cultures . . . have an individual and a collective dimension, because they are developed and shaped by individuals and by communities' (Donders, 2019, p. 69).

This broad notion of culture/s has been consistently alluded to or openly referred to in UNESCO soft law and in UNESCO treaties, consolidating a broad and inclusive understanding of culture and one that supports a capacious understanding of the right itself. In fact, layers of participation are intertwined with different facets of culture as a multifarious concept.

### 2.4. *Progressive Realisation*

A final aspect to be highlighted is that the right to participate in cultural life (as with all economic, social, and cultural rights) is subject to progressive realisation (Corkery & Saiz, 2020; Kaliq & Churchill, 2012). Article 2(1) ICESCR establishes that each State Party undertakes to implement the rights provided for in that treaty 'to the maximum of its available resources, with a view to achieving progressively the full realisation of the rights recognised in the present Covenant'.

The principle of progressive realisation has been a bone of contention since the very beginning, and it has been used as a shield against the justiciability of economic, social, and cultural rights (Kędzia, 2022). However, the CESCR has consistently held that the principle does not remove the obligations under the ICESCR and does not empty rights of their meaningful content. In its General Comment No. 3, the CESCR (1990, para. 9) has indicated that:

> The concept of progressive realization constitutes a recognition of the fact that full realization of all economic, social and cultural rights will generally not be able to be achieved in a short period of time. [. . .] It is on the one hand a necessary flexibility device, reflecting the realities of the real world and the difficulties involved for any country in ensuring full realization of economic, social and cultural rights. On the other hand, the phrase must be read in the light of the overall objective, indeed the

> *raison d'être*, of the Covenant which is to establish clear obligations for States parties in respect of the full realization of the rights in question. It thus imposes an obligation to move as expeditiously and effectively as possible towards that goal.

Consistent with this understanding, the CESCR has generally indicated that States Parties should adopt actions, plans, and policies to realise ICESCR rights, which should be reported adequately to the CESCR (CESCR, 1990).

The CESCR has also indicated that 'retrogressive measures' require 'the most careful consideration' and need to be fully justified 'in the context of the full use of the maximum available resources' (CESCR, 1990, para. 9). It its Statement on Public Debt, Austerity Measures and the International Covenant on Economic, Social and Cultural Rights (CESCR, 2016, para. 4), following earlier statements released in the context of the financial crisis, the CESCR highlighted that when the adoption of 'retrogressive measures is unavoidable, such measures should be necessary and proportionate, in the sense that the adoption of any other policy or failure to act would be more detrimental to economic, social and cultural rights'. However, even in the presence of retrogressive measures, in line with Article 4 ICESCR,[2] the minimum core of the right cannot be undermined (Brems, 2009; Kędzia, 2020, 2022).

### 2.5. *The Relative 'Invisibility' of Disability*

As noted at various junctures in this book, Article 15 ICESCRas well as other articulations of the right to participate in cultural life apply to all individuals including persons with disabilities. This was reiterated by the CESCR in its General Comment No. 5 (1994). However, provisions in human rights instruments do not include an explicit disability dimension. The CRC constitutes the most notable exception. Article 23 CRC on children with disabilities, on the one hand, refers generally to the need to 'facilitate the child's active participation in the community', while, on the other, it only requires States Parties to afford to children with disabilities 'recreation opportunities in a manner conducive to the child's achieving the fullest possible social integration and individual development, including his or her *cultural* and spiritual development' (emphasis added).

Given the dearth of disability references, the CESCR General Comment No. 5 on persons with disabilities had the notable merit of highlighting that the effects of disability-based discrimination have been particularly severe in, *inter alia*,

2 This provision clarifies that ' . . . the State may subject such rights only to such limitations as are determined by law only insofar as this may be compatible with the nature of these rights and solely for the purpose of promoting the general welfare in a democratic society'. Article 4 ICESCR does not speak of the 'essence' of rights and does not mention a minimum core, but according to scholars 'such obligation not to violate the "nature" of rights must be understood as being very similar to protecting their essence' (Thielbörger, 2019).

cultural life as well as access to public places and services (CESCR, 1994, para. 15). In this General Comment the CESCR also highlights the importance of accessibility of physical premises and content (CESCR, 1994, paras. 36–37). It also encourages States Parties to adopt measures 'to dispel prejudices or superstitious beliefs against persons with disabilities' (CESCR, 1994, para. 38). Subsequently, in its General Comment No. 21 on Article 15 ICESCR, the CESCR further cast a light on the needs of persons with disabilities. By recalling the Standard Rules on the Equalization of Opportunities for Persons with Disabilities (Standard Rules) (United Nations, 1993), it affirms that

> persons with disabilities have the opportunity to utilize their creative, artistic and intellectual potential, not only for their own benefit, but also for the enrichment of their community, be they in urban or rural areas, and that States should promote accessibility to and availability of places for cultural performances and services.
>
> (CESCR, 2009, para. 30)

The CESCR also establishes that 'in order to facilitate participation of persons with disabilities in cultural life, States parties should, *inter alia*, recognize the right of these persons to have access to cultural material, television programmes, films, theatre and other cultural activities, in accessible forms' and should have access to monuments and places of cultural importance (CESCR, 2009, para. 31). It moves on to highlight disabled people's 'specific cultural and linguistic identity, including sign language and the culture of the deaf'. However, General Comment No. 21 also unveiled that the cultural rights of persons with disabilities had been neglected for a long time.

The absence of a disability dimension is not only a feature of core UN human rights treaties. In fact, other international treaties and soft law that deal with cultural rights or culture in broad terms are mostly silent with regard to people with disabilities. The 2005 UNESCO Convention on the Protection and Promotion of the Diversity of Cultural Expressions mentions, in Article 7, that States Parties shall endeavour 'to create in their territory an environment which encourages individuals *and social groups*' (emphasis added) *inter alia* 'to create, produce, disseminate, distribute and have access to their own cultural expressions' but does not mention persons with disabilities explicitly. Further, this provision also requires States Parties to pay 'attention to the special circumstances and needs of [. . .] various social groups'. Measures reported under this provision by States Parties, particularly in the most recent reports, refer to persons with disabilities only occasionally.[3]

3 Amongst EU Member States, which represent the geographical scope of this book, see, for example, the Irish periodic report from 2020 that indicates: 'Investments are focused on supporting direct engagement with creativity (e.g. on education, institutions, industry, etc.) as well as creativity as a way of engaging with broader societal issues (e.g. mental illness, social

Against this background, Article 30 CRPD, which will be discussed in the next section, is a key innovation in the landscape of international cultural rights, in that, for the first time, it highlights the specific needs of persons with disabilities when it comes to the cultural domain.

## 3. The Right to Participate in Cultural Life in the CRPD

The Standard Rules (United Nations, 1993) for the first time included an explicit provision on culture and can be considered the forerunner for Article 30 CRPD. In particular, Rule 10 on 'Culture' used 'phraseology and ideas' that influenced the drafting of paragraphs (1) and (2) of Article 30 CRPD (Bantekas et al., 2018, p. 866). In spite of building on the Standard Rules formulation and hinting at the normative content of Article 15 ICESCR, the CRPD *Travaux Préparatoires* showcase a certain uneasiness as regards the notion of cultural rights which were not regarded as a priority during the drafting (Bantekas et al., 2018, p. 867). The idea of dealing in a single provision with participation in culture, as well as in leisure, sports, and recreational activities, was also subject to discussion. Yet, ultimately, the wording of Article 30 CRPD included four paragraphs concerning various facets of cultural participation, followed by a comprehensive paragraph dealing with recreational, leisure, and sporting activities.

### 3.1. *The Normative Facets of Article 30 CRPD and Its Scope*

The first four paragraphs of Article 30 CRPD recognise the right of persons with disabilities to take part in cultural life. As noted earlier in this book, this provision is multifaceted and capacious in that it encompasses the twofold individual dimension of the right – that is, the right to access cultural activities, goods, services and heritage, and the right to active involvement in culture, which includes engagement in the creation of cultural activities, goods, and services (Romainville, 2015; OHCHR, 2020). It also embraces and protects a collective aspect referring explicitly to the 'specific cultural and linguistic identity' of persons with disabilities and mentioning explicitly Deaf culture.

As noted by Bantekas et al. (2018, p. 876) the right of people with disabilities to partake in culture encompasses 'the freedom to enjoy (read: "consume") culture, but also the freedom to pursue and contribute to every aspect of

---

marginalisation, rural isolation, poverty, isolation of the aged, *individuals with disabilities* or special needs, migrant integration, intercultural dialogue, climate action, biodiversity loss, etc.)' (emphasis added). The report can be found at www.unesco.org/creativity/sites/default/files/dce003/QPR_2020_IE_a3a57404-26a0-439e-9228-4a257632f079.pdf. In the latest reports, measures focused on accessibility of culture for persons with disabilities were reported, for example, in Italy, while general measures to support cultural participation without discrimination were reported in several other EU Member States (see e.g. Greece or Austria), and all reports are retrievable at www.unesco.org/creativity/en/policy-and-monitoring/periodic-reports.

cultural life'. In line with well-established interpretations of the right to participate in cultural life, it also implies that States Parties should ensure the participation of people with disabilities in the decision-making processes of cultural policies affecting them through effective and meaningful consultations. This tallies with the general principle of participation articulated in Article 3 CRPD and with the general obligation to 'consult with and actively involve persons with disabilities, including children with disabilities, through their representative organizations' in all matters affecting them provided in Article 4(3) CRPD.

Scholars have highlighted that the material scope of the application of Article 30 CRPD overlaps with that of Article 15 ICESCR, meaning that it embraces a wide understanding of culture as a way of life. In fact, the wording of the provision alludes to what has been defined as 'high culture' when it refers, for example, to theatre and to popular culture, making reference to television programmes or tourism services, as well as to the anthropological meaning of culture when it refers to 'cultural identity'. In this regard, Bantekas et al. (2018, p. 881) suggest that Article 30(1) can contribute to further democratise culture and realise what has been characterised as 'cultural democracy' (Belfiore et al., 2023), in line with the idea that culture is a social good that should be available to everyone in a democratic society (European Commission, 2023; Hadley, 2021).

Article 30 CRPD is subject to progressive realisation, in line with what is generally established for economic, social and cultural rights in Article 4(2) CRPD. As the Office of the High Commissioner of Human Rights (OHCHR, 2007) has stated, progressive realisation is 'a practical device that acknowledge(s) the real world challenges' and aims to avoid 'overburdening states, employers and other duty-bearers' such as, in this case, cultural organisations. As discussed in Chapter 2 of this book, while on the whole cultural rights must be realised progressively, the non-discrimination obligations underpinning them, that is, the duty of States Parties to ensure that the right to participate in culture is enjoyed without discrimination, need to be implemented immediately and without delay. The following subsections first address the right to access cultural life, as provided by Article 30(1) CRPD and further explore the obligation that laws protecting intellectual property rights, particularly copyright, 'do not constitute an unreasonable or discriminatory barrier' to access to cultural materials. Then they examine the obligation of States Parties to take appropriate measures that enable persons with disabilities to develop and use their creative, artistic and intellectual potential, as articulated in Article 30(2) CRPD, moving on to discuss the collective dimension of the right to cultural participation.

### 3.2. *The Right to Access Culture*

Article 30(1) CRPD requires States Parties to recognise 'the right of persons with disabilities to take part on an equal basis with others in cultural life' and to 'take all appropriate measures' to ensure that persons with disabilities can access cultural materials, television programmes, films, theatre and other cultural activities, in accessible formats, as well as access 'places for cultural performances or services, such as theatres, museums, cinemas, libraries and tourism services, and, as far as possible, enjoy access to monuments and sites of national cultural importance'. The list of cultural goods, services, and heritage is not exhaustive (Manca, 2017, p. 544), leaving it to States Parties to ensure that what is considered to have cultural value (tangible or intangible) is rendered accessible to people with disabilities.

This provision alludes to what is defined as the 'passive' facet of the right to participation as it focuses on access. However, 'access', as noted by Laaksonen (2010, p. 17), is a concept 'linked to inclusion, representation and promotion of citizenship' and does not coincide with inaction. Further, it should not be conceived of in a consumeristic way but read through a human rights lens.

The equality obligation stemming from this provision, that is, the duty of States Parties to abolish and refrain from discriminatory practices as well as to actively combat discrimination in the cultural sphere, must be implemented immediately. This obligation also entails redressing the socio-economic disadvantage faced by persons with disabilities through positive measures such as discounts in museums or free entrance for personal assistants. It also entails the duty to afford people with disabilities with reasonable accommodation to access cultural goods, services, and heritage when needed in a particular case and on the basis of a personal and distinct need, taking into account the individualised characterisation of the reasonable accommodation duty (CRPD Committee, 2014, paras. 25–26).

The accessibility obligation, that is, the obligation to dismantle accessibility barriers, is conveyed through overt references to access and accessible formats. Such an obligation links to, and should be read in light of, the general principle of accessibility, mentioned in Article 3 CRPD and set out in Article 9 CRPD, and discussed earlier in Chapter 2. It also connects to Article 21 CRPD, providing for freedom of expression and opinion and access to information. Article 30(1) CRPD is underpinned by the understanding that physical and content inaccessibility (highlighted by extensive literature discussed in Chapter 1 of this book) are key barriers for persons with disabilities in the exercise of their cultural rights.

It is evident from the wording of Article 30 CRPD that accessibility must be realised progressively and, with regard to heritage, as far as is feasible. This is consistent with the CRPD understanding that

> [a] clear distinction should be drawn between the obligation to ensure access to all newly designed, built or produced objects, infrastructure, goods, products and services and the obligation to remove barriers and ensure access to the existing physical environment and existing transportation, information and communication, and services open to the general public.
>
> (CRPD Committee, 2014, para. 24)

In relation to the latter, 'States parties should establish definite time frames and allocate adequate resources for the removal of existing barriers' (CRPD Committee, 2014, para. 24). Further, the CRPD Committee has explicitly recognised that:

> The provision of access to cultural and historical monuments that are part of national heritage may indeed be a challenge in some circumstances. However, States parties are obliged to strive to provide access to these sites. Many monuments and sites of national cultural importance have been made accessible in a way that preserves their cultural and historical identity and uniqueness.
>
> (CRPD Committee, 2014, para. 44)

Article 30(1) CRPD alludes to accessible formats but does not give any further indication of what these formats are. However, Article 21(a) CRPD mentions 'accessible formats and technologies *appropriate to different kinds of disabilities*' (emphasis added), alluding to an array of diverse designs and tools. This provision also cites 'sign languages, Braille, augmentative and alternative communication, and all other accessible means, modes and formats of communication' (Article 21(b) CRPD). In its General Comment No. 2, the CRPD Committee gives some examples of what these formats might be by highlighting the barriers that people with disabilities face in the cultural sphere. In particular, the Committee indicated that

> wheelchair users cannot go to a concert if there are only stairs in the concert hall. Blind persons cannot enjoy a painting if there is no *description* of it they can hear in the gallery. Hard of hearing persons cannot enjoy a film if there are no *subtitles*. Deaf persons cannot enjoy a theatrical play if there is no *sign language* interpretation. Persons with intellectual disabilities cannot enjoy a book if there is no *easy-to-read* version or a version in *augmentative and alternative modes*.
>
> (CRPD Committee, 2014, para. 44) (emphasis added)

The indicators on Article 30 CRPD (OHCHR, 2020) also mention 'Braille, Easy to Read Format, captioning, [and] tactile communication' but connect these formats to the recognition and support of the cultural and linguistic identities of all persons with disabilities.

It is evident that accessible formats and accessibility tools are subject to technological developments, and the open-ended wording of Article 30 CRPD seems to recognise the need for States Parties to embrace technological developments, including digital features, that might enhance access to culture for people with different types of disabilities. In fact, there is a long-standing awareness that the concept of cultural participation is evolving through the use of the internet and new technologies (Laaksonen, 2010) as well as artificial intelligence (AI). Literature discussed in Chapter 1 has highlighted how the use of a range of technologies can enhance the sensory experiences of blind and visually impaired visitors in museums (Vas, 2020), while digitalisation is also considered an important facilitator of cultural participation within archaeological and heritage sites as well as museums (Seale et al., 2021). In this regard, the importance of digital tools is also recognised by persons with disabilities themselves, as will be expounded in Part III of the book.

The CRPD Committee members have not yet had the opportunity to engage with Article 30(1) CRPD, to a great degree, in individual communications. In *Henley v Australia* (CRPD Committee, 2023) the Committee was confronted with measures that provide audio-description content on television, including through trials and budget allocation. In that instance, the CRPD Committee endorsed the complainant's view that the measures adopted by Australia were insufficient and in breach of the principle of progressive realisation. The Committee focused more on Article 9 CRPD (on accessibility) than on Article 30 CRPD. However, in a nutshell, it did confirm that audio description is a fully-fledged accessibility measure that must be provided to comply with CRPD obligations.

Linked to the right to access cultural goods, and to the obligations laid out in Article 30(1) CRPD, is the provision included in Article 30(3) CRPD which addresses the relationship between intellectual property (IP) rights and access rights for persons with disabilities, requiring States Parties to take appropriate steps 'to ensure that laws protecting intellectual property rights do not constitute an unreasonable or discriminatory barrier to access by persons with disabilities to cultural materials'. It is well known that the World Blind Union (WBU) has been one of the most vocal supporters of this provision, on foot of the barriers faced by visually impaired people in accessing printed material in Braille or other formats (Bantekas et al., 2018). It is also well known that this provision has found further specification in the Marrakesh Treaty to Facilitate Access to Published Works for Persons who are Blind, Visually Impaired, or Otherwise Print Disabled (the Marrakesh Treaty) signed in Marrakesh on 27 June 2013 under the auspices of the World Intellectual Property Organisation (WIPO) and which entered into force in September 2016.

The Marrakesh Treaty is generally heralded as one of the most significant steps towards ensuring access to printed material for persons with disabilities and in addressing the 'book famine', that is, the dearth of books available in formats that are accessible. It is regarded as being complementary to the CRPD, and it supports the realisation not only of Article 30(3) CRPD but also of Article 21 CRPD, as well as the right to education included in Article 24 CRPD. The importance of the Marrakesh Treaty has also been emphasised by the CRPD Committee at various junctures in its COs, as will be further examined in Chapter 4. In essence, the Marrakesh Treaty enables people with print disabilities and certain organisations to create accessible copies of publicly available written materials without permission of the copyright holder (Harpur, 2017; Helfer et al., 2020).

Harpur and Suzor (2014) state that the Marrakesh Treaty, overall, aims 'to increase the amount of accessible material available worldwide by creating a standardised framework to ensure that countries around the world introduce exceptions into their copyright regimes'. Without discussing its content in detail, it suffices here to point out that the Marrakesh Treaty covers all literary and artistic works in the form of text, notation, and/or related illustrations, whether published or made available on any media (Ferri, 2024). Further, Article 2 of the Marrakesh Treaty also defines the meaning of an accessible format copy, which is

> a copy of a work in an alternative manner or form which gives a beneficiary person access to the work, including to permit the person to have access as feasibly and comfortably as a person without visual impairment or other print disability.

Notably, the personal scope of the Marrakesh Treaty is delineated by Article 3 which identifies as beneficiaries of the copyright exception: blind persons, visually impaired people, persons with a perceptual or reading disability, and those who are 'otherwise unable, through physical disability, to hold or manipulate a book or to focus or move the eyes to the extent that would be normally acceptable for reading; that cannot access effectively printed material'. Although the definition proffered by the Marrakesh Treaty is wide (Helfer et al., 2020), it is narrower than the scope of the CRPD, which applies to all persons with disabilities who include 'those who have long-term physical, mental, intellectual or sensory impairments which in interaction with various barriers may hinder their full and effective participation in society on an equal basis with others' (Article 1(2) CRPD).

The importance of the Marrakesh Treaty in the context of the implementation of Article 30(3) CRPD also sits within the broader commitment to enhance accessibility (including accessibility of cultural goods, services, and heritage) through international cooperation, envisaged under Article 32 CRPD. The CRPD Committee has further emphasised that international cooperation should constitute 'a significant tool in the promotion of accessibility and universal design' and recommends that international development agencies recognise the significance of supporting projects aimed at improving ICT and other access infrastructure' (CRPD Committee, 2014, para. 47).

On the whole, Article 30(1) and (3) CRPD requires States Parties to adopt a range of legislative and policy instruments that allow and support access to culture for persons with disabilities.

### *3.3. The Right to Actively Participate in and Create Culture*

Article 30(2) CRPD recognises that all persons with disabilities have 'the ability to enjoy culture as well as the potential for creative, artistic, and intellectual pursuits' (Bantekas et al., 2018, p. 885). Article 30(2) CRPD covers both amateur efforts, and the pursuit of cultural activities for leisure or for one's own benefit, and also professional creative endeavours. In that regard, it requires States Parties to enable access to cultural activities for leisure but also to ensure access to professional artistic training.

In addressing the active dimension of cultural participation, this provision has an emancipatory value (Bantekas et al., 2018, p. 873), supporting the view of persons with disabilities as active participants in society. This provision seems to recognise that, as discussed in Chapter 1, people with disabilities can forge and have forged their own cultures (Stober & García Iriarte, 2023). As Bantekas et al. (2018, p. 884) note, Article 30(2) CRPD recognises the aptitude of persons with disabilities 'for achieving high levels of artistic, creative and intellectual attainment', an ability often overlooked or discarded. In fact, literature discussed earlier in this book signals that arts engagement by people with disabilities is not taken seriously and often reduced to a mere therapeutic or educational endeavour (Collins et al., 2022). Further, as noted in Chapter 1 (and as will be discussed in the following chapter), references to the professional employment of people with disabilities within cultural organisations are rare in the reports of States Parties to the CRPD Committee.

All in all, the importance of this provision is linked to its emblematic affirmation that people with disabilities can be makers and shapers of culture in their own right. This provision aligns with the transformative potential of disability art which has been elaborated upon in disability studies literature. As mentioned in Chapter 1, Sandahl (2018, p. 84) contends that 'the break-through' work of artists with disabilities can transform the status quo. Haller (2023), in a recent monograph, highlights the voices of disabled people creating mass media around the world and contends that they transform media culture in all societies. Thus, Article 30(2) CRPD is key in empowering persons with disabilities to challenge majoritarian and ableist views through their art.

### 3.4. *The Protection of the Cultural and Linguistic Identity of Persons with Disabilities*

Article 30(4) CRPD provides that all 'persons with disabilities shall be entitled, on an equal basis with others, to recognition and support of their specific cultural and linguistic identity, including sign languages and deaf culture'. This paragraph alludes to the protection of individual rights of people with disabilities as part of a collective group. However, it can be interpreted as protecting and promoting collective rights of people with disabilities as a cultural group.

Notably, however, the existence of a distinct cultural identity of people with disabilities has been articulated in a multifarious prismatic way by literature in various fields (Kuppers, 2019), as discussed earlier in Chapter 1. In spite of identitarian campaigns such as the *#SaytheWord* movement – a social media call to embrace disability identity (Andrews et al., 2019) – arguments in favour of collective identity (Pierce, 2023) and recent work discussing

Autism as a 'cultural identity' (de Vries, 2022), or Braille as a heritage embodying a culture of visual impairment (Beudaert, 2024), cultural identity claims are somewhat contested (Bantekas et al., 2018). More settled claims and articulations have been made in relation to Deaf people as a cultural group or as a linguistic minority. Deaf people are conceived of as a distinct 'cultural and linguistic community who use sign language as a mother tongue or natural language to communicate' (World Federation of the Deaf, n.d.).

In that connection, while an overall disability culture is questioned, the existence of a Deaf culture is well rooted. In fact, Article 30(4) CRPD specifically singles out Deaf identity. This provision links with Article 24(3) CRPD that provides for the right of Deaf learners to education in a national sign language but does not fully address the debate on whether inclusive education (which is mandated by Article 24 CRPD) is appropriate for them. It has been highlighted that these provisions, however, entail different types of obligations: Article 24 provides for education to be inclusive, and States Parties 'are mandated to "facilitate and promote the linguistic identity" of deaf persons on an equal basis, whereas Article 30(4) provides an individual entitlement to "recognition and support"' (Bantekas et al., 2018, p. 907). On the whole, according to de Beco (2019), the CRPD 'does protect [Deaf people] from the goal of assimilating them into the mainstream'. Yet the CRPD does not articulate sign languages as minority languages and does not go as far as conceptualising Deaf people as a linguistic or cultural minority (Ball, 2011). It navigates a liminal space articulating what Wilks (2022) terms as 'Deaf-disabled rights'. In this regard, Bantekas et al. (2018) posit that the CRPD does allow, but does not require, States Parties to recognise sign languages as minority languages.

Thus far, as will be discussed in the next chapter, the CRPD Committee, in its COs, has urged States Parties to recognise sign languages as national official languages but has mostly addressed sign languages as a matter of accessibility or in the context of reasonable accommodation (CRPD Committee, 2016). This is also the case in the views adopted on the individual communication *Sahlin v Sweden* (CRPD Committee, 2020), which concerned the failure to hire a Deaf lecturer because it would be too expensive to hire a sign language interpreter. In that case, the CRPD Committee focused on the concept of reasonable accommodation in employment contexts. It reached the conclusion that Sweden had failed to fulfil its obligations under Articles 5 CRPD (on equality) and 27 CRPD (on the right to work) but did not consider Article 30(4) CRPD. It is evident that the individual communication revolves around the right to work. However, the CRPD Committee could have engaged with Deaf culture or identity. Only at one juncture does it cursorily limit itself to embracing the view expressed by the complainant that hiring a Deaf lecturer would have promoted diversity in the workplace and facilitated more inclusion in the future (CRPD Committee, 2020, para. 5.11).

On the whole, Article 30(4) CRPD celebrates disability as an identitarian trait and requires States Parties to recognise it and celebrate it as part of human diversity. This tallies with scholarship, examined earlier in this book, that views cultural participation as an enhancement of diversity with the potential to transform how disability is conceived of in society.

## 4. Concluding Remarks

While being essentially legal-doctrinal in its approach, the chapter aims to be more than a merely descriptive account of the legal dimensions of the right to culture for persons with disabilities. It has endeavoured to investigate the normative facets and the complexities of the right to culture of persons with disabilities in light of existing legal scholarship as well as linking Article 30 CRPD to the multidisciplinary literature discussed in Chapter 1. In that regard, it foreshadows the discussion conducted in Chapter 4 and in Part III.

As noted earlier in Chapter 2, the right to participate in cultural life is encompassed by, and essential for, the realisation of the human rights model of disability and to enact inclusive equality. As outlined in Chapter 2, the human rights model revolves around the human dignity of persons with disabilities and values impairments as part of human diversity (Degener, 2017). In that regard, the right to participate in cultural life provided for in Article 30 CRPD connects to the recognition of personhood and dignity of persons with disabilities.

Article 30 CRPD also embeds, and is key to realising, all four dimensions of inclusive equality (i.e. the redistributive dimension, which refers to the need to address socio-economic disadvantages; the recognition dimension, which requires stigma to be combatted and recognition of dignity and intersectionality; the participative dimension, which necessitates the recognition of the social nature of people with disabilities as members of society; and the accommodating dimension, which entails making space for difference as a matter of human dignity). Article 30(1) CRPD, by requiring States parties to ensure access for people with disabilities, embeds and requires a redistributive approach to addressing socio-economic disadvantages. It is also vital to realise the recognition dimension and to combat stigma. Notably, Bergonzoni (2024) contends that, by becoming more 'attentive to inaccessibility' and constantly seeking accessibility tools, we can challenge ableism and 'bring forward a notion of embodied reflexivity that considers social interactions and dynamics through our different embodiments'. The right to access culture is essential in ensuring participation and entails an accommodating dimension, whereby access on an equal basis with others can also be guaranteed by virtue of reasonable accommodations. The freedom of creative activity, which is protected in Article 30(2) CRPD, implies the expression of everyone's identity. Thus, it is as indispensable as access to the recognition of the inherent dignity of persons with disabilities and is essential for the enactment of the recognition dimension of inclusive equality. Literature on participation in different art forms by people with disabilities highlights how art leads to the articulation of identities and experiences that are otherwise overlooked and to greater recognition of them by broader society (Taylor, 2005; Watts & Ridley, 2012).

Article 30(4) CRPD, by protecting disability identities, further connects with the recognition and participatory dimension of inclusive equality.

On the whole, enjoying culture is a vital part of being a citizen, a member of a community, and, more broadly, a member of society, and it is indispensable to furthering the CRPD transformative vision of persons with disabilities as holders of rights.

## References

Andrews, E. E., Forber-Pratt, A. J., Mona, L. R., Lund, E. M., Pilarski, C. R., & Balter, R. (2019). SaytheWord: A disability culture commentary on the erasure of 'disability'. *Rehabilitation Psychology*, *64*(2), 111–118.

Ball, A. (2011). Equal accessibility for sign language under the Convention on the Rights of Persons with Disabilities. *Case Western Reserve Journal of International Law*, *43*(3), 759–798.

Bantekas, I., Stephenson, C. P. Y., Karapapa, S., & Polymenopoulou, E. (2018). Article 30. Participation in cultural life, recreation, leisure, and sport. In I. Bantekas, M. A. Stein, & D. Anastasiou (Eds.), *The UN Convention on the Rights of Persons with Disabilities: A Commentary* (pp. 863–923). Oxford University Press.

Belfiore, E., Hadley, S., Heidelberg, B. M., & Rosenstein, C. (2023). Cultural democracy, cultural equity, and cultural policy: Perspectives from the UK and USA. *The Journal of Arts Management, Law, and Society*, *53*(3), 157–168.

Bergonzoni, C. (2024). In motion: An adaptation of enriched and inclusive audio description practices. *Qualitative Inquiry*, *30*(2), 126–127.

Beudaert, A. (2024). Fifty shades of Braille: Motivations, challenges and cultural significance in visual impairment. *The Journal of Consumer Marketing*, *41*(3), 357–367.

Brems, E. (2009). Human rights: Minimum and maximum perspectives. *Human Rights Law Review*, *9*, 349–355.

Cerqueira, D. (2023). Chapter 27: Article 27 – cultural rights. In H. Cantu Rivera (Ed.), *The universal declaration of human rights* (pp. 710–732). Brill Nijhoff.

Chow, P. Y. S. (2018). *Cultural rights in international law and discourse: Contemporary challenges and interdisciplinary perspectives*. Brill Nijhoff.

Chow, P. Y. S. (2022). Cultural rights. In C. Binder, M. Nowak, J. A. Hofbauer, & P. Janig (Eds.), *Elgar encyclopedia of human rights*. Edward Elgar.

Collins, A., Rentschler, R., Williams, R., & Azmat, F. (2022). Exploring barriers to social inclusion for disabled people: Perspectives from the performing arts. *Journal of Management & Organization*, *28*, 308–328.

Corkery, A., & Saiz, I. (2020). Progressive realization using maximum available resources: The accountability challenge. In J. Dugard, B. Porter, D. Ikawa, & L. Chenwi (Eds.), *Research handbook on economic, social and cultural rights as human rights* (Research Handbooks in Human Rights series) (pp. 275–300). Edward Elgar.

de Beco, G. (2019). The indivisibility of human rights and the Convention on the Rights of Persons with Disabilities. *International & Comparative Law Quarterly*, *68*(1), 141–160.

Degener, T. (2017). A new human rights model of disability. In V. Della Fina, R. Cera, & G. Palmisano (Eds.), *The United Nations Convention on the Rights of Persons with Disabilities: A Commentary* (pp. 41–60). Springer.

de Vries, B. (2022). Should autists have cultural rights? *Human Rights Review*, *23*(2), 205–219.

Donders, Y. (2016). Foundations of collective cultural rights in international human rights law. In A. Jakubowski (Ed.), *Cultural rights as collective rights: An international law perspective* (pp. 87–112). Brill.

Donders, Y. (2019). Cultural rights in international human rights law: From controversy to celebration. *Japanese Yearbook of International Law*, *62*, 61–84.

Donders, Y. (2020). Diversity in Europe: From pluralism to populism? In J. Vidmar (Ed.), *European populism and human rights* (pp. 52–71). Brill Nijhoff.
Donders, Y. M. (2012). Cultural rights in the convention on the diversity of cultural expressions: Included or ignored? In T. Kono & S. Van Uytsel (Eds.), *The UNESCO convention on the diversity of cultural expressions: A tale of fragmentation of international law?* (pp. 165–182). Intersentia.
European Commission, Directorate-General for Education, Youth, Sport and Culture. (2023). *Hammonds, W., Culture and democracy, the evidence – how citizens' participation in cultural activities enhances civic engagement, democracy and social cohesion – lessons from international research*. Publications Office of the European Union.
European Court of Human Rights (ECtHR). (1988, May 24). *Müller and others v. Switzerland*. (Application No. 10737/84).
European Court of Human Rights (ECtHR). (2011). *Cultural rights in the case-law of the European Court of Human Rights*. https://globalfreedomofexpression.columbia.edu/wp-content/uploads/2020/12/Cultural-Rights-in-the-Case-Law-of-the-ECtHR-Artistic-Freedom-RD.pdf
European Court of Human Rights (ECtHR). (2024, May 2). *The J. Paul Getty trust and others v. Italy*. (Application No. 35271/19).
European Parliament Research Service (EPRS). (2017). *Access to culture in the European Union*. https://op.europa.eu/en/publication-detail/-/publication/66f298ec-6840-11e7-b2f2-01aa75ed71a1
Ferri, D. (2008). *La costituzione culturale dell'Unione europea*. CEDAM.
Ferri, D. (2009). La dimensione prescrittiva della cultura. Un'analisi comparata tra significante e significato. *Diritto Pubblico Comparato Ed Europeo*, 12–33.
Ferri, D. (2024). The Marrakesh treaty to facilitate access to published works for persons who are blind, visually impaired or otherwise print disabled in the European Union: Reflecting on its implementation and gauging its impact from a disability perspective. *IIC International Review of Intellectual Property and Competition Law*, *55*, 89–109.
Francioni, F. (2011). The human dimension of international cultural heritage law: An introduction. *European Journal of International Law*, 22(1), 9–16.
Francioni, F., & Vrdoljak, A. F. (Eds.). (2020). *The Oxford handbook of international cultural heritage law*. Oxford University Press.
Guangyu, D. (2023). Cultural heritage rights and rights related to cultural heritage: A review of the cultural heritage rights system. *Santander Art & Culture Law Review*, *9*(2), 167–190.
Hadley, S. (2021). *Audience development and cultural policy*. Palgrave Macmillan.
Haller, B. A. (2023). *Disabled people transforming media culture for a more inclusive world*. Routledge.
Harpur, P. (2017). *Discrimination, copyright and equality: Opening the E-book for the print disabled*. Cambridge University Press.
Harpur, P., & Suzor, N. (2014). The paradigm shift in realising the right to read: How ebook libraries are enabling in the university sector. *Disability & Society*, *29*(10), 1658–1671.
Helfer, L. R., Land, M. K., & Okediji, R. (2020). Copyright exceptions across borders: Implementing the Marrakesh Treaty. *European Intellectual Property Review*, *42*(6), 332–340.
Human Rights Council. (2011). *Report of the independent expert in the field of cultural rights, Farida Shaheed* (UN Doc. A/HRC/17/38).
Kaliq, U., & Churchill, R. (2012). The protection of economic and social rights: A particular challenge? In H. Keller & G. Ulfstein (Eds.), *UN human rights treaty bodies: Law and legitimacy* (pp. 199–260). Cambridge University Press.
Kędzia, Z. (2020). Social rights protection under the ICESCR and its optional protocol – the role of the committee on economic, social and cultural rights. In C. Binder,

J. A. Hofbauer, F. Piovesan, & A. Úbeda de Torres (Eds.), *Research handbook on international law and social rights* (pp. 90–110). Edward Elgar.

Kędzia, Z. (2022). The Committee on Economic, Social and Cultural Rights – The power of subjective rights? *Journal of Human Rights Practice*, *14*(1), 50–74.

Kuppers, P. (Ed.). (2019). *Disability arts and culture: Methods and approaches*. Intellect.

Laaksonen, A. (2010). *Making culture accessible. Access, participation and cultural provision in the context of cultural rights in Europe*. Council of Europe Publishing.

Leckie, S., & Gallagher, A. T. (2006). *Economic, social, and cultural rights: A legal resource guide* (1st ed.). University of Pennsylvania Press.

Logan, W. (2012). Cultural diversity, cultural heritage and human rights: Towards heritage management as human rights-based cultural practice. *International Journal of Heritage Studies*, *18*(3), 231–244.

Manca, L. (2017). Article 30. In V. Della Fina, R. Cera, & G. Palmisano (Eds.), *The United Nations Convention on the Rights of Persons with Disabilities: A Commentary* (pp. 541–555). Springer.

McGoldrick, D. (2007). Culture, cultures, and cultural rights. In M. Baderin & R. McCorquodale (Eds.), *Economic, social, and cultural rights in action* (Online ed.). Oxford University Press.

Office of the High Commissioner for Human Rights (OHCHR). (2020). *Article 30: List of illustrative indicators on participation in cultural life, recreation, leisure and sport*. www.ohchr.org/sites/default/files/article-30-indicators-en.pdf

Office of the High Commissioner of Human Rights (OHCHR). (2007). *From vision to action: The road to implementation of the convention*.

O'Keefe, R. (1998). The right to take part in cultural life under Article 15 of the ICESCR. *International and Comparative Law Quarterly*, *47*(4), 904–923.

Organisation for Economic Co-operation and Development (OECD). (2022). *The culture fix: Creative people, places and industries*. OECD Publishing.

Pierce, K. L. (2023). Bridging the gap between intentions and impact: Understanding disability culture to support disability justice. *The Professional Counselor*, *13*(4), 486–495.

Romainville, C. (2015). On defining the right to participate in cultural life as a human right. *Netherlands Quarterly of Human Rights*, *33*(4), 405–436.

Sandahl, C. (2018). Disability art and culture: A model for imaginative ways to integrate the community. *Alter, European Journal of Disability Research/Revue européenne de recherche sur le handicap*, *12*, 81–95.

Saul, B., Kinley, D., & Mowbray, J. (2014). Article 15: Cultural rights. In B. Saul, D. Kinley, & J. Mowbray, *The international covenant on economic, social and cultural rights: Commentary, cases, and materials*. Oxford University Press.

Seale, J., Garcia Carrizosa, H., Rix, J., Sheehy, K., & Hayhoe, S. (2021). A participatory approach to the evaluation of participatory museum research projects. *International Journal of Research & Method in Education*, *44*(1), 20–40.

Sikora, K. (2021). The right to cultural heritage in international law, with special reference to indigenous peoples' rights. *Santander Art & Culture Law Review*, *2*(7), 149–172.

Stamatopoulou, E. (2007). *Cultural rights in international law: Article 27 of the universal declaration of human rights and beyond*. Brill Nijhoff.

Stamatopoulou, E. (2012). Monitoring cultural human rights: The claims of culture on human rights and the response of cultural rights. *Human Rights Quarterly*, *34*(4), 1170–1192.

Stober, K., & García Iriarte, E. (2023). Intellectual disability, art and identity: A qualitative exploration of the experiences of professional artists with intellectual disabilities. *Disability & Society*, *38*(10), 1871–1894.

Taylor, M. (2005). Self-identity and the arts education of disabled young people. *Disability & Society*, *20*(7), 763–778.

Thielbörger, P. (2019). The 'essence' of international human rights. *German Law Journal*, *20*(6), 924–939.

UNESCO. (2001). *Universal declaration on cultural diversity*. www.unesco.org/en/legal-affairs/unesco-universal-declaration-cultural-diversity

UNESCO. (2009). *UNESCO framework for cultural statistics* (FCS). UNESCO Institute for Statistics. https://uis.unesco.org/sites/default/files/documents/unesco-framework-for-cultural-statistics-2009-en_0.pdf

United Nations. (1993). *Standard rules on the equalization of opportunities for persons with disabilities* (UNGA Resolution 48/96).

United Nations Committee on Economic Social and Cultural Rights (CESCR). (1990). *General Comment No. 3: The nature of states parties' obligations* (UN Doc. E/1991/23).

United Nations Committee on Economic Social and Cultural Rights (CESCR). (1994). *General Comment No. 5: Persons with Disabilities* (UN Doc. E/1995/22).

United Nations Committee on Economic Social and Cultural Rights (CESCR). (2009). *General Comment No. 21: Right of everyone to take part in cultural life* (UN Doc. E/C.12/GC/21).

United Nations Committee on Economic Social and Cultural Rights (CESCR). (2016). *Statement on public debt, austerity measures and the international covenant on economic, social and cultural rights* (UN Doc. E/C.12/2016/1).

United Nations Committee on the Rights of Persons with Disabilities (CRPD Committee). (2014). *General Comment No. 2 on Article 9: Accessibility* (UN Doc. CRPD/C/GC/2).

United Nations Committee on the Rights of Persons with Disabilities (CRPD Committee). (2016). *Lockrey v. Australia* (Communication No. 13/2013, UN Doc. CRPD/C/15/D/13/2013).

United Nations Committee on the Rights of Persons with Disabilities (CRPD Committee). (2020). *Sahlin v. Sweden* (Communication No. 45/2028, UN Doc. CRPD/C/23/D/45/2018).

United Nations Committee on the Rights of Persons with Disabilities (CRPD Committee). (2023). *Henley v. Australia* (Communication No. 56/2018, UN Doc. CRPD/C/27/D/56/2018).

Vas, R. (2020). Blind and visually impaired visitors' experiences in museums: Increasing accessibility through assistive technologies. *The International Journal of the Inclusive Museum*, *13*(2), 57–80.

Vícha, O. (2014). The concept of the right to cultural heritage within the Faro Convention. *International and Comparative Law Review*, *14*(2), 25–40.

Watts, M., & Ridley, B. (2012). Identities of dis/ability and music. *British Educational Research Journal*, *38*(3), 353–372.

Whyatt, S. (2023). *Free to create: Artistic freedom in Europe*. Council of Europe.

Wilks, R. (2022). Developing deaf jurisprudence: The role of interpreters and translators. In C. Stone, R. Adam, R. Müller de Quadros, & C. Rathmann (Eds.), *Routledge handbook on sign language translation and interpretation* (pp. 249–266). Routledge.

World Federation of the Deaf. (n.d.). *The legal recognition of national sign languages*. https://wfdeaf.org/news/the-legal-recognition-of-national-sign-languages

# 4 Implementing the Right of Persons with Disabilities to Participate in Cultural Life

## Trends, State Narratives, and Counter-Narratives

*Delia Ferri and Ann Leahy*

### 1. Introduction

This chapter addresses how, and the extent to which, the right of persons with disabilities to participate in cultural life, provided for in Article 30 of the UN Convention on the Rights of Persons with Disabilities (CRPD), is implemented by States Parties to the CRPD. In doing so, it focuses on whether the human rights model (Degener, 2017; Lawson & Beckett, 2021) is embedded in the practices of States Parties. As outlined already in the introduction and in Chapter 2, the CRPD is underpinned by an understanding of disability as an interactive process between people with impairments and societal barriers. It adopts an all-embracing concept of accessibility in Article 9 CRPD, which, according to Charitakis (2018, 2020), encompasses several dimensions, that is, 'attitudinal accessibility, economic accessibility or affordability, physical accessibility, information accessibility and communication accessibility' (Charitakis, 2018, p. 376). This chapter is premised on this understanding of disability and accessibility and aims to gauge how barriers to, and facilitators of, cultural participation are dealt with by States Parties and the UN Committee on the Rights of Persons with Disabilities (CRPD Committee) and to what extent the multidimensional concept of accessibility extends to and informs the implementation of Article 30 CRPD.

In line with the scope of the project DANCING, of which this book is a core output, the geographical scope of this analysis is European, and it considers the 27 Member States of the European Union (EU), the United Kingdom (UK), as well as the EU itself, which is a party to the CRPD since 2010 (Ferri & Broderick, 2020).

As will be further outlined later, the chapter is based on a systematic analysis of documents pertaining to the reporting procedure provided for in Articles 35 and 36 CRPD, namely States Parties' reports to the CRPD Committee as well as queries raised and recommendations made by the CRPD Committee in response to them, respectively, Lists of Issues (LIs) and Concluding Observations (COs). This was complemented by a review of shadow reports submitted to the CRPD Committee by organisations of people with

DOI: 10.4324/9781032619361-7
This chapter has been made available under a CC-BY-NC-ND 4.0 license.

disabilities (OPDs) or non-governmental organisations (NGOs) where available. As discussed in Chapter 2 of the book, according to Article 35 CRPD, States Parties must submit an initial comprehensive report within two years after the entry into force of the Convention for the State Party concerned and subsequent reports at least every four years thereafter. The reports must set out the legal, policy, and all other measures taken by the state to give effect to the CRPD. They should also indicate any factors that hamper the implementation of the rights provided for in the Convention. These reports should align with the structure and content advised by the Reporting Guidelines released by the CRPD Committee (CRPD Committee, 2009, 2016). Article 36 CRPD, then, enables the CRPD Committee to consider these reports and, further to initial LIs to which States have to respond, the CRPD Committee adopts COs which are transmitted to the State Party concerned and which are also made public on the UN website. COs are considered to assist States Parties in enacting changes in national legislations, policies, and practices at the national level. The reporting procedure as a whole is a tool to monitor States Parties and guide and evaluate their implementation of the CRPD, keeping track of progress achieved. As discussed earlier in Chapter 2 of this book, it is based on a collaborative relationship between the States Parties and the CRPD Committee, in compliance with Article 37 CRPD which requires each State Party to 'cooperate with the Committee and assist its members in the fulfilment of their mandate'.

The thematic analysis of the documents retrieved was informed by the legal analysis conducted in Chapter 3 and will then support the discussion of our empirical research (mainly semi-structured interviews) set out in Part III of the book. Consistent with the approach taken throughout this book and detailed earlier in the introduction, we focus on references to arts practices and heritage within the reviewed documents because they are visible and acknowledged forms of cultural expression (Caust, 2019; European Commission, 2019).

The remainder of this chapter is divided into five main sections. Section 2 outlines the methodology adopted. Section 3 presents a general appraisal of how cultural participation is addressed in the reporting procedure. Section 4 presents our findings in relation to States Parties' reports based on identification of three key themes, and related sub-themes, that link to the obligations laid out in Article 30 CRPD. Section 4 discusses the CRPD Committee approach to the implementation of Article 30 CRPD and its recommendations. The concluding section highlights that there is a rather mixed picture to be seen in States Parties' reports, but there are also some important starting points on which to build in order to dismantle barriers to cultural participation. As noted earlier in this book, bar a few commentaries, limited attention has been paid to Article 30 CRPD, which remains one of the least studied human rights areas (Bantekas et al., 2018), and even less attention has been given to its implementation. Thus, this chapter aims to add to the current debate and to provide a novel contribution to scholarship, with the view of advancing the right to participate in cultural life.

## 2. Methodology

This chapter is based on an extensive document analysis of States Parties' reports and the CRPD Committee's documents (LIs and COs). It relates to EU Member States plus the UK and the EU itself, and the reference period was between January 2008, when the CRPD came into force, and the end of May 2024.

As we referred to briefly in the introduction to this book, document analysis is a form of qualitative research that uses a systematic procedure to analyse documentary evidence and answer specific research questions (Gross, 2018). It is a method for reviewing or evaluating documents combining elements of content analysis and thematic analysis (Bowen, 2009, pp. 27–32). A qualitative approach requires examination and interpretation to elicit meaning, gain understanding, and develop empirical knowledge, although documents may be treated in a variety of ways, depending on the focus of the study (Bowen, 2009). Thus, qualitative document analysis seeks to make explicit the implications of various formulations and presentation strategies (Wolff, 2004, p. 289). Since qualitative research can be enriched by critical attention to the gathering and analysis of documents of various kinds (Coffey, 2013), we have reviewed a selection of shadow reports submitted under the CRPD to support our analysis of the selected documents. In this regard, we attempted to reflect what Wolff (2004, p. 289) characterises as the 'conversation' between the document(s) being investigated. Our analysis also embeds and is underpinned by the legal analysis of Article 30 CRPD conducted in Chapter 3.

We accessed reports on the UN Treaty Body Database of progress reports,[1] for the 27 EU countries, the UK, and the EU, which has concluded the CRPD alongside its Member States (Council of the EU, 2010). All EU countries had submitted their initial reports, in compliance with Article 35 CRPD, and twelve of those countries had submitted subsequent reports, usually combining second and third reports. In addition, the UK had submitted its initial report and the EU had submitted an initial report as well as a subsequent report, bringing the total number of States Parties' reports reviewed to 42. In addition to states' reports, we reviewed 70 documents comprised of LIs and COs (published up until 31 May 2024), which are detailed in **Table 4.1.**

1 The website of the UN Treaty Body database is accessible at https://tbinternet.ohchr.org/_layouts/15/TreatyBodyExternal/Home.aspx

*Table 4.1* Reports Reviewed: Periodic Reports of States Parties, Lists of Issues, and Concluding Observations

| *Countries* | *Reports of States Parties* | *Lists of Issues (LIs)* | *Concluding Observations (COs)* |
|---|---|---|---|
| EU countries (x1 = one state report filed; x2 = 2 two states' reports filed): Austria (x2), Belgium (x2), Bulgaria (x1), Croatia (x2), Cyprus (x1), Czechia (x2), Denmark (x2), Estonia (x1), Finland (x1), France (x1), Germany (x2), Greece (x1), Hungary (x2), Ireland (x1), Italy (x1), Latvia (x2), Lithuania (x2), Luxembourg (x1), Malta (x1), Netherlands (x1), Poland (x1), Portugal (x1), Romania (x1), Slovakia (x2), Slovenia (x1), Spain (x2), Sweden (x2). | 39 | 37 | 28 |
| European Union | 2 | 2 | 1 |
| UK | 1 | 1 | 1 |
| Total | 42 | 40 | 30 |

In total, therefore, the documents reviewed consisted of 42 reports of States Parties,[2] as well as 40 LIs[3] and 30 COs[4] issued by the CRPD Committee.

We conducted a thematic analysis which involves examining the data collected and identifying recurrent themes (Tight, 2019) or, as Braun and Clarke (2006) suggest, it involves searching across a dataset (including a range of texts) to find repeated patterns of meaning. Taking into account the different types of documents and their function in the reporting process, recalled in Chapter 2 of this book, we examined the documents for references to 'culture', 'arts' and 'heritage' in relation to Article 30 CRPD, as well as Articles 9

2 Initial reports were submitted for all 28 countries as well as the EU and, in addition, 12 countries and the EU had submitted subsequent reports. Those 12 countries were Austria, Belgium, Croatia, Czechia, Denmark, Germany, Hungary, Latvia, Lithuania, Slovakia, Spain, and Sweden.

3 There were Lists of Issues (LIs) raised for 26 of the 28 countries and also for the EU. In addition, there was a second set of LIs raised in the case of 12 countries and also in the case of the EU, bringing the total number of LIs reviewed to 40. The two countries in respect of which none had been raised at the time of our review were Ireland and Romania.

4 Concluding Observations (COs) had been issued for 24 countries plus the EU itself, and, in addition, a second set of COs had been issued for five of them (Austria, Germany, Hungary, Spain, and Sweden) bringing the total reviewed to 30. The countries for which no COs were available at the time of our review were Finland, Ireland, the Netherlands, and Romania.

CRPD (accessibility) and 21 CRPD (freedom of expression and communication). In that regard, we reviewed any related comments or recommendations made by the CRPD Committee. We then indexed the data and searched for themes that identified patterns (Bowen, 2009; Braun & Clarke, 2006; Coffey, 2013), taking into account the various obligations laid out in Article 30 CRPD as well as the different dimensions of the right to participate in cultural life. With regard to the EU, in our analysis, we took note of the fact that it has 'supporting competences in the area of participation in cultural life' (Article 6 TFEU; CRPD/C/EU/1, para. 171).

As cautioned by Coffey (2013), we cannot treat records – however 'official' – as firm evidence of what they report, but we must approach them for what they are and for what they are used to accomplish. In that regard, as noted at the outset of this chapter, our thematic analysis was supported by a thorough legal understanding of the CRPD, as an international human rights treaty, of its normative dimensions, and of the nature and rationale of the reporting procedure. The reports of States Parties allow them to conduct a comprehensive review of national laws and policies to highlight conformity with the CRPD but also to monitor the actual situation with respect to each of the rights and to identify gaps. However, States Parties tend to focus on efforts made arising from cultural projects or to emphasise the allocation of budgetary resources or specific actions taken in the field of disability. By contrast, the CRPD Committee tends to place emphasis on gaps, challenges, and lack of progress, albeit in a constructive and dialogic manner. The comments and recommendations of the CRPD Committee are, in fact, designed to improve compliance and are informed by a broader set of inputs, including shadow reports from OPDs and civil society organisations.

In this chapter, documents from the reporting procedure are referred to using their official UN document code/number, which is set out at the outset of each UN document and includes the acronym of the treaty (CRPD), and acronyms indicating the type of document and the State party. The documents are all referred to in the text of the chapter but not included in the list of references as they are retrievable on the UN Treaty Body Database.

## 3. Cultural Participation of Persons with Disabilities in the CRPD Reporting Procedure: General Trends

Before delving into the thematic analysis, this section gives an overview of the general trends in relation to how States Parties on the one hand and the CRPD Committee on the other deal with Article 30 CRPD and, more broadly, how they address cultural participation.

As highlighted in Chapter 2, and as noted in the introduction to this chapter, the CRPD Committee has released Reporting Guidelines (CRPD Committee, 2009, 2016) to ensure that States Parties' reports are not only complete but also compiled in a uniform manner, and in a way that is appraisable by members of the CRPD Committee. These guidelines add to the multiple toolkits and general guidelines for reporting to human rights treaty bodies of the United Nations (United Nations, n.d.), as well as human rights indicators (OHCHR, 2020). Relevant legal provisions and policies should be described but also placed in adequate context, including information on the factual situation and data. Under Article 30 CRPD, the CRPD Committee (2016, para. 32) requires States Parties to report, *inter alia*, on the measures adopted to ensure that both public and private cultural facilities, television programmes, films, theatre and other cultural activities, and cultural materials and content are accessible to persons with disabilities. They should also indicate all of the measures that have been adopted to enable persons with disabilities to develop and utilise their creative, artistic, and intellectual potential, as well as the measures adopted to recognise and support the specific cultural and linguistic identity of persons with disabilities, including sign languages and Deaf culture. Further, the ratification of the Marrakesh Treaty to Facilitate Access to Published Works for Persons Who Are Blind, Visually Impaired or Otherwise Print Disabled (Marrakesh Treaty) adopted within the remit of the World Intellectual Property Organisation (WIPO) (2013) should be reported along with other measures to ensure that intellectual property laws do not become a barrier for persons with disabilities in accessing cultural materials in compliance with Article 30(3) CRPD. Measures related to accessibility of facilities and information should also be reported under Articles 9 and 21 CRPD. In relation to the latter provision, the Reporting Guidelines (CRPD Committee, 2016, para. 23(d)) require for measures 'adopted to recognize sign language(s) as official language(s)' and 'to promote the learning of sign language, the availability of qualified sign language interpreters and the use of sign language in all settings' to be highlighted.

Notwithstanding these guidelines, our review reveals that States Parties' reports varied a lot in the degree of attention that they gave to Article 30 CRPD and to the aspects of cultural participation mentioned or emphasised. While many reports included lengthy sections addressing arts and heritage, others did so to a much lesser extent, and sometimes there can be a sense that participation in culture is less important than other areas of life. For example, a report filed by Romania in 2022 refers to arts and tourism but focuses overwhelmingly on sports participation in its section dealing with Article 30 (CRPD/C/ROU/1, paras 331–340). Likewise, a report from Portugal largely deals with sport in its section addressing Article 30, devoting 11 paragraphs to it and only one brief paragraph to culture (CRPD/C/PRT/1, para. 273)[5]. More limited attention paid to cultural participation was also acknowledged in a shadow report from Croatia (Disability Ombudsman of Croatia, 2014), which suggested that cultural activities are not considered 'vital'. As will be discussed in the subsequent section, there seems to be an increasing awareness of the different facets of accessibility and a growing focus on accessibility

5 Portugal subsequently filed information in response to a query raised in a LIs from the CRPD Committee on the accessibility of 'tourism, recreation and leisure' (CRPD/C/PRT/Q/1: para. 28), which mainly addresses tourism issues (CRPD/C/PRT/Q/1/Add.1; paras 163–165).

of content beyond physical accessibility. Given that Article 30(3) CRPD explicitly obliges States Parties to 'take all appropriate steps, in accordance with international law, to ensure that laws protecting intellectual property rights do not constitute an unreasonable or discriminatory barrier to access by persons with disabilities to cultural materials', reports of many countries referenced copyright laws, and exceptions to reproduction restrictions provided therein.

Of the 30 COs from the CRPD Committee reviewed (which relate to 24 countries plus the EU, with two sets of COs issued for five countries), there was an Article 30 recommendation in all but five of them. Action in respect of copyright and the Marrakesh Treaty was the sole feature of 11 recommendations made under Article 30 CRPD. A further 14 COs, particularly the most recent ones, featured recommendations to address issues of cultural participation more broadly than copyright issues or the Marrakesh Treaty (as set out in **Table 4.2**). Given the ratification of the Marrakesh Treaty by the EU on behalf of all its Member States in 2018 and the enactment of related EU implementing legislation (Ferri, 2024; Ferri & Donnellan, 2022; Sganga, 2020), this is somewhat expected in the latest documents. It is, in fact, evident that the CRPD Committee has moved its focus, giving more attention to the implementation of obligations other than that included in Article 30(3) CRPD.

It is telling that recommendations made in relation to Article 30 CRPD for Estonia (CRPD/C/EST/CO/1, paras 58–59), released in 2021, Hungary (CRPD/C/HUN/CO/2–3, paras 58–59), released in 2021, Austria (CRPD/C/AUT/CO/2–3, paras 67–68) and Germany (CRPD/C/DEU/CO/2–3, paras 67–68), both published in 2023, and Sweden (CRPD/C/SWE/CO/2–3, paras 63–64)) released in 2024, make no reference to the Marrakesh Treaty or copyright exceptions. It is also interesting to see wider recommendations in more recent documents. So, for example, the COs for Greece, released in October 2019, included recommendations to address the fact that people with disabilities face 'barriers in their participation in cultural life, recreation, leisure and sport on an equal basis with others', which is said to be due, *inter alia*, to 'limited access to cultural materials and activities in accessible formats, cultural performances and services . . . monuments and sites of national cultural importance' (CRPD/C/GRC/CO/1, paras 44–45). COs to the Maltese report specify that a budget is needed to promote and protect the right to participate in cultural life (CRPD/C/MLT/CO/1, para. 44) as do COs for France, which suggest that this is especially required in respect of children with disabilities (CRPD/C/FRA/CO/1, para. 61(b)). Interestingly the most recent COs for Germany, issued in October 2023, contain a rather comprehensive list of recommendations relating to culture, which include references to accessibility of venues and to promoting 'inclusion in and the accessibility of all creative arts studies' (CRPD/C/DEU/CO/2–3, paras 67–68). The latter, relating to creative arts studies, is not one that is commonly made, but it is worth noting, given that people with disabilities are often excluded from education and training opportunities in the arts, as discussed in Chapter 1

*Table 4.2* Concluding Observations from the CRPD Committee: How They Address Article 30 CRPD

| *How Article 30 is addressed* | *State Parties in respect of which Concluding Observations have been issued* |
|---|---|
| **No recommendations made** | Latvia (CRPD/C/LVA/CO/1).<br>Poland (CRPD/C/POL/CO/1).<br>None in Concluding Observations on initial reports of Austria (CRPD/C/AUT/CO/1), Hungary (CRPD/C/HUN/CO/1), and Spain (CRPD/C/ESP/CO/1). |
| **Recommendations focus only on copyright exceptions and/or ratification or implementation of the Marrakesh Treaty** | Belgium (CRPD/C/BEL/CO/1, paras 40–41).<br>Cyprus (CRPD/C/CYP/CO/1, paras 59–60).<br>Czechia (CRPD/C/CZE/CO/1, paras 59–60).<br>Denmark (CRPD/C/DNK/CO/1, paras 62–63).<br>Germany (CRPD/C/DEU/CO/1, paras 55–56).<br>Italy (CRPD/C/ITA/CO/1, paras 75–56).<br>Portugal (CRPD/C/PRT/CO/1, paras 57–58).<br>Slovenia (CRPD/C/SVN/CO/1, paras 51–52).<br>Spain (CRPD/C/ESP/CO/2–3, paras 56–57).<br>Sweden (CRPD/C/SWE/CO/1, paras 53–54).<br>European Union (CRPD/C/EU/CO/1, paras 70–71). |
| **Recommendations are broader in scope, while they may also focus on copyright exceptions and/or ratification of the Marrakesh Treaty** | Austria (CRPD/C/AUT/CO/2–3, paras 67–68).<br>Bulgaria (CRPD/C/BGR/CO/1, paras 63–66).<br>Croatia (CRPD/C/HRV/CO/1, paras 47–48).<br>Estonia (CRPD/C/EST/CO/1, paras 58–59).<br>France (CRPD/C/FRA/CO/1, paras 60–61).<br>Germany (CRPD/C/DEU/CO/2–3, paras 67–68).<br>Greece (CRPD/C/GRC/CO/1, paras 44–45).<br>Hungary (CRPD/C/HUN/CO/2–3, paras 58–59).<br>Lithuania (CRPD/C/LTU/CO/1, paras 59–62).<br>Luxembourg (CRPD/C/LUX/CO/1, paras 52–53).<br>Malta (CRPD/C/MLT/CO/1, paras 43–44).<br>Slovakia (CRPD/C/SVK/CO/1, paras 79–82).<br>Sweden (CRPD/C/SWE/CO/2–3, paras 63–64).<br>UK (CRPD/C/GBR/CO/1, paras 62–63). |

and as will be outlined in the presentation of the empirical analysis in Part III. Notably, there is also a recommendation that relates to the cultural and linguistic identity of Deaf people (CRPD/C/DEU/CO/2–3, para. 68(c)). The most recent COs for Sweden includes a recommendation to ensure access at no cost to personal assistance 'to practise sport and attend cultural and social activities' (CRPD/C/SWE/CO/2–3, para. 64(b)).

Notably, the need to enhance the range of accessible formats – sign language interpretation, Braille, subtitles, Easy Read, augmentative and alternative modes of accessible communication for people with intellectual or psychosocial disabilities – is often raised by the CRPD Committee in COs under Article 21 CRPD (dealing with freedom of expression and access to communication). A common recommendation is for more access to sign language interpretation or investment in training of sign language interpreters, an issue which also features within the indicators related to Article 30 CRPD (OHCHR, 2020). Typically, these recommendations cross a range of areas of life such as access to justice, media communications, or public information. Only rarely are there specific Article 21 CRPD recommendations on the need for interpretation or other accessible formats in accessing arts and heritage.

## 4. The Implementation of Article 30 CRPD: Patterns and Narratives in States Parties' Reports

After giving a general overview in which we sketched the 'big picture' of how cultural participation has been, thus far, addressed in the reporting process, we move on to discuss common trends and recurring narratives in relation to cultural participation and with regard to how barriers to participation are understood and said to be addressed by States Parties.

We identified three overall themes that recur in States Parties' reports. The first theme highlights the blurred awareness on the part of States Parties when it comes to barriers to cultural participation, with an emphasis on physical accessibility. This theme links particularly (albeit not exclusively) to Article 30(1) CRPD and to individual passive dimension of the right to participate in culture. The second theme presents instances where people with disabilities were constituted as holders of cultural rights or where there was a recognition of disability culture(s) or identities. This theme connects with the 'active' dimension of cultural participation and the implementation of Article 30(2)(4) CRPD. The third theme is a more general one that evidences a throwback to the medical model in how people with disabilities are constituted in many States' reports. The analysis also shows that there can be different, somewhat contradictory, understandings of disability and of the right to participate in culture even within the same report.

### *4.1. A Blurred Awareness of Environmental and Social Barriers to Cultural Participation*

The first main theme correlates with the multidimensional concept of accessibility (Charitakis, 2018) and, as mentioned, with the implementation of Article 30(1) CRPD and is articulated in three sub-themes. The first is concerned with barriers to physical accessibility, which was common across reports reviewed. This is consistent with the wealth of scholarship highlighting the need for physically accessible environments for people with motor and sensory impairments (Mastrogiuseppe et al., 2020; Universidad de Deusto, 2019) and with literature addressing barriers to cultural participation by people with disabilities discussed in Chapter 1. The second sub-theme relates to accessibility of cultural content intended to be inclusive of a diverse range of people with disabilities. The third sub-theme concerns social, attitudinal, and financial barriers.

#### 4.1.1. *Emphasis on Physical Barriers*

It is considered that physical barriers may be easier to recognise than attitudinal barriers (Bickenbach, 2011), and this is consistent with the findings of our empirical research (based mainly on semi-structured interviews), where several participants felt that cultural organisations focused more on physical barriers to participation, rather than other types of barriers, as will be further discussed in Chapter 5. In terms of identifying specific barriers in States' reports, there is often a focus on physical access to venues and/or an indication of steps taken or being planned to address this. Our review shows that this is frequently a primary issue addressed in how states approach Article 30 CRPD, although it is treated with different degrees of depth across the reports reviewed. Amongst many such references is, for example, the following one in the report from Bulgaria (CRPD/C/BGR/1, para. 225):

> To create conditions for physical access to buildings of cultural institutions the Ministry of Culture engaged cultural institutions in the field of theatre, museums, music and dance, permanent and removable ramps were created in 14 buildings, bathrooms in 8 sites were adapted and elevators were installed in 2 sites.

A few reports quantify the physical accessibility of certain types of venues. For example, according to the report from France, fully accessible cinemas account for 73% of admissions (in 2014) (CRPD/C/FRA/1, para. 300). The initial report from Germany suggests that 84% of cinemas participating in a study were 'accessible' but that only 6% could provide aids for Deaf or hearing-impaired people (in 2009) (CRPD/C/DEU/1, footnote 66 to para. 263). The same report, however, admits that 'not all buildings which serve cultural purposes are barrier-free, and hence they are not accessible for all people equally' and that the lack of accessibility had been highlighted by associations of persons with disabilities (para. 263). The initial Latvian report suggests that accessibility measures have been put in place at 54% of accredited museum visitor sites (or in 76 museums), and this includes accessibility mainly for people with 'functional impairments' but also accessibility for people with other kinds of impairments (CRPD/C/LVA/1, para. 364). A report from Croatia (2nd, 3rd, and 4th report) outlines the accessibility of libraries from the 'network of public libraries', suggesting that, out of 318 libraries, '118 of them have access for [persons with disabilities] and 95 are partially accessible. 17 libraries have additional equipment for the blind, while 13 have electronic magnifying glasses for the partially sighted, and 316 of them provide Internet access' (CRPD/C/HRV/2–4, para. 190).

Sometimes States Parties specifically refer to addressing the needs of wheelchair users in a cultural venue. For example, the Estonian report (CRPD/C/EST/1, para. 220) states that the construction and renovation of cultural buildings take 'maximally' into consideration the needs of wheelchair users. However, and much less positively, that report goes on to say that 'if access to some halls is hindered due to absence of elevators, the staff in theatres is trained to help with lifting the wheelchairs' (para. 220). Also, reports sometimes mention challenges around the removal of barriers in older or heritage buildings. For example, the report from Romania refers to adaptation in heritage and historical buildings, being 'hampered by the need to respect the architectural features' (CRPD/C/ROU/1, para. 54; see also report from Poland CRPD/C/POL/1, para. 525). Furthermore, shadow reports from civil society organisations sometimes take issue with the type of access provided even for wheelchair users (see, for example, *Alliantie voor het VN-verdrag*, 2019, p. 13; *Defensor Del Pueblo De España – Institución Nacional de Derechos Humanos* – INDH, 2017, p. 7), something that is also consistent with the findings discussed in Part III.

#### 4.1.2. *Moving Towards a Multidimensional Approach to Accessibility of Cultural Content*

As the literature reviewed in Chapter 1 evidences, access to culture can be complex and require a range of measures informed by different groups of people with disabilities (Mastrogiuseppe et al., 2020). It can be made up of many complex factors, which significantly influence the possibility of benefiting from products, environments, and services (Aquario et al., 2017). States Parties' reports show that, alongside an emphasis on physical accessibility, there is a growing awareness of a broader approach to accessibility intended to be inclusive of a range of people with disabilities, and this awareness is, we suggest, more limited but developing. In this regard, legislation, policies, and various initiatives are cited, designed to make cultural products like films, audio-visual products, theatres, exhibitions, the content of libraries, and museum sites accessible, as well, sometimes, as making information about them accessible. Some states' reports emphasise the accessibility of certain cultural products or services such as films or libraries or interpretive information in heritage sites. The initial EU report also places an emphasis on accessibility of audio-visual media services for all EU citizens, which is regulated at the EU level (CRPD/C/EU/1, para. 172)[6]. Likewise, the 2nd and 3rd report from the EU refers to a number of EU rules adopted to make the EU more accessible for persons with disabilities. These include the 'EAA [European

6 The report refers to Directive 2010/13/EU on the coordination of certain provisions laid down by law, regulation, or administrative action in Member States concerning the provision of audio-visual media services (Audiovisual Media Services Directive (AVMSD)), [2010] OJ L 95/1, 15.4.2010. Most recently the directive has been modified and recast (Directive (EU) 2018/1808 on the coordination of certain provisions laid down by law, regulation, or administrative action in Member States concerning the provision of audio-visual media services (Audiovisual Media Services Directive) in view of changing market realities OJ L 303, 28.11.2018, pp. 69–92).

Accessibility Act] covering products and services, the WAD [Web Accessibility Directive], the Electronic Communications Code, the Audiovisual Media Services Directive (AVMSD) and copyright legislation, and the Digital Services Act (DSA)' (CRPD/C/EU/2–3, in reply to the issues raised in paragraph 23 of the list of issues, point (b)).

Given that Article 30(1) CRPD alludes to accessible formats but does not give any further indication of what these formats are, examples of initiatives to support accessibility of cultural content given in States Parties' reports vary. For example, in the case of art galleries and other cultural venues, the initial report from Czechia states that museums are progressively making 'all expositions and exhibitions accessible' (CRPD/C/CZE/1, para. 449). That report also mentions a venue with a tactile exposition and the digitalisation of content, and it instances the Museum of Puppet Culture as enabling visitors to engage by touch (CRPD/C/CZE/1, paras. 456–460). A festival of Pantomime and Motion Theatre is also referenced where Deaf or hearing-impaired people are said to constitute over half of the participants (CRPD/C/CZE/1, paras. 456–460). Other examples are seen in the Estonian report, which refers to theatres using text strips and sign language interpretation, loop systems, the subtitling of films, and the inclusivity of cultural sites, museums, and art galleries (CRPD/C/EST/1, paras 220–228). The initial report of Latvia outlines measures within museums to make the content available to people with a broad range of impairments (CRPD/C/LVA/1, paras 365–370). The initial EU report mentions *Europeana*, as a portal that 'brings together digitised content from Europe's museums, archives, libraries and audiovisual collections' and features content 'designed to be universally accessible' with a post-prototype version to be produced for blind people (CRPD/C/EU/1, para. 175). Furthermore, the European Commission is said to be committed to ensuring that accessibility criteria are taken into account in the context of the European Capitals of Culture award (CRPD/C/EU/1, para. 175). The subsequent 2nd and 3rd report from the EU refers to a range of initiatives taken (including the Europe Beyond Access and the Accessible Resources for Cultural Heritage EcoSystems-Arches projects). It further mentions the fact that the Creative Europe programme explicitly refers to the CRPD 'and supports actions towards the inclusion of persons with disabilities, both in the creative process and as part of the audience' (CRPD/C/EU/2–3, in reply to the issues raised in paragraph 31 of the LIs, points (c) and (d)).

References, under Article 30 CRPD, to efforts to make library material more accessible for people with visual impairments were common. For example, the initial report from Denmark refers to a state-owned library producing audio books, e-books, and Braille for visually impaired and dyslexic people (CRPD/C/DNK/1, para. 337), and a report from Croatia refers to actions taken under a national strategy (National Strategy for Equalization of Opportunities for Persons with Disabilities from 2017 to 2020) to ensure the accessibility of information, libraries, and 'other contents of cultural life' (CRPD/C/HRV/2–4, para. 187). Much less common were references to sign language libraries, but the Finnish report refers to one (CRPD/C/FIN/1, para. 444). Also unusual were references to visual arts being made accessible for people with visual impairments. However, the Estonian initial report highlights improvements to the accessibility of the Art Museum of Estonia for 'mobility, visual, hearing and intellectually impaired people' (CRPD/C/EST/1, para. 224).

Film and/or broadcasting, which is explicitly mentioned in Article 30(1) CRPD, is another area of focus in some reports. For example, the initial report from Germany highlights that the Film Promotion Act (*Filmförderungsgesetz*) supports audio description and subtitling, as well as providing for incentives 'for the creation of barrier-free versions of cinema films' (CRPD/C/DEU/1, para. 262) and the 2nd and 3rd report also refers to measures related to films (CRPD/C/DEU/2–3, paras 188–189). The 2nd and 3rd report from Denmark (CRPD/C/DNK/2–3, Annex 1, para. 17) mentions funding being made conditional on films having subtitles and an experimental scheme involving audio description. Other reports also highlight initiatives to support the accessibility of film (e.g. reports from Slovakia, CRPD/C/SVK/1, paras 382–384; and France, CRPD/C/FRA/1, para. 300). A report from Croatia mentions legislation requiring public media companies to make their content more accessible to blind and Deaf people, referring to the fact that HRT (Croatian Radio-Television) has greatly increased the amount of content with audio description but also conceding that 'content adapted to people with visual impairments remains a rarity' (CRPD/C/HRV/2–4, para. 123).

### *4.1.3. Social, Attitudinal, and Financial Barriers*

As some of the scholarly work presented in Chapter 1 shows, the important role of arts practices as visible forms of cultural expression makes them an area of unique value when it comes to disability, with potential for challenging how the social order is communicated and reproduced. However, this potential remains untapped, not least because of social and attitudinal barriers and because of stigma (Bariffi, 2018). Our analysis of states' reports suggests a limited and rather patchy approach by States Parties to social, attitudinal, and financial barriers to cultural participation.

These barriers are acknowledged in States Parties' reports, but not to a great extent. Examples include the Estonian initial report, which refers to trainings and seminars about disability for museum staff (CRPD/C/EST/1, para. 226; see also Latvian report, CRPD/C/LVA/1, para. 368), and the initial Slovakian report, which acknowledges efforts to educate people working in the cultural sector to 'eliminate mental and physical barriers' (CRPD/C/SVK/1, para. 386; see also Greek report, CRPD/C/GRC/1, para. 274). The initial report from Latvia refers to radio programmes that promote 'public awareness on disability' (CRPD/C/LV/2–3, para. 224), and the initial Belgian report mentions the need for measures to increase accessibility of infrastructure and also to increase 'receptiveness to sign language or subtitling at cultural events' (CRPD/C/BEL/1, para. 173).

States Parties' reports often refer to funding for specific projects that are accessible. Less common was a commitment to an integrated approach across all areas of culture, including funding, such as that anticipated in the initial report from Sweden that a 'disability perspective must be integrated in the regular granting of subsidies within the field(s) of culture' (CRPD/C/SWE/1, para. 283). However, it is also notable that the subsequent LIs raised by the CRPD Committee for Sweden prior to the submission of its 2nd and 3rd report sought information 'on the national strategy to protect the right to participate in leisure, sports and cultural activities in an inclusive manner' and on 'the extent to which austerity measures affected this right' (CRPD/C/SWE/QPR/2–3, para. 23).

It was also not common for States' reports to specify that schemes of social care or support covered participation in cultural events. Exceptions include the initial report from Germany, which referred to the availability of assistance to attend events, and aids facilitating access to information on cultural events (CRPD/C/DEU/1, paras. 264, 172), something that was rare to find referenced even in this degree of detail (but see also reports from Cyprus, CRPD/C/CYP/1, para. 235; Slovakia, CRPD/C/SVK/1, para. 170; and Latvia, CRPD/C/LVA/1, para. 362). However, it is interesting that, in the case of Germany, this issue was also addressed by the CRPD Committee in subsequent COs, which, *inter alia*, recommend ensuring access to 'personal assistance at no cost to practise sport and attend cultural and social activities' (CRPD/C/DEU/CO/2–3, para. 68(b)) (see also COs for Sweden, CRPD/C/SWE/CO/2–3, para. 64(b)).

Finally, reports often identify measures providing for free or discounted entry to museums or other venues and/or to companion passes. For example, the initial report from Belgium observes that 'persons with disabilities are often obliged to be accompanied, increasing the cost of their participation' (CRPD/C/BEL/1, para. 169). To address this, some local authorities in Belgium are said to issue companion cards enabling companions to take part free of charge. The Finnish initial report refers to free admission to many museums (CRPD/C/FIN/1, paras. 439–440). Sometimes these measures are said to be limited to specific venues, sectors, or by reference to degrees of impairment. For example, the Estonian report refers to free access to state museums, but only for children and people aged 16+ with 'a profound disability' and their companions (CRPD/C/EST/1, para. 223), and the initial report from Romania mentions adults with disabilities receiving 'tickets to shows, museums, arts and sports events under certain conditions' (CRPD/C/ROU/1, paras 334 and 347).

### 4.2. *People with Disabilities as Holders of Cultural Rights*

The second theme identified concerns the recognition of people with disabilities as holders of cultural rights, for which there was some evidence in the State Parties' reports under Article 30 CRPD. This implies the full embracement of the ethos of the CRPD, and an acknowledgement that persons with disabilities should have not only the right to access culture, but also the right to create culture, and to shape culture as amateur or professional artists, as workers in the cultural sphere, and as decision-makers at management and governance levels. This also means developing supports for disability culture and disability identities. In this respect, this theme links to the 'active' participation in culture and to the implementation of Article 30(2)(4) CRPD.

### 4.2.1. *People with Disabilities as Cultural Creators*

The need for cultural participation as a means of self-expression or as an amateur activity was evident in the reports of many countries. For example, the Latvian report (CRPD/C/LVA/1, para. 370) refers to various opportunities for Deaf people, citing 'a variety of creative self-expression measures: free time activities . . . educational and informative measures . . . and amateur performances which is one of the most popular area[s] of leisure for deaf people'. The Lithuanian report mentions 'artistic ability development classes' to provide 'the opportunity to express their abilities in a variety of forms' (CRPD/C/LTU/1, para. 305), and the initial Slovakian report discusses the availability of 'active and passive culture' (CRPD/C/SVK/1, para. 390). There are also references to events or festivals organised by people with disabilities. Examples come from reports from Latvia (CRPD/C/LVA/1, para. 370), which mentions performances in sign language, and from Lithuania, where persons with disabilities are said to 'hold exhibitions of their work and take part in contests' (CRPD/C/LTU/1, para. 305). A report from Croatia refers to financial support for projects 'that affirm the creative and artistic possibilities of PWD' (CRPD/C/HRV/2–4, para. 188) and another highlights projects that 'sensitise the public for artistic work of persons with disabilities and specific theatres of persons with disabilities' (CRPD/C/HRV/1, para. 217).

There is also awareness shown in some States Parties' reports of people with disabilities as creators of culture in their own right at a professional level, and this is an aspect that appears to be developing. Thus, some reports (or their annexes) refer to Deaf artists or to artists or actors with disabilities. Notable amongst them was the UK report where there were several references to artists with disabilities or Deaf artists, including references to grants that promote the work of artists with disabilities (CRPD/C/GBR/1, para. 328) and to an Arts Council England scheme centring on 'prominence' for people with disabilities (para. 328). Several reports are explicit about the need to develop both amateur and professional participation, and/or mention arts organisations that include disabled and non-disabled artists. For example, the initial report from Ireland makes mention of a national development organisation (Arts & Disability Ireland) that promotes 'engagement with the arts at all levels – as professional artists, audience members and arts workers' (CRPD/C/IRL/1, para. 422). A report from France refers to 'equal access to cultural practices and amateur activities and to artistic training and practice for persons with disabilities' (CRPD/C/FRA/1, para. 301). Somewhat similarly, the initial report from Sweden recognises 'personal creation' and opportunities to share in 'professional artistic creation' (CRPD/C/SWE/1, para. 282). That report also states that it 'is becoming increasingly common for professional theatre and dance groups to include actors and dancers both with and without disabilities' (para. 289). It instances the National Theatre, within which the Quiet Theatre produces drama in sign language (para. 287). Sometimes references to artists with disabilities are cursory references, without much elaboration. For example, the Portuguese report addresses arts and culture briefly in one paragraph (CRPD/C/PRT/1, para. 273), mentioning services 'for persons with disabilities, both as an audience and as artists'.

Other reports, albeit only implicitly, suggest that the professional engagement of artists and performers may be envisaged. Examples include references to 'cultural production', which occurs in the Italian report along with a reference to 'the development and implementation of creative, artistic and intellectual potential' said to be 'guaranteed by laws 285/97 and 328/00, and by means of specific public tenders' (CRPD/C/ITA/1, para. 168). There were also references to 'practising art' (Netherlands report, CRPD/C/NLD/1, para. 335) or to assistance for 'persons with disabilities in the media and artistic productions' (2nd and 3rd German report, CRPD/C/DEU/2–3, para. 62). In these cases, the use of the terms 'production' or 'practice/practising' may be referring to professional engagement, but this is not made explicit. Many other reports talk generally about initiatives fostering the cultural participation of people with disabilities, and it is possible that those may, in fact, include professional artists with disabilities, but this is unclear (see, for example, the Luxembourg report, CRPD/C/LUX/1, paras 393–394).

However, we found very few explicit references within the states' reports reviewed to the employment of people with disabilities as arts workers or professionals within arts and cultural industries or to their participation in governance or decision-making roles. The Irish report referred to already is one of the exceptions – with its reference to 'arts workers' (CRPD/C/IRL/1, para. 422). The Slovenian initial report (CRPD/C/SVN/1, para. 236) was also an exception, referring to 'projects to improve the employability of vulnerable groups in the field of culture' characterised as a means to support social inclusion. The Estonian report also mentions 'several' people with disabilities having qualified as data entry clerks in museums (CRPD/C/EST/1, para. 226). Related to this, references to the input of people with disabilities into governance or decision-making in cultural organisations were also extremely limited. However, the establishment of 'a user council for disability organizations' to act as an ongoing forum for discussion is said to be required of the Danish Broadcasting Corporation under its public service contract (CRPD/C/DNK/1, para. 339).

On the whole, there is evidence that States Parties are beginning to appreciate people with disabilities as contributors and shapers of culture. However, there is much still to be done to realise the provisions of Article 30(2) CRPD, and this involves ensuring that measures are taken that enable people with disabilities to 'develop and utilize their creative, artistic and intellectual potential, not only for their own benefit, but also for the enrichment of society'.

### 4.2.2. *Cultural Identities of People with Disabilities*

As discussed already, especially in Chapter 3; Article 30(4) CRPD recognises the specific cultural and linguistic identity of people with disabilities, explicitly protecting sign language and Deaf culture. The formulation of this provision tallies with Article 21(e) CRPD, which requires States Parties to take measures 'recognizing and promoting the use of sign languages'. In fact, States Parties' reports from many countries make reference to steps taken, or to be taken, towards the recognition of sign language. This is expressed in various ways, involving, for example, references to sign language as a 'language in its own right' (see reports from Austria, CRPD/C/AUT/1, para. 31; and the UK, CRPD/C/GBR/1, para. 208) or as a 'separate', 'independent', or 'official' language' (see reports from Estonia, CRPD/C/EST/1, para. 218; Ireland, CRPD/C/IRL/1, para. 265; Germany, CRPD/C/DEU/1, paras 21, 167, 259), or as 'the mother tongue specific to deaf and/or deaf people' (report from Romania CRPD/C/ROU/1, para. 246).

There are also references to users of sign language or Deaf people as a language or linguistic or cultural minority (e.g. reports from Belgium, CRPD/C/BEL/1, para. 97; Finland, CRPD/C/FIN/1, para. 259; Hungary, CRPD/C/HUN/1, para. 17; and Lithuania, CRPD/C/LVA/1, para. 158). Other reports do not refer to sign language recognition at all or refer to the lack of legislative instruments recognising and protecting sign language, or they emphasise measures providing for the *use* of sign language. Amongst them, the report from Luxembourg mentions that sign language enjoys 'de facto recognition' (CRPD/C/LUX/1, para. 237). However, subsequent COs for Luxembourg recommend expediting the enactment of legislation to recognise German sign language and 'promoting other sign languages to respect the multilingual character of the State party' as well as measures to increase access to sign language interpretation (CRPD/C/LUX/CO/1, para. 39).[7] Somewhat similarly, while the initial report from France refers to an Act from 2005 that 'recognises French Sign Language as a language in its own right' (CRPD/C/FRA/1, para. 181), COs addressed to France, under Article 21 CRPD, note that sign language is recognised only in certain areas, such as in education, and call for recognition of French sign language as an official language, including at the constitutional level, as well as the promotion of its use (CRPD/C/FRA/CO/1, paras 44–45). Examples of reports referring

7 Information subsequently filed by Luxembourg suggests that an Act of 23 September 2018, amending an Act of 24 February 1984 on language policy, was approved by the Chamber of Deputies in July 2018, providing for the recognition of German sign language and establishing, *inter alia*, the right to communicate with the authorities in sign language ('Information received from Luxembourg on follow-up to the Concluding Observations [Date received: 14 November 2018]' CRPD/C/LUX/CO/1/Add.1, para. 41).

to measures providing for the *use* of sign language occur in reports from Croatia (CRPD/C/HRV/2–4, para. 120), Latvia (CRPD/C/LVA/1, para. 21); and Poland (CRPD/C/POL/1, para. 246). However, in the case of Croatia, an earlier (that is, initial) report had referred to the preparation of 'legal regulation' to, *inter alia*, recognise sign language as a 'minority language' (CRPD/C/HRV/1, para. 17).

Interestingly, several reports deal with sign language most extensively under the implementation of Article 21 CRPD, rather than under Article 30 CRPD. This seems to hint at a conception of sign language as a mode of communication or an accessible format rather than a language *per se*. However, some reports do highlight the promotion of Deaf culture and research exploring the history or culture of Deaf people within education. The Finnish report represents an interesting case in its level of detail. It refers to sign language users as a 'language and cultural minority' (CRPD/C/FIN/1, para. 259). A consciousness of different linguistic groups amongst Deaf people is shown in references to Sámi and sign language users, who are said to represent minorities amongst persons with disabilities (para. 257). It also refers to measures needed to protect the endangered Finnish-Swedish sign language (para. 266). It also recognises that sign language can be considered a native language if a parent or older sibling is a sign language user and if sign language has been used with a child since birth (para. 261).

References to Braille and to other alternative forms of communication were common in reports from states, often in responses to Article 21 CRPD and in relation to access to information and communications, and were not framed in terms of cultural or linguistic identity. This is perhaps unsurprising given that Deaf people and sign language users are the sole group specified in Article 30 CRPD in the context of linguistic identity and the only group that has advocated for recognition as a minority. However, there was a small number of references to events that seem designed to highlight or celebrate the lives or achievements of people with visual impairment. For example, the Lithuanian report refers to events organised by the Lithuanian Library to mark 'important dates in the lives of public figures who were blind' (CRPD/C/LTU/1, para. 294). The initial Slovakian report had some references to the 'culture of persons with sight disabilities' and, in the context of museums and galleries, to the development of 'the culture of the disabled' (CRPD/C/SVK/1, paras 379, 385).

On the whole, in some reports it is possible to detect an understanding of Deaf people as having a distinct cultural or linguistic identity even if that is not always fully supported in practice, but there is a much more limited sense of people with disabilities as characterised by a cultural identity.

### 4.3. *Throwback to the Medical Model: Cultural Participation as Therapy or Education*

The third theme identified in our analysis deals with how people with disabilities are constituted in the cultural sphere. The measures articulated under Article 30 CRPD by States Parties' responses suggest a patchwork in terms of how participation in culture is understood and in relation to what the motivation for this is – including motivations based on educating others, promoting health, compensating for health challenges, or fostering social inclusion. Thus, a medical, or therapeutic, or charitable understanding of disability is evident in several States Parties' reports. The Polish report refers to 'library therapy and art therapy' for blind people and characterises a 'series of workshops in various arts' as 'Creative Therapy' (CRPD/C/POL/1, paras 514 and 516), and the report from Czechia includes reference to 'art-therapy' and to a programme of support for projects focused on exploiting the 'therapeutic function of culture in order to compensate for disadvantages on account of health' (CRPD/C/CZE/1, para. 452). Another report refers to public libraries organising home deliveries for people unable 'to visit the library due to health reasons' (Estonian report, CRPD/C/EST/1, para. 230; see also Slovakian report CRPD/C/SVK/1, para. 379). Sometimes a therapeutic approach was linked to ideas of rehabilitation or tackling social exclusion. A Lithuanian report links 'social rehabilitation services' to 'artistic self-expression and cultural activities for persons with disabilities' (CRPD/C/LTU/2–3, para. 248). Another mentions the 'National Programme of Social Integration of the Disabled', listing a range of arts and cultural activities supported, including 'social rehabilitation services' and referring also to cultural events aimed at 'improvement of the status of the people with disabilities in the society and reduction of their social exclusion' (CRPD/C/LTU/1, paras 304–6). While art therapy may be beneficial in its own right, it is not the same thing as artistic practice and can seem like discrimination to artists with disabilities (Solvang, 2018).

Sometimes, states' reports refer to cultural activities in terms of education about disability issues amongst the general public or people working in cultural sectors. There may, of course, be valuable aspects to such awareness-raising initiatives, but some of these references seem to suggest that disability is still constituted as an individual problem or an issue requiring a charitable response. For example, Hungary's initial report mentions support for people with disabilities 'with regard to public education programmes', and public education conferences are described as opportunities for people with disabilities 'to report their own problems' (CRPD/C/HUN/1, para. 236). Similarly, in a report from Croatia, broadcasts adapted for Deaf people and hearing-impaired people are described as aiming 'to educate society about the behaviour towards PWD and sensitize society to their problems' (CRPD/C/HRV/2–4, para. 124). There can also be explicit links made between cultural events and charitable donations or fundraising efforts (e.g. Bulgarian report, CRPD/C/BGR/1, para. 242; Latvian report CRPD/C/LV/2–3, para. 225).

Overall, the references to therapy, rehabilitation, education, or of other references to the 'problems' of persons with disabilities or charitable aims reveal a lingering understanding of disability within the responses to Article 30 CRPD that is anchored to a medical understanding of disability, instead of the social-contextual and rights-based approach embodied in the CRPD's human rights model of disability. This is also consistent with comments contained in shadow reports from civil society organisations, which often highlight a continued focus on medicalised approaches or the lack of a social-contextual understanding of disability or the human rights model in their countries (see, amongst others, Autistic Minority International, 2015, p. 8; Human Rights Monitoring Institute and Mental Health Perspectives, 2023; Northern Ireland Civil Society, n.d., para. 1). Furthermore, States Reports do not seem to reflect the shift envisaged in disability studies to problematising what is perceived as 'normal' or 'mainstream' culture (see, amongst others, Davis, 2013; Goodley & Bolt, 2010; Riddell & Watson, 2003).

## 5. The CRPD Committee Concluding Observations: Shallow Counter-Narratives

The CRPD Committee has dedicated limited attention to the implementation of Article 30 CRPD. As noted earlier, it has often (and definitely, in relation to the European States considered up to 2018) focused on ratifying or implementing the Marrakesh Treaty, which provides for copyright exceptions for the benefit of blind, visually impaired, or otherwise print disabled people.

In relation to the 'narratives' purported by States Parties, the CRPD Committee has not always proffered distinct counter-narratives or comprehensive recommendations. Thus, the CRPD Committee has traditionally tended to provide limited guidance in the field of culture (as discussed earlier). For example, even when there are recommendations that are broader than copyright issues or the Marrakesh Treaty, they can still be framed in quite brief and general terms, although there is variation across the COs reviewed. An example of these general and rather vague terms comes from the COs for Bulgaria, which (as well as addressing the Marrakesh Treaty) state as follows (CRPD/C/BGR/CO/1, para. 66): 'The Committee recommends that the State party take steps to support and encourage the participation of persons with disabilities, including children, in cultural, recreational, leisure and sporting activities.'

Even if this approach is changing, and some specific recommendations have been included, especially in COs of recent years (see, for example, the COs for Germany released in 2023, CRPD/C/DEU/CO/2–3, paras. 67–68; and, to some extent, those for Sweden, released in 2024, CRPD/C/SWE/CO/2–3, paras. 63–64), there is still room for the CRPD Committee to consistently demonstrate a more comprehensive approach to cultural participation.

The CRPD Committee has, however, addressed reports of States Parties that represent a throwback to medical models, although not always with specific reference to Article 30 CRPD. Thus, it has mentioned the absence of a human rights approach in reports of States Parties or recommended the adoption of such a model, and the Committee sometimes refers to the continuance, instead, of medicalised approaches. For example, COs issued in 2021, in response to the initial report from France, refer to the need for a review of legislation and policies to harmonise them with the CRPD 'including by transposing into domestic law the human rights model of disability' (CRPD/C/FRA/CO/1, para. 8(b). COs for Hungary recommend as follows:

> Reorient its disability assessment systems by replacing elements of the medical model of disability with principles of the human rights model of disability and by establishing systems aimed at the assessment of legal and environmental barriers to persons with disabilities and the provision of the necessary support and assistance to promote the independent living of persons with disabilities and their full social inclusion. (CRPD/C/HUN/CO/2–3, para. 7(a), see also para. 15(a))

In a similar vein, LIs for Slovenia (CRPD/C/SVN/QPR/2–4, para. 1(a)) enquire about reforms

> aimed at shifting from medical and charity approaches to disability to a human rights model of disability in all legislation, plans and practices, and on the harmonization of the various divergent definitions of disability, based on the human rights model of disability.

Similarly, COs on the initial report from Austria highlight how Austrian society has not seen 'a complete understanding of the paradigm shift created by the human rights-centred approach in the Convention' and recommend awareness-raising 'to effectively transform the old-fashioned charity model of disability' (CRPD/C/AUT/CO/1, paras 21–22; see also COs for Belgium, CRPD/C/BEL/CO/1, para. 17). As another example, and in a somewhat similar vein, COs for Estonia refer to the continued use of 'derogatory concepts and terminology' in laws and policies, 'which emphasize persons' impairments, reflect the medical and paternalistic approaches to disability that exist in the State party and reinforce stigma against persons with intellectual or psychosocial disabilities' (CRPD/C/EST/CO/1, para. 7(b)).

## 6. Concluding Remarks

As indicated earlier, the approach of the States Parties under consideration varies when it comes to Article 30 CRPD. However, a lengthy report relating to culture, with multiple references to arts and heritage, is not necessarily representative of a thoroughgoing approach to addressing cultural participation. For example, there are many initiatives referred to under Article 30 CRPD in the report from Bulgaria (CRPD/C/BGR/1) and, to a lesser extent, in the report of Croatia (CRPD/C/HRV/1). However, the degree to which this might represent a comprehensive approach at a national level to meet the objectives of Article 30 CRPD is unclear. In fact, in the case of those two countries, subsequent COs express concern about the levels of participation of persons with disabilities in cultural life and contain recommendations aimed at increasing participation (CRPD/C/BGR/CO/1, paras 65–66; CRPD/C/HRV/CO/1, paras 47–48).

Our analysis shows that the implementation of the right to participate in cultural life is lagging behind. States' reports present a mixed picture, or patchwork, in terms of how they realise the obligations laid out in Article 30 CRPD. A systematic, mainstreamed approach to culture informed by the potential for cultural transformation that the CRPD represents (Scully, 2012) is yet to be realised. This need for mainstreaming was articulated comprehensively in a document accompanying a shadow report from the National Confederation of Disabled People of Greece (NCDP) (2019, p. 20), which recommended:

> To mainstream the disability dimension in every cultural policy, process, action, measure and program to ensure the human right of persons with disabilities and chronic diseases to full and equal participation as public, employees and/or creators-artists in the cultural heritage, sites, material, services as well as in the modern culture.

Our analysis of States Parties' reports suggests that there is a developing (yet insufficient) sense of the need for a broader approach to accessibility, such as access to the contents of cultural products for people with a broad range of disability types. Reports mention to varying degrees diverse accessible formats, including tactile and sound signage elements, Braille, Easy Read, pictograms, captioning, or audio description. Such a developing awareness is somewhat counterbalanced by a far more bittersweet picture emerging from our empirical research, which will be discussed in Part III, and from shadow reports submitted to the CRPD Committee by OPDs and NGOs or other civil society groups, which, where they deal with culture, often detail inadequate accessibility of cultural offerings. For example, in their shadow report, the Belgian Disability Forum (2014) suggests that, while the accessibility of cultural activities is guaranteed under regional regulations, implementation is lacking. A report coordinated by the Disabled People's Organisations Denmark (DPOD) (2019, para. 48) suggests that many cultural institutions – such as theatres, museums, and cinemas – are not accessible in terms of either physical accessibility of buildings or the digital accessibility of apps, websites, or content. Similarly, the shadow report from the German CRPD Alliance (BRK-Allianz, 2013, pp. 90–91) suggests that both physical accessibility and accessibility of content are inadequate across a range of cultural and heritage venues and for people with different kinds of impairments.

Our analysis also ascertained limited explicit recognition that each person with a disability is unique and may require specific and diverse supports in order to access culture. In that regard, the value of reasonable accommodation when it comes to cultural rights is not recognised.

References to social, attitudinal, or financial barriers to participation in culture were quite sparse, as was recognition of a potential role for people with disabilities in transforming arts practices and hence for challenging how the social order is communicated and reproduced. Relatedly, in our analysis of States Parties' reports, we detected a rather limited (if developing somewhat) understanding of people with disabilities as makers and shapers of culture in their own right. In addition, references to the employment of people with disabilities within cultural organisations and to their involvement at decision-making levels were also almost non-existent.

Furthermore, States Parties often recognise the linguistic identity of sign language users or suggest that measures are planned towards that recognition. However, shadow reports frequently contend that, in practice, support for Deaf culture is inadequate. For example, the German BRK-Allianz (2013) report refers to insufficient support for the cultural identity of people who use plain language or German sign language, and a report from France suggests that sign language is not as broadly recognised as the government report purports (*Fédération Nationale des Sourds de France*, 2019; see also, amongst others, reports from the British Deaf Association, 2017, para. 6(c); PanCyprian Alliance for Disability, 2017). There is little evidence that recognition of cultural identity is apprehended more broadly as applying to other groups of people with disabilities. As mentioned in Chapter 3, the issue of the existence of a 'disability identity' (other than one that relates to Deaf people) is a contested issue even within disability studies (Davis, 2013; Siebers, 2008, p. 11) as is the conceptualisation of disability culture(s) (Johnson, 2020). However, Article 30(4) CRPD may support the recognition of various cultural perspectives of people with disabilities and of the role of a range of art forms in articulating those shared cultures already emphasised by scholarly work (Johnson, 2020). For Jakubowicz and Meekosha (2003, p. 190), disability culture seeks to revalorise disability experiences and turn upside down the devaluation that society accords people with disabilities, arguing that disability culture affirms 'different embodiments through literature, drama, sport and music'. Our review shows that these issues have yet to be reflected to any extent in how reports of States Parties from EU countries address Article 30 CRPD and (for the most part) in how the CRPD Committee responds to them.

On the whole, the continued narrow approach to accessibility, the limited awareness shown in the States Parties' reports about disability identities, and the evident focus on people with disabilities as consumers of culture or participants at an amateur level fall short of the obligations of Article 30 CRPD. Medical or charitable models of disability are still influential, and engagement with culture is sometimes linked to the mere desire to promote health, enhance rehabilitation, or foster social inclusion. In that regard, we contend that States Parties still problematise disability, rather than locating it within mainstream culture (Waldschmidt, 2018, p. 74), which hampers the implementation of Article 30 CRPD.

## References

Alliantie voor het VN-verdrag. (2019). *VN-Vertelpunt (UN Listening Post) Stories of disability experiences Appendix to the Shadow Report CRPD*. https://tbinternet.ohchr.org/_layouts/15/treatybodyexternal/Download.aspx?symbolno=INT%2FCRPD%2FICO%2FNLD%2F47915&Lang=en

Aquario, D., Pais, I., & Ghedin, E. (2017). Accessibilità alla conoscenza e universal design. Uno studio esplorativo con docenti e studenti universitari. *Italian Journal of Special Education for Inclusion*, *5*(2), 93–106.
Autistic Minority International. (2015). *Written submission to the 14th session of the Committee on the Rights of Persons with Disabilities: Review of the European Union: About Autism, Without Autistics*. https://tbinternet.ohchr.org/_layouts/15/treatybodyexternal/Download.aspx?symbolno=INT%2FCRPD%2FCSS%2FEUR%2F21278&Lang=en
Bantekas, I., Stephenson, C. P. Y., Karapapa, S., & Polymenopoulou, E. (2018). Article 30: Participation in cultural life, recreation, leisure, and sport. In I. Bantekas, M. A. Stein, & D. Anastasiou (Eds.), *The UN Convention on the Rights of Persons with Disabilities: A Commentary* (pp. 863–923). Oxford University Press.
Bariffi, F. (2018). Article 8: Awareness-raising. In I. Bantekas, M. A. Stein, & D. Anastasiou (Eds.), *The UN Convention on the Rights of Persons with Disabilities: A Commentary* (pp. 863–923). Oxford University Press.
Belgian Disability Forum. (2014). *Position of the associations and advisory structures representing persons with disabilities. Shadow Report Initiated and Coordinated by the Belgian Disability Forum*.
Bickenbach, J. (2011). The world report on disability. *Disability & Society*, *26*(5), 655–658.
Bowen, G. A. (2009). Document analysis as a qualitative research method. *Qualitative Research Journal*, *9*(2), 27–40.
Braun, V., & Clarke, V. (2006). Using thematic analysis in psychology. *Qualitative Research in Psychology*, *3*(2), 77–101.
British Deaf Association. (2017). *BDA response to the list of issues in relation to the initial report of the United Kingdom of Great Britain and Northern Ireland: Government response*. https://tbinternet.ohchr.org/_layouts/15/treatybodyexternal/Download.aspx?symbolno=INT%2FCRPD%2FCSS%2FGBR%2F28469&Lang=en
BRK-Allianz/Alliance of German Non-Governmental Organizations (Eds.). (2013). *First civil society report on the implementation of the UN Convention on the Rights of Persons with Disabilities in Germany*. BRK-Allianz.
Caust, J. (2019). Cultural rights as human rights and the impact on the expression of arts practices. *Journal of Citizenship and Globalisation Studies*, *3*(1), 17–30.
Charitakis, S. (2018). *Access denied: The role of the European Union in ensuring accessibility under the United Nations Convention on the Rights of Persons with Disabilities*. Intersentia.
Charitakis, S. (2020). Accessibility of goods and services. In D. Ferri & A. Broderick (Eds.), *Research handbook on EU disability law* (pp. 221–242). Edward Elgar.
Coffey, A. (2013). Analysing documents. In U. Flick (Ed.), *The SAGE handbook of qualitative data analysis* (pp. 367–369). SAGE.
Council of the European Union. (2010). Council decision of 26 November 2009 concerning the conclusion, by the European Community, of the United Nations Convention on the Rights of Persons with Disabilities. *Official Journal of the European Union*, *23*, 35–36.
Davis, L. J. (2013). The end of identity politics: On disability as an unstable category. In L. J. Davis (Ed.), *The disability studies reader* (pp. 263–277). Routledge.
Defensor Del Pueblo De España (INDH). (2017). *Contribución Escrita Lista de Preguntas que deben Adoptarse sobre España en la 17ª Sesión del Comité de Derechos de las Personas con Discapacidad* (20 de marzo – 12 de abril). https://tbinternet.ohchr.org/_layouts/15/treatybodyexternal/Download.aspx?symbolno=INT%2FCRPD%2FIFR%2FESP%2F34071&Lang=en
Degener, T. (2017). A new human rights model of disability. In V. Della Fina, R. Cera, & G. Palmisano (Eds.), *The United Nations Convention on the Rights of Persons with Disabilities: A Commentary* (pp. 41–60). Springer.

Disability Ombudsman of Croatia. (2014). *Parallel report: On the implementation of the UN Convention on the Rights of Persons with Disabilities in the Republic of Croatia on the occasion of the review of the initial report of the government of the republic of Croatia before the UN committee on the rights of persons with disabilities*. Republic of Croatia Disability Ombudsman.

Disabled People's Organisations Denmark (DPOD). (2019). *Civil society's suggestions to the UN committee on the rights of persons with disabilities regarding the 'List of issues prior to reporting' on the kingdom of Denmark*. Disabled People's Organisations Denmark.

European Commission, Directorate-General for Education, Youth, Sport and Culture. (2019). *From social inclusion to social cohesion – The role of culture policy*. Publications Office of the European Union.

Fédération Nationale des Sourds de France. (2019). *Convention des Nations Unies relative aux droits des personnes handicapée: État des lieux préparatoire à la rédaction du rapport alternatif de la société civile, dans le cadre du suivi du rapport initial du gouvernement sur l'application de la convention*. https://tbinternet.ohchr.org/_layouts/15/treatybodyexternal/Download.aspx?symbolno=INT%2FCRPD%2FICO%2FFRA%2F35655&Lang=en

Ferri, D. (2024). The Marrakesh treaty to facilitate access to published works for persons who are blind, visually impaired or otherwise print disabled in the European Union: Reflecting on its implementation and gauging its impact from a disability perspective. *IIC International Review of Intellectual Property and Competition Law*, *55*(1), 89–109.

Ferri, D., & Broderick, A. (2020). Introduction to research handbook on EU disability law. In D. Ferri & A. Broderick (Eds.), *Research handbook on EU disability law* (pp. 1–10). Edward Elgar.

Ferri, D., & Donnellan, K. (2022). The implementation of the Marrakesh Treaty in the European Union: An important piece in the accessibility jigsaw? *Legal Issues of Economic Integration*, *49*(3), 269–292.

Goodley, D., & Bolt, D. (2010). Introduction. In D. Goodley & D. Bolt (Eds.), Special issue theorizing culture and disability: Interdisciplinary dialogues. *Review of Disability Studies: An International Journal*, *6*(3).

Gross, J. M. S. (2018). Document analysis. In B. Frey (Ed.), *The SAGE encyclopedia of educational research, measurement, and evaluation* (Vol. 4, pp. 545–548). SAGE.

Human Rights Monitoring Institute and Mental Health Perspectives. (2023). *Alternative report submitted to the UN CRPD 17th pre-sessional working group on the occasion of the review of Lithuania's combined second and third report under the UN Convention on the Rights of People with Disabilities*. https://tbinternet.ohchr.org/_layouts/15/treatybodyexternal/Download.aspx?symbolno=INT%2FCRPD%2FICO%2FLTU%2F51798&Lang=en

Jakubowicz, A., & Meekosha, H. (2003). Can multiculturalism encompass disability? In S. Riddell & N. Watson (Eds.), *Disability, culture and identity* (pp. 180–199). Pearson Education.

Johnson, K. (2020). Recognising cultural diversity: Implications for persons with disabilities. In E. J. Kakoullis & K. Johnson (Eds.), *Recognising human rights in different cultural contexts* (pp. 63–78). Palgrave Macmillan.

Lawson, A., & Beckett, A. E. (2021). The social and human rights models of disability: Towards a complementarity thesis. *The International Journal of Human Rights*, *25*(2), 348–379.

Mastrogiuseppe, M., Span, S., & Bortolotti, E. (2020). Improving accessibility to cultural heritage for people with intellectual disabilities: A tool for observing the obstacles and facilitators for the access to knowledge. *Alter, European Journal of Disability Research/Revue européenne de recherche sur le handicap*, *15*(2), 113–123.

National Confederation of Disabled People of Greece (NCDP). (2019). *Human rights and persons with disabilities: List with recommendations for the 22 session* (August 26 – September 20). National Confederation of Disabled People of Greece.
Northern Ireland Civil Society. (n.d.). *Draft response from Northern Ireland Civil Society to the List of Issues relating the forthcoming examination of the UK State by the UN Committee on the Rights of Persons with Disabilities.* https://tbinternet.ohchr.org/_layouts/15/treatybodyexternal/Download.aspx?symbolno=INT%2FCRPD%2FCSS%2FGBR%2F28465&Lang=en
Office of the High Commissioner for Human Rights (OHCHR). (2020). *Article 30: List of illustrative indicators on participation in cultural life, recreation, leisure and sport.* www.ohchr.org/sites/default/files/article-30-indicators-en.pdf
Pancyprian Alliance for Disability. (2017). *Submission of the Pancyprian Alliance for Disability in response to the list of issues of the committee on the rights of persons with disabilities in relation to the initial report of Cyprus.* Pancyprian Alliance for Disability.
Riddell, S., & Watson, N. (2003). Disability, culture and identity: Introduction. In S. Riddell & N. Watson (Eds.), *Disability, culture and identity* (pp. 1–18). Pearson Education.
Scully, J. L. (2012). The Convention on the Rights of Persons with Disabilities and cultural understandings of disability. In J. Anderson & J. Philips (Eds.), *Disability and universal human rights: Legal, ethical, and conceptual implications of the Convention on the Rights of Persons with Disabilities* (pp. 71–84). Utrecht University Netherlands Institute of Human Rights.
Sganga, C. (2020). Disability in EU copyright law. In D. Ferri & A. Broderick (Eds.), *Research handbook on EU disability law* (pp. 201–220). Edward Elgar.
Siebers, T. (2008). *Disability theory.* University of Michigan Press.
Solvang, P. K. (2018). Between art therapy and disability aesthetics: A sociological approach for understanding the intersection between art practice and disability discourse. *Disability & Society*, *33*(2), 238–253.
Tight, M. (2019). *Documentary research in the social sciences.* SAGE.
United Nations. (n.d.). *Guidelines and tools for treaty body reporting.* https://www.ohchr.org/en/treaty-bodies/guidelines-and-tools-treaty-body-reporting
United Nations Committee on the Rights of Persons with Disabilities (CRPD Committee). (2009). *Guidelines on treaty-specific document to be submitted by States parties under article 35, paragraph 1, of the Convention on the Rights of Persons with Disabilities* (UN Doc. CRPD/C/2/3).
United Nations Committee on the Rights of Persons with Disabilities (CRPD Committee). (2016). *Guidelines on periodic reporting to the CRPD, including under the simplified reporting procedures adopted by the Committee at its 16th session* (UN Doc. CRPD/C/3).
Universidad de Deusto. (2019). *Manifiesto por un ocio inclusivo.* Publicaciones de la Universidad de Deusto.
Waldschmidt, A. (2018). Disability – culture – society: Strengths and weaknesses of a cultural model of dis/ability. *Alter, European Journal of Disability Research/Revue européenne de recherche sur le handicap*, *12*(2), 65–78.
Wolff, S. (2004). Analysis of documents and records. In U. Flick, E. von Kardorff, & I. Steinke (Eds.), *A companion to qualitative research* (pp. 284–289). SAGE.
World Intellectual Property Organisation (WIPO). (2013). *Marrakesh treaty to facilitate access to published works for persons who are blind, visually impaired or otherwise print disabled.* www.wipo.int/treaties/en/ip/marrakesh/

Part III

# Realising the Right of Persons with Disabilities to Participate in Cultural Life

## Barriers and Facilitators

# 5 Barriers to Cultural Participation of People with Disabilities

*Ann Leahy and Delia Ferri*

## 1. Introduction

Having outlined the core obligations set out in Article 30 of the UN Convention on the Rights of Persons with Disabilities (CRPD), and the extent to which they have been implemented by States Parties, this chapter focuses on the barriers experienced by persons with disabilities in the exercise of their right to participate in cultural life. Specifically, this chapter presents the results from an empirical study which sought to identify which barriers to cultural participation persist and cut across different types of disability and geographical areas across Europe. It links the discussion of these barriers to the obligations laid out in Article 30 CRPD and to the human rights model of disability, which constitutes the theoretical framework of the book. In doing so, the chapter aims to identify what has thus far hampered the realisation of Article 30 CRPD, juxtaposing the experiences of people with disabilities with the narratives of States Parties discussed in Chapter 4.

As discussed earlier in Part II, barriers – societal, environmental, and attitudinal – are central to how disability is defined in the preamble and in Article 1(2) CRPD, which states that disability results from 'the interaction between persons with impairments and attitudinal and environmental barriers that hinder their full and effective participation in society on an equal basis with others'. The UN Committee on the Rights of Persons with Disabilities (CRPD Committee) has also recognised that disability is a social construct and has emphasised the role of barriers in creating disability (CRPD Committee, 2018a). In this chapter, in particular, the term 'barriers' is used in a way that is consistent with the CRPD to mean 'factors in a person's environment that, through their absence or presence, limit functioning and create disability' (World Health Organization (WHO) & World Bank, 2011, p. 302), with reference to both active and passive forms of cultural participation (Chow, 2018, p. 111; see also Bantekas et al., 2018). In that regard, this chapter discusses barriers to the exercise of the right to access cultural activities, goods, services and heritage, and the right to active involvement in culture, which includes engagement in the creation of cultural activities, goods, and services (EPRS, 2017; Romainville, 2015).

DOI: 10.4324/9781032619361-9

This chapter has been made available under a CC-BY-NC-ND 4.0 license.

After these introductory remarks, Section 2 presents the methodology employed. Section 3 then discusses the results from this empirical research and examines a range of intertwined barriers identified that limit the lives of people with disabilities and hamper their enjoyment of the right to participate in cultural life, as provided for in Article 30 CRPD. Being interlinked, these barriers prevent the enjoyment of the twofold individual dimension of the right – that is, the right to access cultural activities, goods, services and heritage, and the right to active involvement in culture – and also hamper the exercise of its collective aspect – that is, the 'specific cultural and linguistic identity' of persons with disabilities. The barriers identified tally (or overlap) with structural barriers that persons with disabilities face beyond the cultural context, signalling that the implementation of Article 30 CRPD must go hand in hand with the realisation of other provisions of the Convention. Section 4 concludes with some final remarks.

## 2. Methodology

As noted in the introduction, this book encompasses a socio-legal analysis of the right of people with disabilities to participate in cultural life, focusing on barriers to, and facilitators of, its realisation, entailing an examination of Article 30 CRPD within the social situations in which it applies. Consistent with this approach, alongside the blending of legal analysis and the study of relevant cultural studies and disability studies literature, this book is based on a large qualitative study that sought to identify the main barriers to cultural participation as perceived by key stakeholders, namely organisations of persons with disabilities (OPDs) and organisations working on disability rights or in disability arts across Europe.

We pursued a purposeful sampling strategy and recruited representatives of 64 organisations drawn from 28 European countries (27 EU Member States and the UK). We identified the target organisations through online searches, through existing contacts, and, in some cases, through snowball sampling whereby participants suggested others (Taylor et al., 2015). In particular, those invited to participate were drawn from three types of organisations: umbrella OPDs working at national level within their countries and representing people with a range of disability types (n = 28), national organisations of Deaf people (n = 11), and organisations that work in the cultural field, where we prioritised organisations that were disability-led (n = 25) (see **Table 5.1**). Participants from at least two organisations from each country participated.

The decision to include representatives of organisations of Deaf people is underpinned by the acknowledgement that they are sometimes organised separately to OPDs and sometimes pursue a 'somewhat separatist ideology' (Bagenstos, 2009, p. 3), and links to the prominence given to Deaf culture in Article 30(4) CRPD as well as to the importance afforded to sign languages throughout the text of the CRPD (Batterbury, 2012). In a few cases, where a

*Table 5.1* Participating Organisations

| *Type of Organisation* | *Number of Participant Organisations* |
|---|---|
| Organisations of People with Disabilities | 28 |
| Arts and Disability Organisation | 25 |
| Organisation of Deaf People | 11 |
| **Total** | **64 (28 countries)** |

national umbrella OPD did not agree to participate, we engaged with other organisations in that country such as umbrella organisations of blind people or an organisation working on independent living.

We prioritised organisations primarily governed by people with disabilities based on the definition in General Comment No. 7 of the CRPD Committee (CRPD Committee, 2018b, para. 11). As mentioned in the introduction to this book, according to this General Comment, OPDs are 'those that are led, directed and governed by persons with disabilities' which entails that 'a clear majority of their membership should be recruited among persons with disabilities themselves' (CRPD Committee, 2018b, para. 11). The vast majority of participant organisations characterised themselves in a way that is consistent with a disability-led approach, with those few that did not characterise themselves either as an organisation of parents and families of children with disabilities or as an organisation engaged in advocacy on the rights of persons with disabilities. While organisations working on arts and disability are multifaceted, due to nuanced meanings of terms and diversified aims and approaches (Hadley & McDonald, 2019), we prioritised associations of artists with disabilities or companies where artists with disabilities engage in professional practice, not those pursuing therapy or social services. To the maximum extent possible, we aimed for organisations in which agency lies with people with disabilities. However, some participants represented inclusive companies of performers, including people with disabilities – sometimes people with intellectual disabilities – and are not necessarily governed by people with disabilities.

In line with best practices in qualitative research, we adopted a flexible approach which evolves in response to context (Foley, 2021; Taylor et al., 2015). This flexibility was particularly necessary in the present study, which involved participants using a range of different languages, as well as requiring reasonable accommodations (such as sign-language interpretation) to facilitate their participation. Furthermore, we started our empirical research during the Covid-19 pandemic, which ruled out face-to-face interviews (Lobe et al., 2020) and resulted in a series of challenges for people with disabilities (European Disability Forum, 2021). We carried out online interviews allowing for maintaining the face-to-face element of interviewing (Foley, 2021). As an alternative, we provided qualitative questionnaires that sought open-ended or free-text answers and enabled participants to respond in writing in English or in a language of their choice as a way to reasonably accommodate them. It has already been highlighted that such questionnaires can be combined in a complementary way with interviews enabling extensive research over a large or geographically dispersed population (McGuirk & O'Neill, 2016). While written questionnaire can limit the depth and richness of responses, in our case they allowed for open-ended responses that contributed to an in-depth study of individual cases (Blaxter et al., 2010). In our study, the quality of data from many questionnaires compares favourably with qualitative interviewing on the same topic (Denz-Penhey & Campbell Murdoch, 2009).

We typically recruited representatives of organisations in senior roles. Representatives of 41 organisations participated in interviews; and representatives of 23 organisations completed written questionnaires (64 organisations represented in total). All participants received information on the study in advance and gave written consent to participate. The study received approval from the relevant Maynooth University ethics committee. The interviews were conducted from May 2021 until August 2023.

The interviews were transcribed verbatim. Transcripts and questionnaires were analysed using a reflexive approach to thematic analysis involving familiarisation; systematic coding; generating initial themes; developing and reviewing themes; refining, defining, and naming themes; and writing up (Braun & Clarke, 2020). Thematic analysis is a flexible method for 'identifying and analysing patterns in qualitative data' and involves analytic processes common to most forms of qualitative research (Clarke & Braun, 2013, pp. 120–123, 2017). We pursued an initial coding process that was open, unstructured, and largely inductive, albeit taking into account the normative content of Article 30 CRPD and being informed by the human rights model of disability. Themes were afterwards developed from codes. We ultimately organised initial themes on the subject of barriers according to the overall classification we had already identified from an initial literature review (Leahy & Ferri, 2022a). These themes were in turn developed from the eight categories of barriers presented in the World Report on Disability (WHO & World Bank, 2011) and linked to the obligations of Article 30 CRPD.

This chapter presents extracts from participants' interviews and questionnaires, identifying from which country they were drawn, sometimes using the standard abbreviations for countries used in the EU[1] and the type of organisation involved: organisation of people with disabilities (OPD), organisation working on arts and disability (A&D), organisation of Deaf people (D). When more than one of these organisation types in any country participated, we indicate that by adding a number (i.e. IE A&D 1). We use the pronoun 'they' and the corresponding 'them', 'their/theirs' as gender-neutral third-person pronouns when referring to participants as an additional layer of anonymisation.

1 See https://ec.europa.eu/eurostat/statistics-explained/index.php?title=Glossary:Country_codes

## 3. Barriers to Cultural Participation

All of the participants in our study identified a series of ingrained barriers to the cultural participation of people with disabilities in their countries, while often pointing to improvements in access to culture in more recent years. Participants also pointed to a piecemeal approach to cultural participation. This tallies with the findings of the analysis of States Parties' reports, set out in Chapter 4, which highlighted a rather patchy implementation of Article 30 CRPD with limited awareness of, and attention to, social, attitudinal, and financial barriers experienced by persons with disabilities.

Notwithstanding social and economic differences across Europe, barriers encountered by persons with disabilities were common or comparable across the States Parties considered, even if some participants perceived that the cultural participation of people with disabilities was not a priority in their countries or, indeed, that the position of people with disabilities generally in their countries was not well advanced in comparison with other countries. We identified five interlinked, and somewhat overlapping, types of barriers that hamper the realisation of the right to participate in cultural life in all its facets: (1) lack of adequate or effective laws and policies; (2) lack of adequate services; (3) negative attitudes; (4) lack of accessibility; (5) lack of consultation with, and involvement of, persons with disabilities in cultural organisations.

### 3.1. *Lack of Adequate or Effective Laws and Policies*

Article 30 CRPD, read in conjunction with Article 4(1) CRPD, requires States Parties to adopt all appropriate measures (legislative, policy, and all other measures) to ensure that persons with disabilities can access cultural goods, services, materials, and heritage and can actively participate in culture as creators. While subject to progressive realisation, as outlined earlier in Chapter 3, Article 30 CRPD does require a proactive attitude, and the adoption of legislation is certainly one of the first steps to support cultural participation. Yet a key barrier perceived by participants from many countries relates to lack of effective laws, as well as inadequate approaches to public policies, with cultural policy-making insufficiently involving people with disabilities.

#### 3.1.1. *Adequate Legislation Is Not Enough*

Some participants felt that the existing national laws in their countries were insufficient or did not sufficiently include specific provisions to facilitate cultural participation of persons with disabilities. A lack of adequate legislative provisions was mentioned in relation to access to cultural content (including exhibitions or performances), and also sometimes in relation to access to cultural buildings. For example, for a Dutch participant (NL OPD), the relevant legislation was a kind of 'framework' that left 'a lot of space and interpretation to self-regulation', and current laws did not ensure that accessible guided tours were provided to Deaf people, to blind people, or to people who need easy-to-read language. A Polish participant said that the theatre was one of the least accessible aspects of culture and, talking about recent legislation on accessibility,[2] suggested that it was yet to become fully evident if and how it would be applied to the cultural field (PL A&D).

However, for many participants, the greatest barriers did not lie in the way legislation was set out or in legislative gaps but rather in the lack of effectiveness of existing laws. Even when national legislation was deemed reasonably comprehensive, participants highlighted that legal provisions were not complied with. Such failure to comply was not challenged or sanctioned. As one participant from Portugal put it: 'our legislation prohibits discrimination and defends accessibility to all aspects of life; however, the legislation is not applied in its entirety and there is a lot of permissiveness with the breaches' (PT OPD). Similarly, another participant suggested that Latvia has the necessary legislation for the inclusion of persons with disabilities in cultural and artistic life but stated that 'another issue is how this legislation is complied with' (LV OPD 1). A Slovenian participant characterised the 'Equalisation of Opportunities for Persons with Disabilities Act' as 'rather far reaching and ambitious' but added that 'there are often laws that are excellent on paper, but they are not necessarily implemented' (SI OPD). Other participants put it even more strongly, suggesting that laws existed only 'on the paper', as one Romanian participant said and are 'not reflected in reality' (RO A&D) and participants from Cyprus made similar points (CY A&D). A Polish participant instanced a law from several decades ago establishing a Central Library of the Blind, which had never been fully implemented, to support access to cultural material for blind people (PL OPD). In a similar vein, participants also raised concerns that legal requirements for physical access to cultural buildings could be ignored or only partially implemented in practice with minimal or no consequences. For example, a participant from Czechia perceived that legislation relative to wheelchair access to auditoria is 'completely ignored' (CZ OPD). A Danish participant suggested that nobody checks compliance despite laws requiring full physical accessibility of cultural institutions receiving public funding (DK A&D). Similarly, a participant from Germany indicated that even new or renovated museums do not always comply with the prescribed standards and that 'nobody is really checking; nobody is really controlling this' (DE A&D).

Another aspect of the problem identified by participants was that there was ambiguity and considerable room for 'self-regulation' by cultural organisations. For example, for an Estonian participant, cultural institutions did not know what legal requirements applied to them (EE A&D). Similarly, a Latvian

2 Dz. U. 2019 poz. 1696 USTAWA z dnia 19 lipca 2019 r. o zapewnianiu dostępności osobom e szczególnymi potrzebami.

participant (LV OPD 1) suggested that, as regards culture, there 'is no common understanding of the observance of legal norms'. Similarly, an Irish participant talked about 'a gap between law and policy', which meant that the law was not 'specific enough to support its implementation in cultural contexts' (IE A&D 3).

Participants sometimes highlighted that problems with enforcement were exacerbated because the burden fell to individual people with disabilities to bring a case to the courts, which is costly and daunting. For example, an Italian participant (IT OPD) highlighted the difficulty for individuals of challenging inaccessibility, because the justice system is 'complicated' and persons with disabilities simply 'give up'. Likewise, a participant from the UK highlighted how ensuring compliance tended to fall to individuals and suggested that the Equality Act 2010 was 'a good piece of legislation' but that problems have arisen from lack of enforcement of it:

> [I]t is for the individual disabled person to decide to take up the case and I think that is where often it falls down. Because if you are one individual challenging an institution it can be quite difficult and that is even before you think about how much it might end up costing.
>
> (UK OPD)

This is consistent with some research that found that in many ways the Equality Act is 'acting as a token instrument' (Berghs et al., 2019).

With regard to sign language, participants often perceived that, despite laws recognising or promoting sign-language, access to cultural content for Deaf people continued to be intermittent and problematic. An organisation from Finland (FI D) suggested that, despite the Sign Language Act from 2015, cultural organisations did not integrate sign language and were not even 'very aware of it', while also acknowledging that, especially in the area of visual art, there were now more signed guided tours. A Lithuanian organisation (LT D) suggested that, while there were some good sign-language projects, access depended on 'goodwill' with only 'recommendations and informal communication' being applied to cultural organisations.

### *3.1.2. Inadequate Policies*

In addition to specific legislation, participants pointed to a range of broader policies across different areas of life, including those operating in relation to the cultural sector, education, employment and social protection, as barriers to cultural participation in both its passive and active facets.

Where cultural policies were concerned, participants often perceived that they did not include input by people with disabilities, that there was a lack of expertise to ensure development and implementation of good policies, and that these factors resulted in barriers to cultural participation. For example, the views of a German participant that disability issues were 'not part of the national cultural policy' (DE A&D), were consistent with perceptions of many participants. Similarly, an Estonian participant suggested the country lacked 'a structure, a framework from the national level' and a concrete strategy to support greater accessibility even within publicly funded organisations (EE OPD). They highlighted the need for auditing for compliance, as well as training within the arts/cultural sector to embed greater knowledge.

Sometimes participants stated that lack of input into policies by people with disabilities could be linked to overly medicalised approaches to disability. For example, a Bulgarian participant felt that 'the whole policy framework is based on the medical model', that people with disabilities were framed as 'sick', which meant that 'they may participate in their treatment . . . but not participate generally in social life . . . not support or development because they cannot develop by definition' (BG OPD). This accords with the analysis of states' reports that, as discussed in Chapter 4, shows in many respects, a throw-back to a medical, therapeutic, or charitable understanding of disability.

In contrast with the obligation provided for in Article 30(2) CRPD, according to which persons with disabilities must be given 'the opportunity to develop and utilize their creative, artistic and intellectual potential', general policies on education provided to people with disabilities were often perceived as not inculcating an interest in culture due to stereotypes and stigma. For example, an Irish participant suggested that, within state organisations offering training for people with disabilities, 'there is no section on art. There is nothing there to develop a person [with] disability's artistic anything. You are on your own' (IE A&D 2). In that regard, a participant from Belgium felt that continuing segregation in education, which is contrary to the CRPD (particularly top Article 24 CRPD), had consequences in terms of the marginalisation of people with disabilities within all aspects of life, including in culture, and that segregated education did not cultivate artistic tastes (BE OPD). Similarly, participants from Greece and Croatia highlighted how the quality of the education received did not cultivate and promote involvement in culture 'either in mainstream schools or special education schools' (EL OPD).

The explicit exclusion of people with disabilities from performing arts schools was reported by participants from Croatia and Greece, who suggested that an explicit requirement for able-bodiedness had operated until challenged by advocates in recent years. Other participants also pointed to similar requirements and to exclusionary practices operating against people with disabilities. For example, a participant from Lithuania had been told, when they wished to become a performer, that the educational programme of an academy 'is not adapted for people like me' (LT OPD). In addition, participants often felt that exclusion happened in more indirect ways such as through inaccessible buildings or curricula or by unspoken prejudice or discrimination. For example, a Bulgarian participant mentioned that people who wanted to train as musicians, actors, or painters could not do so because of physical barriers and the exclusion of guide dogs in university buildings or because learning materials were largely inaccessible for people with visual impairments and Deaf people (BG A&D). That participant suggested that this meant that the artists with disabilities who were associated with their organisation and who had formal training were those who experienced impairment later in life, after having had the opportunity for third-level education earlier on (BG A&D).

Attitudes of academics could also operate as a barrier. As one Portuguese participant put it: 'the idea teachers in those schools have of who can be an artist, what kind of bodies can be present on stage, is very limited or perhaps non-existent' (PT A&D). Some participants linked such exclusion from access to third-level education in the arts to broader attitudes towards people with disabilities and to the lack of representation of people with disabilities. For example, a Finnish participant felt that formal theatre training was highly valued amongst actors but access for people with disabilities was extremely difficult, adding: 'And the representation on the stage affects what kind of art you can see, and this is huge' (FI OPD).

Participants highlighted that welfare policies also created barriers to working in creative industries because of the risk of loss of disability payments, something widely reported across countries. For example, a participant from Sweden described the issue as follows: 'The professionality is limited by the system, you can be an artist but perhaps you can't get paid for your contribution in the normal way.' Similarly, a Danish artist (DK A&D) discussed how they are unable to take up residencies or grants because it would represent a form of income, saying 'when it comes to working life . . . I feel boxed in'. This accords with scholarly work discussed in Chapter 1 (Arts Council England, 2017; Finn, 2023; Yoon et al., 2021).

### 3.2. *Lack of Adequate Services*

The second thematic category of barriers identified by participants refers to the lack of adequate services, broadly conceived. Participants referred generally to structural issues such as financial barriers and the lack of services exacerbating poverty and marginalisation and operating as ingrained obstacles for people with disabilities to partake in cultural life, in particular, as audience. In that regard, they also pointed to the lack of funding for cultural organisations to provide adequate services to people with disabilities and facilitate their access to culture.

#### 3.2.1. *Financial Barriers and Lack of Adequate Disability Services*

Participants often highlighted inadequate disability payments or supports that resulted in reduced opportunities to participate in all areas of life and hampered cultural participation, particularly the right to access cultural goods, services, and heritage. In terms of living conditions, a stark position was outlined by participants from a range of countries in which lack of cultural participation was the consequence of deficient income supports and inadequate services. In this respect, the study confirms the existence of structural barriers faced by persons with disabilities, as well as the fact that they often face extreme poverty (see Braithwaite & Mont, 2009; Groce et al., 2011; Pinilla-Roncancio, 2015; WHO and World Bank, 2011).

A Croatian participant saliently stated that 'disability and poverty goes really hand in hand' (HR A&D). For a Cypriot participant, income support and basic services (such as education and health) were so deficient, especially for people with severe levels of impairment, that cultural participation was 'a luxury' (CY OPD). A Bulgarian participant (BG OPD) instanced cases of people with disabilities attending theatres and cinemas for free, but a personal assistant or family member being asked to pay, which, they added, 'is totally the opposite to the common sense and equal treatment'. They also highlighted unemployment amongst people with disabilities and the fact that the 'disability pension, disability allowances are really very, very low' such that regular attendance at cultural events was not possible for many. An Irish participant suggested that 'lots of us won't be able to afford' to go to the theatre (IE OPD 1). In a similar vein, a Latvian participant characterised disability payments as only sufficient for 'basic needs', leaving cultural and artistic activities 'in the background' (LV OPD 1). Likewise, a Bulgarian participant from an arts and disability organisation felt that there was much to do relative to the rights of people with disabilities (highlighting problems accessing healthcare, employment, and education). They added that 'even if we don't like to state this, the participation of people with disabilities in our cultural life is a very last problem of our country' (BG A&D).

Even where access to events or venues was free, there could be additional costs of participating for which support was perceived to be absent. For example, a Portuguese participant highlighted extra costs of participating in cultural activities if you experience disability such as needing to take a taxi due to not being able to access public transport (PT A&D). Similarly, an Irish participant said that 'the biggest issue for many people with disabilities is not necessarily the venues themselves, it is getting there, and it is getting home', referring to transport issues, especially for people for whom cultural participation meant having to travel into large urban areas (IE A&D 3).

Other participants highlighted a lack of personal assistance. For example, as one participant put it, the lack of personal assistance could 'prevent the full participation in cultural life' (AT OPD) and an Irish participant suggested that a lack of personal assistance prevented participation as both audiences and as artists (IE OPD 1). A Cypriot participant highlighted both the lack of income and the lack of assistance in leaving their home, suggesting that if they wished to attend any performance, there is 'no mechanism of including me or of supporting me to get out of the house – we have nothing' (CY A&D). Furthermore, even if personal assistance was available, it was not always sufficient for cultural participation. One participant suggested that, given restrictions on availability of personal assistance, people with disabilities could not always choose to use it for cultural participation (MT A&D). For a Danish participant, austerity measures resulted in supports being unavailable that would facilitate leading 'a full life' (DK OPD). They suggested that limited availability of personal assistance meant that participating in cultural life 'is considered a luxury and not a basic need', highlighting how a great deal now depends on the decisions of individual municipalities, and that it was people with the highest levels of impairment and those with the least financial resources who were most negatively affected by these economic decisions.

### *3.2.2. Lack of Adequate Cultural Services Due to Lack of Funding*

As well as financial problems faced by individuals, participants sometimes highlighted that cultural organisations were not well supported financially to offer cultural services that are accessible to people with disabilities. In that regard, several participants indicated that obtaining the budget necessary to facilitate even occasional projects that were accessible could be challenging. As one participant put it: '[cultural institutions] don't have funding, they don't have people, they don't know how to do the accessibility' (RO A&D). Another referred to how, if there is no accessibility budget, the accessibility officer 'has to fight' to make cultural goods and services accessible (NL OPD). Regarding this, the interviews evidenced an approach to the accessibility of cultural goods, services, and heritage that is linked to single projects or a series of initiatives, rather than an ongoing mainstream approach to accessibility. This was reported even in France by participants who perceived that funding overall for culture was quite good, but that participation of people with disabilities often relied on intermittent projects (FR A&D). In addition, organisations of Deaf people and others highlighted a paucity of funding for sign-language interpretation of events, which a Finnish participant characterised as 'very scarce' (FI D), and which could mean that, as one Irish participant put it, sign language is 'barely used' in cultural events (IE OPD 1).

On the whole, participants highlighted that a lack of funding is a key barrier to making cultural events and performances accessible, as would be required by Article 30(1) CRPD. In some cases, participants instanced that, even when funding is available, it is not sufficient to fully cover costs associated with providing accessible formats. For example, a participant from Germany suggested that 'the way in which funding itself is structured doesn't really meet the real cost of access needs'. For them, addressing this 'is actually the key to real change' (DE A&D). Other participants highlighted that funders had little understanding of the real costs of creating accessible performances.

Notably, the lack of, or inadequate, funding is underpinned by medicalised understandings of disability, which focus on therapeutic or social aims of cultural participation. This acts as a distinct barrier in supporting not only access but also the cultural production of people with disabilities. In that regard, a participant from a theatre company from Czechia outlined difficulties obtaining money from cultural budget lines, as the Ministry of Culture assumes that 'they are people with disabilities so just go and ask the social field' (CZ A&D). Similarly, a German participant (DE A&D) felt that access is merely seen 'as a social initiative rather than something that should be embedded in the arts all the time'. Thus, a key issue was that participants felt that the funding for their work could fall between funding agencies with different remits – whether that was between cultural funding, funding to facilitate access or social funding (BE OPD 1; FI A&D; SK D). This, again, was evident, to a certain degree, in States Parties' reports, discussed in Chapter 4, whereby several cultural initiatives were seen as a form of social engagement or therapy.

### 3.3. *Negative Attitudes*

Attitudinal barriers, or negative attitudes, or ableism were identified as key barriers by many participants. As outlined earlier, attitudes cut across, link to, or underpin other barriers. In this respect, the study confirms the existence of attitudinal barriers within the cultural sector as discussed in the literature reviewed in Chapter 1 (see, amongst others, Argyropoulos & Kanari, 2015; Ludwig, 2012; Renel, 2019). It is also consistent with the emphasis on prejudice and on the withholding of social and cultural recognition from people with disabilities often highlighted in disability scholarship (see, amongst others, Campbell, 2013; Reeve, 2012; Watson, 2003) and with the concept of 'disablism', defined as practices in contemporary society that exclude, eradicate, and oppress people with sensory, physical, or intellectual impairments (Scully, 2020; see also Thomas, 2007, p. 13). As Bê (2016) puts it, the effects of disablism can be 'onerous, widespread and compound'.

Negative attitudes were the 'biggest obstacle' (CZ A&D) to cultural participation in both its passive and active dimensions for several participants. Many perceived that attitudes were not so much 'negative', as 'ignorant', 'charitable' or 'medicalised' rather than based on ideas of equality or human rights. As a Portuguese participant put it, the first barrier to cultural participation is people's 'mentality . . . what we think some people can or cannot do' (PT A&D). Likewise, a Slovenian participant perceived that despite the existence of legislation, 'the mentality of people is not there yet' (SI OPD) and a Cypriot participant talked about their country having signed up to commitments such as the CRPD, adding that 'we still have no dream or vision to include people with disabilities' (CY A&D). In terms of prejudicial approaches towards audiences in cultural venues, a Slovenian participant instanced a front-of-house person not addressing someone in a wheelchair and talking instead to their companion – out of 'ignorance' (SI OPD). A Romanian participant linked exclusion from cultural centres to lack of knowledge and fear, especially of some types of disability such as intellectual disabilities, and talked about staff being 'very afraid to welcome people with disabilities' (RO A&D) and an Irish participant, also talking about experiences of people with intellectual disabilities, made a similar point in relation to fear, also suggesting that even navigating the box-office or booking tickets could be obstacles and that an element of 'handholding' was absent (IE A&D1).

With particular reference to the right of people with disabilities to cultural participation as makers and shapers of culture in their own right, provided for in Article 30(2) CRPD, several participants felt that their creative work was not understood or supported because of assumptions that art made by people with disabilities had mere therapeutic or social aims, not artistic ones, as touched upon already. For example, a participant from a performance company in Czechia outlined audience assumptions that their performances would lack artistic merit, which they related to fear of people perceived as different, who 'should be somehow isolated or excluded', but they also felt that audiences were becoming more open to their performances (CZ A&D). A Lithuanian participant highlighted how people with disabilities were not always valued as equal participants in the arts 'with whom you create together', which they related to the issue of disability having been associated with 'shame' in the past (LT OPD). They felt that those attitudes were hard to change, which meant that society in general continued to be influenced by ideas of pity or charity. Some participants characterised attitudes in the arts not so much as negative as 'not open'. This was the view of a participant from an Irish organisation, working in a theatre that included people with intellectual disabilities, who perceived that people pre-judged the capacities of performers with intellectual disabilities and consequently limited what they could do (IE A&D 1). Similarly, a Finnish participant suggested that while people working in culture think that they are very open-minded, this is not always the case:

> disablism or ableism that can be a part of cultural field as well even though the people, I think they tend to think that they are very open-minded but sometimes when they are actually confronted with disability issues it can be seen that they are not that open minded.
>
> (FI OPD)

Given the prevalence of limited and often negative cultural representations of disability (Hadley, 2015; Mitchell & Snyder, 2000; Shakespeare, 1994), the findings confirm that the contributions of artists with disabilities are perceived by participants as indispensable to the recognition of the inherent dignity of all people with disabilities as required by the CRPD.

However, there were also perceptions that attitudes had improved especially in the last few years with regard to certain groups. Although participants did not always point to the CRPD specifically, it seems evident that the Convention has started to have an impact on the way that people with disabilities are viewed. For example, participants from Latvia and Germany (DE OPD; LV OPD 2) felt that attitudes had especially improved towards wheelchair users. However, typically, participants perceived that people with intellectual or psychosocial disabilities, and neurodivergent people, continued to be more affected by negative attitudes. Several participants attributed examples of good practice that exist to particular institutions or to individuals within certain institutions that have engaged and learnt about disability and about access. For example, an Estonian participant (EE OPD) referred to several cultural organisations, which they characterised as 'pioneers', that sought funding to engage in training delivered by people with disabilities aimed at upskilling their staff. Moreover, a few participants felt that mainstream audiences had started to become more open to engaging with culture that features, or is produced by, people with disabilities. One participant from the UK pointed to high-profile performers and actors with 'a greater penetration of mainstream work by disabled artists than we have ever seen before' (UK OPD). Overall, however, and as already mentioned, good examples tended to be perceived as occasional or fragmentary in many countries.

### 3.4. *Lack of Accessibility*

The fourth theme identified in our analysis relates to lack of accessibility of cultural venues, services, and products and which manifests in physical barriers for audiences as well as artists and cultural workers, barriers in accessing cultural content, and difficulty accessing information about cultural opportunities, events, goods, and services. As noted earlier, the accessibility obligation, that is, the obligation to dismantle accessibility barriers, is conveyed by Article 30(1) CRPD through overt references to access and accessible formats, but it is relevant to the overall provision in light of the general principle of accessibility, mentioned in Article 3 CRPD and set out in Article 9 CRPD.

#### 3.4.1. *Barriers to Physical Access*

As Chapter 4 showed, an analysis of state reports submitted to the CRPD Committee found that they emphasise physical accessibility in the cultural sphere, often with reference to heritage, highlighting improvements in relation to physical access (Leahy & Ferri, 2022b). However, participants reported that many cultural buildings – even publicly owned ones – continue to be inaccessible, or to be only partly accessible for audiences and visitors, something also reported by scholarly work reviewed in Chapter 1. For example, according to a participant from Bulgaria, most 'museums, galleries, theatres . . . are physically not accessible' and 'libraries are equally inaccessible' (BG OPD), and an interviewee from Cyprus suggested that the lack of accessibility continued to be a problem, suggesting that accessibility is absent in theatres and exhibition venues and also in other aspects of life such as in hospitals or supermarkets (CY A&D). For a Polish participant, 'architectural barriers are well preserved' (PL OPD) and a Greek one considered that while gradual improvements have occurred for wheelchair users in accessing heritage sites and museums, theatres and cinemas often continue to be inaccessible (EL OPD).

Several participants, including one from Finland (FI OPD), reported that accessibility for wheelchair users was improving, but a lack of access to older buildings or to smaller venues continued to be a problem. In the experience of a Danish participant, only one visual art museum in Copenhagen was truly accessible for someone using a wheelchair and smaller art galleries were often inaccessible due to being in basements (DK A&D). In several cases, even new or renovated buildings were experienced as inaccessible. For example, Latvian and Romanian participants (LV OPD; RO OPD) highlighted that what were intended to be accessibility features were in fact unusable, such as overly steep ramps recently installed in cultural buildings. As one said:

> The focus is on the physical environment and sometimes the actions are not coherent – ramp, but you can enter the lobby, but not the performance room. . . . Usually, there are no accessible toilets.
>
> (RO OPD)

Participants who mentioned ineffective accessibility measures sometimes attributed this inadequacy to lack of knowledge on the part of those engaged in design and construction. As a participant from Germany explained, accessibility often depends on the expertise of the architectural firm concerned (DE A&D). Similarly, a Danish participant suggested that 'there is a lack of awareness amongst architects, builders, the ones who build the buildings and there is still a tendency in Denmark that you don't build universally' (DK OPD). An Estonian participant suggested that, while in recent times accessibility as a topic had become 'more mainstream', there was a lack of expertise around how to create spaces that were accessible for people with a wide range of disabilities, instancing cases where the local municipality had approved a building for its accessibility, but people with disabilities had afterwards experienced inadequate access and 'very weak spots' (EE OPD). Difficulties with physical access to buildings for people with other kinds of impairments were also reported. In the experience of a Lithuanian participant, for people who are blind or visually impaired, the aesthetic pursued in new buildings tended to be even 'more exclusionary' than in traditional buildings (LT OPD). They referred to lack of tactile guides, as well as signs on walls and doors that blink, have low contrast, or are otherwise hard to see. Likewise, in the account of a participant from Germany (DE A&D), even new buildings were sometimes difficult to access for people with sensory impairments (as well as for people using wheelchairs). They explained:

> [I]n one space we went to they had thought of tactile flooring and they poured the tactile flooring in concrete but they poured it in the wrong spot in relation to where you descend a set of stairs.
>
> (DE A&D)

Another issue commonly reported was that even if there was compliance with laws in cinemas, theatres, or museums, the experience provided, even for people using wheelchairs, was not optimal, such as different and less attractive paths through a museum or, typically, separating wheelchair users from companions in a theatre or cinema and/or placing them in an undesirable position, often in the front row. For example, an Italian participant said that cultural organisations may comply with the legislation but 'do not give the maximum satisfaction to the person', instancing how separate museum paths for wheelchair users may be limited or not entirely usable (IT OPD), and a Danish participant outlined how this occurred even in new buildings, suggesting that designers and builders may try to comply with the law, 'but they don't ask themselves are we giving the same experience to people with disabilities' (DK OPD). Addressing the issue of being separated from others, a Swedish participant (SE OPD) said: 'You are only counted as a person with a disability and not as a member of a family or a couple or a mother or father. So it is very stereotyped' (SE OPD).

These negative experiences can be contrasted with more positive statements from some participants from the UK, Luxembourg and Slovenia – at least concerning access for audiences and in new buildings. The first felt that basic access for audiences in theatres, concert halls, and galleries was 'well addressed' and that there was now 'a greater commitment to changing-places, toilets and the provision of more specialist access' (UK OPD). Similarly, a Slovenian participant perceived that, through legislation and awareness raising, it had become 'a matter of decency to ensure accessibility' with regard to buildings and physical premises (SI OPD).

Hence, when it comes to the right of persons with disabilities to access culture (as audiences), the picture is mixed, with some improvements in physical access being reported, somewhat in line with the trends discussed in Chapter 4. By contrast, participants sometimes also indicated that, for artists, performers, or employees with disabilities, physical accessibility to cultural buildings, theatres, and premises is still an afterthought. Participants from many countries reported that, even in buildings or institutions that had been made accessible for audiences, physical barriers were still present in the backstage, artists' spaces, and entrances. As a UK participant put it, 'there is a real barrier for access to backstage areas and organisation administration areas' (UK OPD), and a Swedish participant talked of a theatre having had to remodel a dressing room to accommodate their company (SE A&D). A Portuguese participant described how cultural bodies would engage their organisation to identify barriers in the public areas, but they often had not thought about access to offices, rehearsal rooms, and dressing rooms (PT A&D). Participants connected this to the way disability is still thought of in stereotypical ways. For example, a Croatian participant commented that access to stages, toilets, and rehearsal spaces continues to limit their work and that people still didn't perceive that: 'somebody who is disabled could actually take the centre space and have the voice' (HR A&D), and a participant from the Netherlands linked these issues to lack of awareness of the capacity of people with disabilities, saying: 'it is not thought out that you can be an artist in a wheelchair' (NL OPD).

### *3.4.2. Barriers in Access to Cultural Content*

Participants also addressed barriers constituted by inaccessible content of museums, theatres, cinemas, libraries, and events, while often also highlighting improvements in recent years. For instance, a UK participant spoke positively about improvements, stating that things are 'definitely moving along' adding, however, that they ware 'perhaps not moving along as fast as the more physical access, but in terms of Braille interpretations and the provision of much more specific access is being improved [. . .] across the arts' (UK OPD). Somewhat similarly, a Portuguese participant (PT A&D) perceived that, notwithstanding recent improvements, accessibility of content continued to be a problem across 'all the programming that cultural organisations have to present' (instancing museum exhibitions, performances, and libraries).

Participants provided some good examples of accessible formats (some of those are explicitly mentioned in Article 21 CRPD) being used. Nonetheless, for the most part, they highlighted that these remained fragmentary or project-based and outside the mainstream. Thus, access to exhibitions and performances tended to be facilitated from time to time or by way of special events or projects rather than being part of mainstream offerings. Participants also indicated that there could be significant regional or geographical divergences within their countries, with smaller venues in smaller cities failing to provide accessible content. For example, a Greek participant (EL OPD) characterised positive access measures to cultural content as 'fragmented', and a Polish participant outlined that, while there were cultural events that included people with disabilities, they added that this did not happen on a regular basis and referred to 'many festivals or many performances' funded with EU funds that had come and gone (PL OPD). A participant from a Bulgarian organisation of Deaf people made a similar argument stating that good practice in cultural access was associated with short-term projects funded by EU funds or charitable foundations (BG D). A participant from Estonia used the vivid metaphor of 'islands' to characterise this fragmentation in the cultural participation of blind and visually impaired people:

> In Estonia, there are . . . quite good examples of accessible museums, films, performances and major events, which are equipped with, for example, a descriptive translation. . . . It can be figuratively said that there are fantastic islands, but there are no bridges or boats/ships that will bring [you] to them. And this fragmentation does not favour the visits to these islands and the enjoyment of what is offered on them.
>
> (EE A&D)

Some participants referred specifically to the dearth of accessible formats. For example, a Slovenian participant highlighted that libraries did not, in general, make audio books available on the internet and that 'nothing is digitalised yet' (SL OPD). An Estonian participant felt that museums lacked a focus on accessibility for a broad range of people and instanced how many museums presented information in text that was not accessible for blind and visually impaired people (EE OPD), although they suggested that there had been some improvements in how locally made films were produced with closed captions and audio descriptions. Another Estonian participant highlighted that major films generally did not come with 'descriptive translations' which meant that blind people were 'unable to keep up with the times' (EE A&D). Consistent with this, a Polish participant suggested that films remained largely inaccessible for a broad range of people with disabilities because (despite some individual projects) the movie industry failed to provide audio description and subtitles (PL A&D), and a representative of a Lithuanian organisation suggested that, in their country, they generally lacked technologies that would provide audio descriptions for movies and, thus, that access to cinema remained unusual for blind and visually impaired people (LT OPD). Some participants mentioned that opportunities for people with intellectual or psychosocial disabilities were particularly limited. For example, a Romanian participant felt that cultural venues failed to offer alternatives for people with intellectual disabilities (RO OPD), and a Greek participant suggested that cinemas made no provision for people with autism (EL OPD).

Furthermore, a lack of sign language interpretation was frequently highlighted by participants from a range of countries. For example, an Italian participant referred to problems associated with lack of sign language interpreters and a lack of understanding on the part of cultural organisations about interpretation (IT OPD). A Lithuanian participant emphasised examples of good practice (such as performances with subtitles or sign language interpretation; museum exhibitions with technological adaptations) but suggested that overall 'museums, exhibitions, libraries or theatres in Lithuania are still very minimally adjusted to people with hearing impairments' (LT D). Representatives of several organisations suggested that they themselves had to arrange to have sign language interpretation in the field of culture (AT D; SI D). A Bulgarian participant outlined difficulties for Deaf and Deaf-blind people both in travelling to, and in using, libraries and other venues due to a lack of use of sign language (BG D). Another issue related to the quality of the sign language. For example, a representative of an organisation of Deaf people from Finland indicated that the quality of sign language was crucial to the experience, requiring interpreters to be 'included in the performance' and that 'often the best interpreters are native sign language users, so that the language that is used is correct but also culturally expressive' (FI D).

An underlying issue related to the dearth of accessible cultural content is the lack of knowledge and skills of staff of cultural organisations. Making content accessible was perceived as more challenging than physical access. For instance, even though an Estonian participant felt that the cultural sector had shifted and now know 'that accessibility is good', but that lack the competence and expertise on accessibility is still a major issue amongst cultural professionals (EE OPD). A Polish participant (PL A&D) highlighted how accessibility was not treated as a central issue throughout cultural organisations and, instead, responsibility is allocated as an add-on to other responsibilities of someone without specialist knowledge. Further, there were also examples of attempts to make content accessible that were not successful. For example, one participant (IE A&D 2) instanced production of a large-print book to accompany an exhibition in which the ordering was out of synch with the order of the actual exhibits, making navigation impossible for visually impaired people.

### *3.4.3. Barriers to Accessing Information Relevant to Cultural Participation*

Several participants perceived that obtaining information about cultural events or cultural venues, especially from websites, could be difficult and off-putting. Specifically, they discussed how websites of cultural bodies often remained inaccessible for some groups or inadequate in terms of the information provided. This evidences that the implementation of Article 30 CRPD is inextricably linked to the implementation of other provisions of the CRPD, such as Article 21 CRPD (freedom of expression and communication) and Article 9 CRPD (accessibility). Again, in some cases, participants acknowledged that things had somewhat improved in this area, which tallies with the improvements acknowledged as being effects of the implementation of the Web Accessibility Directive (European Commission, 2022).

Generally, participants reported shortcomings in the 'information environment' (LV OPD 1) or a lack of 'informational accessibility' (MT OPD; RO OPD). Specifically, they reported that websites continued to be inaccessible for some groups of people with disabilities. An Austrian participant instanced a lack of accessible formats on the websites of cultural bodies such as easy language, sign language, and incompatibility with screen readers for blind people (AT OPD). Speaking about their experience, a Cypriot participant suggested that even public websites tended not to be accessible: 'we don't have accessible websites especially in the public sector at all; they are not even user friendly for me' (CY A&D).

In addition, there were perceptions that the information provided was not always well considered or organised for people with disabilities. For instance, from the perspective of blind and visually impaired people, a participant from Estonia (EE A&D) felt that websites often did not bring together information on accessibility, suggesting that home pages often lacked a link to a section on accessibility that 'will concentrate all the information concerning the institution and services'. Somewhat aligned with this, another participant from Sweden felt that the information provided can be 'really poor' because it fails to provide the requisite details such as the accessibility of the buildings or the availability of accessible parking, and they linked this to a lack of mainstreaming (SE OPD). In the absence of easily accessible information, attendance could require research and effort. In that regard, an Estonian participant argued that blind people and people with visual impairments had to do 'a lot of preliminary work' to find out what the possibilities were (EE A&D) and a Belgian participant made a similar point in respect of people with different types of disabilities (BE OPD). A related issue raised was a lack of liaison with people with disabilities or Deaf people in order to publicise the accessibility of events. For example, a participant from an organisation of Deaf people in Luxembourg suggested that, while more events were now accessible for Deaf people, knowledge about them was not available in a timely fashion (LU D).

### 3.5. *Lack of Consultation with, and Involvement of, Persons with Disabilities in Cultural Organisations*

As discussed in Chapter 2, participation is a general principle and features in the general obligations of the CRPD, with Article 4(3) requiring for people with disabilities to be involved in all 'decision-making processes concerning issues relating to persons with disabilities'. Yet one further barrier identified in our analysis relates to how the cultural sector often fails to consult people with disabilities in a meaningful way. In that regard, participants also emphasised the lack of employment of people with disabilities as artists or arts professionals and lack of input by them into management and decision-making.

#### 3.5.1. *Inadequate Consultation*

Explicit or implicit in the statements of many participants addressing the lack of knowledge on the part of designers and staff of cultural institutions when it comes to how to facilitate access is the sense that there was also a failure to adequately consult with people with disabilities. This was perceived to occur at many stages, including during the planning of buildings, in programming and in creating content. For example, a Danish participant (DK OPD) linked incapacity to provide good experiences to people with disabilities to a lack of understanding: 'they don't have the ideas or the ability to put themselves in the shoes of people with disabilities' (DK OPD). As one Romanian participant put it, because people with disabilities 'are not consulted and involved', there are only 'superficial measures' effected by 'professionals that do not really have expertise in the field' (RO OPD). Despite 'good intentions', projects are planned 'from the perspective of the person without the disability' without 'any person with a disability as an organiser' and, thus, without the knowledge to create something interesting or accessible for people with disabilities (PL A&D).

Moreover, the experience of some participants in consultative or inclusion processes was that they were inadequate. For example, an Irish participant talked about the agency of people with disabilities being ignored, about cursory consultation but no opportunities to be employed in cultural organisations to work on accessible programming, such that cultural organisations were speaking from the 'point [of view] of non-disabled people . . . making things accessible *for* [persons with disabilities]' (IE A&D 2). Relatedly, a German participant talked about consultation happening almost as an afterthought, instancing a new museum consulting with their organisation 'too late' when programming was already in place – so 'access was added at the end' (DE A&D). That participant flagged the need to move to a more mainstream approach to facilitating access for a wide range of people with disabilities – rather than focusing on specific impairments – and felt there was very little understanding of this within cultural organisations (DE A&D).

In sum, even where cultural organisations attempted to create greater accessibility, their efforts often fell short because of lack of knowledge underpinned by a failure to adequately consult persons with disabilities. These findings signal that there is still some way to go in realising the ambition, which informs the CRPD, of centring the personal experience of people with disabilities as primary sources of knowledge.

### *3.5.2. Lack of Employment as Artists, Arts Professionals, and Leaders*

A related point concerned the lack of employment of people with disabilities within cultural organisations – as artists, arts professionals, managers, leaders, and decision-makers, something that is also evidenced by the review of States Parties' reports to the CRPD Committee, outlined in Chapter 4. Participants mentioned a range of ways in which people with disabilities are excluded from opportunities to create art or to be employed in cultural organisations. This links back to negative attitudes, ableism, or lack of openness on the part of people working in the cultural sector, which was highlighted earlier. Thus, participants from a range of countries suggested that cultural professionals often failed to understand that people with disabilities could work in various capacities in cultural organisations, including as artists. For example, a Greek participant felt that medicalised notions meant that people with disabilities were considered 'only as visitors and/or consumers of cultural products [and] services' (EL OPD). That participant added that working as a museum 'curator, designer, educator . . . looks like as an unreachable expectation' (EL OPD). Similarly, a Swedish participant argued that cultural organisations of various types, and even artists themselves, 'do not think to hire people with disability' (SE OPD). Several participants highlighted how people with disabilities were not thought of as artists or performers. As one Slovakian participant said, 'quite deep prejudices' make it 'hard for a blind person to become a professional actor' (SK A&D). Another participant recalled that, while a funding scheme to support artistic directors required them to include artists with disabilities, such a requirement was complied with only in a limited fashion as a 'tick box' exercise (MT A&D).

Where opportunities for the employment of artists with disabilities exist, they were still perceived as limited or inadequate. For example, a Finnish participant highlighted that 'people tend to look at your art through the disability whether you are yourself disability politically minded or not' (FI OPD). Thus, even when people with disabilities were employed as artists, this tended to involve a focus on disability itself, and, as one participant suggested, not to involve people with disabilities as ordinary artists (DK OPD). A related issue was that art created by people with disabilities often continues to be less valued than that of others or tends, as discussed earlier, to be viewed through a reductive medicalised lens or assumptions that it is purely social in nature and that it often continues to be segregated. As a Lithuanian participant put it, art created by people with disabilities 'is valued differently' adding that 'if people know that something [was] made . . . by a blind person or a person sitting in a wheelchair they would give a lower price to that art' (LT OPD 1). Similarly, a Polish participant felt that the lack of visibility of artists with disabilities meant that 'we are not shown that it is also culture and it is not as valued as the mainstream culture' (PL OPD) – highlighting how art made by people with disabilities has not yet been incorporated in the mainstream and so their perspectives and expressions continue to be at one remove. Consistent with this, a Finnish participant (FI OPD) anticipated a time when it was understood that 'art is not something special for special people who all have beautiful and functioning bodies' and when artists with disabilities initiated projects themselves from 'scratch' (FI OPD). Thus, participants echo the challenge identified in scholarship on disability art and aesthetics, discussed earlier in this book, of how to move 'out of the ghetto' and into the mainstream world of high art (Solvang, 2018, p. 243) while refusing to recognise the representation of 'the healthy body . . . as the sole determination of the aesthetic' (Siebers, 2006, p. 64). Furthermore, consequences were perceived in terms of limitations on artistic and cultural expression more broadly, depriving societies of important perspectives and of challenges to stereotypical or medicalised ideas about disability.

Finally, and directly linked to lack of employment as just discussed, participants sometimes pointed to a lack of involvement by people with disabilities in leadership or decision-making roles in cultural sectors. It is worth noting, however, that participants in several countries perceived that improvements were occurring, especially relating to individual artists or companies that had achieved recognition or prominence. A UK participant perceived that, while there was 'greater integration of the disabled experience on stage and also on television and on film' (UK OPD), a key barrier continued to relate to a lack of people with disabilities in leadership positions. Crucially, this participant felt that people with disabilities were not given 'the reins of organisational power to change things . . . whether that is broadcasting, film or the arts' (UK OPD). Again, this lack of influence within the cultural sector is consistent with the findings of the review of States Parties' reports, discussed in Chapter 4.

## 4. Concluding Remarks

While barriers to the participation of persons with disabilities in society can differ considerably between countries and communities (WHO and World

Bank, 2011), the analysis reported on in this chapter shows that, across Europe (and arguably beyond), there are similar experiences of barriers that hamper the enjoyment and exercise of the right to participate in culture provided in Article 30 CRPD. Interestingly, participants across Europe emphasised similar patterns of exclusion, comparable practices that are in breach of the accessibility obligations set out in the CRPD, and views of disability that are at odds with the social-contextual understanding embedded in the Convention and with the human rights model of disability. Even if some participants perceived that disability issues were not as advanced in their countries as in others and pointed at certain states as being more progressive and aligned with the CRPD, our analysis signals analogous experiences and a somewhat generalised lack of prioritisation of cultural participation. Further, our findings, while often consistent with the findings of scholarly work reviewed in Chapter 1, showcase how certain barriers are widely experienced across Europe, across different disability types and different types of cultural engagement.

The chapter identifies five interlinked categories of barriers which hamper cultural participation in all the facets protected and promoted by Article 30 CRPD: (1) lack of effective/adequate laws and policies; (2) lack of adequate services; (3) negative attitudes; (4) lack of accessibility; (5) lack of consultation with, and involvement of, persons with disabilities in cultural organisations. These barriers are not only interlinked but also partially overlapping, as well as underpinned by general structural barriers faced by persons with disabilities. In this respect, the chapter signals that the implementation of Article 30 CRPD and its realisation cannot be separated from the implementation of other provisions of the CRPD. Participants' experiences evidence the interdependence and indivisibility of the rights provided for in the CRPD and make even more obvious that Article 30 must be read and implemented taking into account the overall texture and fabric of the Convention.

Participants did point to legislative gaps but often emphasised that the lack of implementation of existing laws and the difficulty in enforcing existing provisions is a major hurdle. This finding confirms that the implementation of Article 30 CRPD (and of the whole Convention) must go beyond adopting comprehensive legislation. Further, the lack of input into cultural policies and into decision-making processes in cultural venues subsists in many countries, notwithstanding the requirements of Article 4(3) and Article 33(3) CRPD for persons with disabilities and their representative organisations to participate fully in implementation of the CRPD and constitutes a barrier that greatly impacts on cultural participation. This validates what some studies have already claimed and points to the need for greater consultation by cultural organisations (European Blind Union, 2012; Ludwig, 2012; Lid, 2016). It also confirms how organisations specialising in accessibility and in working with people with disabilities may be important to support the realisation of the right to participate in cultural life (British Council, 2021).

With regard to access to cultural venues, goods, services, and heritage for people with disabilities as audience and to the obligations laid out in Article 30(1) CRPD, participants in our study highlighted that barriers to physical access to buildings and sites persist. The provision of cultural content in accessible formats, and accessibility in goods, services, and heritage is, however, still lagging behind. Participants signal fragmentary and ad hoc approaches to accessibility, which also are visible in the States Parties' reports discussed in Chapter 4. Access to cultural content tends to be afforded in an intermittent way and, despite some good initiatives, often fails to become part of the mainstream, which in turn militates against participation becoming more of a norm. This is consistent with the scholarship reviewed in Chapter 1 that presents practices related to accessibility which are narrowly focused and often engaged with in relation to one type of impairment. In addition, participants in our study also tend to confirm that the 'hierarchy of impairments' that is identified in general approaches to societal participation (Waltz & Schippers, 2020, p. 9) also operates in the cultural field, with least attention having been paid to date to what it means to facilitate access for certain groups such as people with intellectual disabilities, neurodiversity, or cognitive impairments.

With regard to the participation of people with disabilities as artists, creators, and performers and in connection with the obligations set forth in Article 30(2) CRPD, the range of barriers to cultural production by people with disabilities tend to link back to stigma, negative attitudes, and overly medicalised views of disability. Participants have underlined how disablism operates widely in person-to-person interactions as well as how it manifests in institutionalised and other socio-structural forms (Thomas, 2007, 2010). In that regard, negative attitudes also militate against a wider recognition of disability identities as cultural identities and their contribution to the mainstream in line with Article 30(4) CRPD. However, participants showed a tension between, on the one hand, the artistry of people with disabilities being recognised as art regardless of their disability and being included in the mainstream, and, on the other, disability art being acknowledged as a specific contribution to be made to the cultural scene outside the mainstream.

This chapter outlines, at various junctures, that participants did perceive improvements to have occurred, especially in some countries, and particularly as regards physical access, and participation as audiences in new buildings. Nonetheless, as noted earlier, fragmentation and patchy approaches were highlighted. Linked to this, good practices can depend on an individual staff member within a cultural venue and may be lost as projects end. This, as Weisen (2012) contends, has been happening for decades and is so despite the publication of many guidelines and checklists in different countries (see British Council, 2021, pp. 81–87).

On the whole, this chapter showcases that there is a long way to go to fully implement the CRPD and Article 30 in particular. It further points to a fundamental challenge for policy-makers, which is to embrace the human rights model of disability and reject medicalised views of disabilities, as well as to build on good practices developed within individual projects and institutions and to move to more systematic approaches. It also points to the need for a change in the knowledge base and ethos of cultural bodies, one that aligns with the CRPD.

## References


Argyropoulos, V. S., & Kanari, C. (2015). Re-imagining the museum through 'touch': Reflections of individuals with visual disability on their experience of museum-visiting in Greece. *Alter, European Journal of Disability Research/Revue européenne de recherche sur le handicap*, *9*(2), 130–143.

Arts Council England. (2017). *Making a shift report: Disabled people and the arts and cultural sector workforce in England: Understanding trends, barriers and opportunities*. https://www.artscouncil.org.uk/making-shift

Bagenstos, S. (2009). *Law and the contradictions of the disability rights movement*. Yale University Press.

Bantekas, I., Stephenson, C. P. Y., Karapapa, S., & Polymenopoulou, E. (2018). Article 30: Participation in cultural life, recreation, leisure, and sport. In I. Bantekas, M. A. Stein, & D. Anastasiou (Eds.), *The UN Convention on the Rights of Persons with Disabilities: A Commentary* (pp. 863–923). Oxford University Press.

Batterbury, S. C. E. (2012). Language justice for sign language peoples: The UN Convention on the Rights of Persons with Disabilities. *Language Policy*, *11*, 253–272.

Bê, A. (2016). Disablism in the lives of people living with a chronic illness in England and Portugal. *Disability & Society*, *31*(4), 465–480.

Berghs, M., Atkin, K., Hatton, C., & Thomas, C. (2019). Do disabled people need a stronger social model: A social model of human rights? *Disability & Society*, *34*(7–8), 1034–1039.

Blaxter, L., Hughes, C., & Tight, M. (2010). *How to research*. McGraw-Hill Education.

Braithwaite, J., & Mont, D. (2009). Disability and poverty: A survey of world bank poverty assessments and implications. *Alter, European Journal of Disability Research/Revue européenne de recherche sur le handicap*, *3*(3), 219–232.

Braun, V., & Clarke, V. (2020). One size fits all? What counts as quality practice in (reflexive) thematic analysis? *Qualitative Research in Psychology*, *18*(3), 328–352.

British Council. (2021). *Time to act: How lack of knowledge in the cultural sector creates barriers for disabled artists and audiences*. (Final report November 2021. A research report authored by On the Move, commissioned by the British Council). www.disabilityartsinternational.org/wp-content/uploads/2022/01/TIMETO2.pdf

Campbell, F. K. (2013). Ableism: A theory of everything. In *Keynote for International Conference on Linking Concepts of Critical Ableism and Racism Studies with Research on Conflicts of Participation*, University of Hamburg.

Chow, P. Y. S. (2018). *Cultural rights in international law and discourse: Contemporary challenges and interdisciplinary perspectives*. Brill Nijhoff.

Clarke, V., & Braun, V. (2013). Teaching thematic analysis: Overcoming challenges and developing strategies for effective learning. *The Psychologist*, *26*(2), 120–123.

Clarke, V., & Braun, V. (2017). Thematic analysis. *The Journal of Positive Psychology*, *12*(3), 297–298.

Denz-Penhey, H., & Campbell Murdoch, J. (2009). A comparison between findings from the DREEM questionnaire and that from qualitative interviews. *Medical Teacher*, *31*(10), 449–453.

European Blind Union. (2012). *Summary report: EBU access to culture survey 2012. Mapping current levels of accessibility to cultural venues and activities in Europe*. www.kulttuuriakaikille.fi/doc/research_and_reports/SUMMARY-REPORT-OF-THE-EBU-Access-to-Culture-Survey-2012-and-EBU-call-for-action.pdf

European Commission. (2022). *Study supporting the review of the application of the Web Accessibility Directive (WAD) VIGIE 2020-0656*. Publications Office of the European Union.

European Disability Forum. (2021). *European human rights report Issue 5–2021 impact of COVID-19 on persons with disabilities*. www.edf-feph.org/publications/human-rights-report-2021-impact-of-covid19-on-persons-with-disabilities/

European Parliament Research Services (EPRS). (2017). *Access to culture in the European Union*. https://op.europa.eu/en/publication-detail/-/publication/66f298ec-6840-11e7-b2f2-01aa75ed71a1

Finn, P. (2023). *Artists at the intersection of work and welfare: Disabled artists navigation of welfare – short interim report*. ALL Institute and School of Law and Criminology, Maynooth University.

Foley, G. (2021). Video-based online interviews for palliative care research: A new normal in COVID-19? *Palliative Medicine*, *35*(3), 625–626.

Groce, N., Kett, M., Lang, R., & Trani, J. F. (2011). Disability and poverty: The need for a more nuanced understanding of implications for development policy and practice. *Third World Quarterly*, *32*(8), 1493–1513.

Hadley, B. (2015). Participation, politics and provocations: People with disabilities as non-conciliatory audiences. *Participations: Journal of Audience and Reception Studies*, *12*(1), 154–174.

Hadley, B., & McDonald, D. (2019). Introduction: Disability arts, culture and media studies. In B. Hadley & D. McDonald (Eds.), *The Routledge handbook of disability arts, culture, and media* (pp. 1–18). Routledge.

Leahy, A., & Ferri, D. (2022a). Barriers and facilitators to cultural participation by people with disabilities: A narrative literature review. *Scandinavian Journal of Disability Research*, *24*(1), 68–81.

Leahy, A., & Ferri, D. (2022b). The right to participate in cultural life of persons with disabilities in Europe: Where is the paradigm shift? *Alter, European Journal of Disability Research/Revue européenne de recherche sur le handicap*, *16*(4), 5–29. http://journals.openedition.org/alterjdr/1430

Lid, I. M. (2016). Access to cultural heritage: A multiscaled approach. In A. Arenghi, I. Garofolo, & O. Sørmoen (Eds.), *Accessibility as a key enabling knowledge for enhancement of cultural heritage* (pp. 77–89). Franco Angeli.

Lobe, B., Morgan, D., & Hoffman, K. A. (2020). Qualitative data collection in an era of social distancing. *International Journal of Qualitative Methods*, *19*.

Ludwig, E. (2012). Stigma in the arts: How perceptual barriers influence individuals with disabilities participation in arts organizations. *The Journal of Arts Management, Law, and Society*, *42*(3), 141–151.

McGuirk, P. M., & O'Neill, P. (2016). *Using questionnaires in qualitative human geography* (Faculty of Social Sciences – Papers, 2518). https://ro.uow.edu.au/articles/chapter/Using_questionnaires_in_qualitative_human_geography/27691062?file=50428593

Mitchell, D., & Snyder, S. (2000). *Narrative prosthesis: Disability and the dependencies of discourse*. University of Michigan Press.

Pinilla-Roncancio, M. (2015). Disability and poverty: Two related conditions. A review of the literature. *Revista de la Facultad de Medicina*, *63*, 113–123.

Reeve, D. (2012). Psycho-emotional disablism: The missing link? In N. Watson, A. Roulstone, & C. Thomas (Eds.), *Routledge handbook of disability studies* (pp. 78–92). Routledge.

Renel, W. (2019). Sonic accessibility: Increasing social equity through the inclusive design of sound in museums and heritage sites. *Curator: The Museum Journal*, *62*(3), 377–402.

Romainville, C. (2015). On defining the right to participate in cultural life as a human right. *Netherlands Quarterly of Human Rights*, *33*(4), 405–436.

Scully, J. L. (2020). Disability, disablism, and COVID-19 pandemic triage. *Bioethical Inquiry*, *17*, 601–605.

Shakespeare, T. (1994). Cultural representation of disabled people: Dustbins for disavowal? *Disability & Society*, *9*(3), 283–299.

Siebers, T. (2006). Disability aesthetics. *Journal for Cultural and Religious Theory*, *7*(2), 63–73.

Solvang, P. K. (2018). Between art therapy and disability aesthetics: A sociological approach for understanding the intersection between art practice and disability discourse. *Disability & Society*, *33*(2), 238–253.

Taylor, S. J., Bogdan, R., & DeVault, M. (2015). *Introduction to qualitative research methods: A guidebook and resource* (4th ed.). John Wiley & Sons.

Thomas, C. (2007). *Sociologies of disability and illness: Contested ideas in disability studies and medical sociology*. Palgrave Macmillan.

Thomas, C. (2010). Medical sociology and disability theory. In G. Scambler & S. Scambler (Eds.), *New directions in the sociology of chronic and disabling conditions: Assaults on the lifeworld* (pp. 37–56). Palgrave Macmillan.

United Nations Committee on the Rights of Persons with Disabilities (CRPD Committee). (2018a). *General Comment No. 6 on equality and non-discrimination* (UN Doc. CRPD/C/GC/6).

United Nations Committee on the Rights of Persons with Disabilities (CRPD Committee). (2018b). *General Comment No. 7 on the participation of persons with disabilities, including children with disabilities, through their representative organizations, in the implementation and monitoring of the Convention* (UN Doc. CRPD/C/GC/7).

Waltz, M., & Schippers, A. (2020). Politically disabled: Barriers and facilitating factors affecting people with disabilities in political life within the European Union. *Disability & Society*, *36*(4), 517–540.

Watson, N. (2003). Daily denials: The routinisation of oppression and resistance. In S. Riddell & N. Watson (Eds.), *Disability, culture and identity* (pp. 34–51). Pearson Education.

Weisen, M. (2012). International perspectives on the cultural accessibility of people with disabilities (European Centre for cultural accessibility; art beyond sight). In J. Berding & G. Matthias (Eds.), *The inclusive museum – proceedings of the come-in thematic conference* (pp. 12–17). Berichte des Instituts Verkehr und Raum.

World Health Organization & The World Bank. (2011). *World report on disability*. World Health Organization.

Yoon, J. H., Ellison, C., & Essl, P. (2021). Shifting the perspective from 'incapable' to 'capable' for artists with cognitive disability; case studies in Australia and South Korea. *Disability & Society*, *36*(3), 443–467.

# 6 Facilitators of Cultural Participation of People with Disabilities

*Delia Ferri and Ann Leahy*

## 1. Introduction

The legal exploration of the core obligations set out in Article 30 of the UN Convention on the Rights of Persons with Disabilities (CRPD), and the discussion of their implementation, has supported the analysis of the barriers experienced by persons with disabilities in the exercise of their right to participate in cultural life. Following that analysis, this chapter moves on to consider what factors were perceived as being facilitative of cultural participation by participants in the empirical study that informs this book, some of which have been cursorily mentioned in Chapter 5 (see also Leahy & Ferri, 2024). As with the term 'barrier', this chapter uses the term 'facilitator' in a way that is consistent with the World Report on Disability (WHO & World Bank, 2011, p. 304), where facilitators are 'factors in a person's environment that, through their absence or presence, improve functioning and reduce disability'. Notably, this chapter links the discussion of such facilitators to the obligations laid out in Article 30 CRPD and to the human rights model of disability, which constitutes the theoretical framework of the book. In doing so, the chapter complements the socio-legal analysis of the book by identifying what supports the realisation of Article 30 CRPD and by looking at the social situations in which it applies.

As discussed in Chapter 1, our review of the literature found that barriers to, and facilitators of, cultural participation by people with disabilities appear to be a growing focus of research, especially in recent years, and in a range of scholarly fields, including not only disability studies but also cultural and museum studies, leisure and management studies, and other fields. Yet research focusing specifically on what facilitates cultural participation by people with disabilities or identifying how cultural policies should be formulated and implemented to operate as facilitative is more limited. Nonetheless, the studies reviewed in Chapter 1 refer to a broad range of factors that are facilitative of participation by different groups of people with disabilities. Facilitative factors include good design of buildings and various approaches to making the content of museums and other cultural venues accessible, in line with the wording of Article 30 CRPD

DOI: 10.4324/9781032619361-10

This chapter has been made available under a CC-BY-NC-ND 4.0 license.

which mentions accessible formats and the right to access films and theatre and other cultural activities. In fact, scholarly work often has a narrow focus and tends to look at people with disabilities as audience. A range of studies highlight measures that provide enhanced logistical access to venues (Hadley, Paterson et al., 2022), including audio description, touch tours, sign-language interpretation, technologies, and digitisation (see, amongst others, Agostiano, 2016; Argyropoulos & Kanari, 2015; Cachia, 2013; Mesquita & Carneiro, 2016; Renel, 2019; Seale et al., 2021). Other studies mention input from stakeholder groups and co-production, involving disabled users from an early stage of design, as well as carrying out assessments with them, and outreach programmes and training for people working in cultural sectors (see, amongst others, Lazar & Briggs, 2015; Levent & Pursley, 2013; Lid, 2016; Vas, 2020). Scholarly work on the participation of people with disabilities as artists is more limited, yet burgeoning in the last few years. This tallies with our analysis of reports by States Parties to the CRPD Committee discussed in Chapter 4, which showed a limited, yet developing, awareness of people with disabilities as artists and performers. This chapter builds on these findings and moves beyond them to look holistically at facilitators of all the different aspects of cultural participation covered by Article 30 CRPD such as cultural consumption (participating as audience or visitor), cultural creation (including as artists and performers) as well as being employed in cultural industries, and, in addition, the collective aspect of cultural participation and the protection of disability identities.

The methodology of the empirical study informing this chapter has been described in the introduction to this book and further detailed in Chapter 5. It suffices here to recall that the participants in the study were representatives of 64 organisations in 28 European countries (27 EU Member States and the UK). In particular, those invited to participate were drawn from three types of organisations: umbrella organisations of persons with disabilities (OPDs) working at national level within their countries and representing people with a range of disability types (n = 28), national organisations of Deaf people (n = 11), and organisations that work in the cultural field, where we prioritised organisations that were disability-led (n = 25). Representatives from at least two organisations from each country participated. We prioritised organisations primarily governed by people with disabilities based on the definition in General Comment No. 7 of the CRPD Committee (CRPD Committee, 2018, para. 11). In line with Chapter 5, this chapter presents extracts from participants' interviews and questionnaires, identifying from which country they were drawn, using the standard abbreviations for countries used in the EU,[1] and the type of organisation involved: OPD, A&D, or

1 See https://ec.europa.eu/eurostat/statistics-explained/index.php?title=Glossary:Country_codes

D. Consistent with the approach adopted in the previous chapter, when more than one of these organisation types in any country participated, we indicate that by adding a number (e.g. IE A&D 1). We use the pronoun 'they' and the corresponding 'them' and 'their/theirs' as gender-neutral third-person pronouns when referring to participants as an additional layer of anonymisation.

After these introductory remarks, this chapter is divided into three main sections. Section 2 highlights a range of good practices that support increased cultural participation. Section 3 discusses what *in practice* is perceived as facilitative of cultural participation by people with a broad range of disabilities across European countries. In many ways, facilitative factors are somewhat implicit in the views of participants in relation to barriers discussed already in this book. However, Section 3 expounds four interlinked facilitators that can contribute to the realisation of Article 30 CRPD and can address the intertwined barriers discussed earlier in Chapter 5: (1) disability-inclusive cultural funding mechanisms; (2) meaningful consultation and engagement with OPDs; (3) employment of people with disabilities within the cultural sector; and (4) changes to professional training and education to include people with disabilities. In line with Chapter 5, Section 4 concludes by highlighting the need for a shift in policies and practices to encompass, not just greater accessibility but also a change in the ethos of cultural bodies.

## 2. Some Steps Forward: Good Practices in the Cultural Sphere

While highlighting facilitative tools or approaches, there was a perception amongst many participants of an improvement in access to the arts and an increased focus on participation by people with disabilities and Deaf people in the cultural sector in their countries, even if there was a perception that much more needed to be done and even if this perception was quite limited in some instances. Participants, notably from the UK, Slovenia, and Luxembourg were quite positive about improvements in physical access to cultural spaces for audiences. As a Slovenian participant put it, 'the standard is being raised' (SI OPD). More positively still, a UK participant said: 'I think basic access for audiences in theatres and concert halls and galleries by and large have been pretty well addressed in the UK,' suggesting that there was now 'a greater commitment to changing-places, toilets and the provision of more specialist access' (UK OPD). Participants provided many good examples of accessible content, sometimes also highlighting that access measures (such as easy-to-read approaches) made exhibitions more accessible for a broad range of groups, such as children and tourists, in addition to the groups of people with disabilities who the measures specifically targeted (LU OPD; LV OPD). Innovative practices were referenced by a few participants that made theatre performances more accessible to blind people – such as tactile tours or engagement being facilitated (before or during the performance) through the senses (EL A&D; LT OPD). A Portuguese participant listed a series of positive initiatives on the part of museums:

> There are more and more museums, for instance, with audio guides that include audio description, there are museums with video guides that have tours in Portuguese sign language. Some also do live tours with audio description and sign language. We have now a museum . . . first time in Portugal . . . with relaxed visits.
>
> (PT A&D)

Various technologies were referenced as improvements when it comes to films or museum exhibitions through adaptations for audiences who are blind or visually impaired or Deaf or hard of hearing. For example, a Finnish participant (FI OPD) felt that a 'movie reading App' was making more movies accessible to blind people, although there was still room for improvement. A participant from Luxembourg described mobile phone/tablet technologies that translated exhibitions into words for blind people and into sign language for Deaf people (LU OPD), and a participant from Slovenia (SI D) talked about a mobile app that can be used to scan a QR code included in print media which then 'plays a video of the interpreter in sign language'. For hearing-impaired people, several participants referred to induction or loop systems (HU D; SI D). Less common were discussions of technologies that translated sound frequencies into vibrations. But in a city in Luxembourg, that was European Capital of Culture in 2022, music performances were made accessible to Deaf people through a vibrating pack. Extensive consultation and trialling in advance were perceived as central to the success of this initiative (LU D; LU OPD).

Such improvements and new focus reflect the renewed attention to disability rights stemming from the CRPD and the commitments undertaken by States Parties under the Convention. In fact, most improvements and examples of good practice seem to have arisen following the adoption and entry into force of the CRPD. Tellingly, the CRPD was sometimes credited by participants with leading to change or improvements. For example, a representative of an organisation of Deaf people from Luxembourg felt that the CRPD had brought 'movement' in the area of culture, suggesting that, as a result, 'more and more artists and institutions implement inclusion or at least more accessibility' in their programmes (LU D). For a Swedish participant, the CRPD had established a baseline that helped with international contacts and cross-border working, saying that 'the Convention is very helpful and I think it is very good that the whole world can rely on the same founding documents . . . it is like a common starting point' (SE A&D). Furthermore, participants sometimes linked improvements in the approaches of cultural organisations to changes in how disability is positioned or understood in recent times, which can also be seen as a consequence of the human rights model of disability embedded in the CRPD, as well as being linked to advocacy on the part of people with disabilities over decades. For example, an Italian participant suggested that, in recent years, 'attention regarding access to culture and the usability of culture and people with disabilities has increased' which they associated with a shift from medical model thinking, which focused attention on a narrow set of issues, to an approach involving an 'awareness of the person with disabilities as a person, with all their own interests, even beyond the primary ones' (IT OPD). A participant from the Netherlands felt that people working in government departments were beginning to 'understand this principle that if you take away the barriers you don't need to assist anyone in going into society' (NL OPD). Further, perceived improvements may well mirror general trends identified within cultural policies internationally related to audience development and emancipatory initiatives (see Glow et al., 2021; Hadley, 2021).

Participants sometimes referred to equality laws or legislation mandating accessibility as the baseline for supporting cultural participation but pointed to the need to support the mainstreaming of good practices, as well as to the need for staff members who are knowledgeable about access issues or willing to involve people with disabilities in the life of their organisations. For example, a Romanian participant felt that the books in libraries were not, in general, accessible except where there was a staff member who had some experience and took a particular interest: 'it is not about the law; it is about the personal willingness and the personal approach' (RO A&D). While often highlighting positive instances of access or inclusion, their intermittent nature was also frequently underlined, and most participants felt that there was a lot more that needed to be done and pointed to facilitative tools and approaches which will be discussed in the subsequent sections.

## 3. Facilitators of Cultural Participation of People with Disabilities

Alongside identifying a series of improvements in access to culture in the last few years, in particular in relation to physical access, participants in this study also discussed facilitators of cultural participation of people with disabilities in their countries. However, they often perceived that these facilitators were operating, if at all, in a piecemeal fashion. Participants pointed to four general types of facilitators that overlap and interlink and jointly address and counteract the interweaved identified barriers and hint at the indicators for the implementation of Article 30 CRPD (OHCHR, 2020): (1) disability-inclusive cultural funding mechanisms; (2) meaningful consultation and engagement with OPDs; (3) employment of people with disabilities within the cultural sector; and (4) changes to professional training and education to include people with disabilities.

### 3.1. *Disability-Inclusive Funding Schemes*

While participants often highlighted the lack of availability of funding for the participation of people with disabilities in culture –at the level of both organisations and individuals with disabilities, as discussed in Chapter 5 – there were also some perceptions that funding availability and certain funding mechanisms had operated to support the enjoyment of the right to partake in cultural life. These could support both engagement as audiences and professional engagement as artists or performers, with funding criteria considered supportive if they incorporated requirements relative to disability. Most notable in this regard were the views of participants from a small number of countries, especially Sweden and the UK, who highlighted the facilitative role played by public funding mechanisms that mandated accessibility for organisations that they fund. For example, a Swedish participant referenced requirements put in place by the Swedish Arts Council that mandate accessibility in funding applications, saying:

> That made a lot of difference. So now everybody, every organisation that applies for money must have a plan for accessibility in every sense. So, when that law passed in 2017 it was also a game changer because otherwise you won't get any money.
>
> (SE OPD)

Similarly, a UK participant (UK OPD) pointed to funding policies pursued by the Arts Councils in the UK over decades, pointing to how Arts Council England facilitated access and participation by ensuring that 'the organisations that it funds understand the implications of the Equality Act' (UK OPD). They credited these policies with leading to the considerable proportion of audiences for national portfolio organisations represented by people with disabilities (UK OPD). They also felt that there were more artists with disabilities involved in mainstream arts work than ever before. Availability of funding and facilitative funding processes were also identified by another UK participant from an integrated performance company who talked about having moved from project-to-project funding to obtaining three-year funding from the Arts Council ('the same as any mainstream company'), which 'makes a massive difference because it makes it easier to find matched funding . . . and you can plan' (UK A&D). Other participants spoke positively about national funding mechanisms. One from France (FR A&D) mentioned that certain funding schemes for culture 'allow for a lot of great things to be done' and highlighted the establishment of regional arts and disability hubs, which engage in a variety of actions, including supporting amateur and professional engagement, but they still felt that the participation of people with disabilities often relied on intermittent funding for projects (FR A&D).

A few participants referred to somewhat recent developments in relation to arts funding mechanisms. It was anticipated that they would start to effect change. For example, a Portuguese participant talked about their Arts Council having initiated (from 2020) 'specific funding for projects' to be led by people with disabilities or involving artists with disabilities, and they looked forward to seeing 'where it will take us now in the coming years' (PT A&D). A German participant (DE A&D) pointed to changes amongst funding bodies at state level in recent years, suggesting that there is now 'more awareness in the mainstream arts sector in terms of disabled artists and what their needs are', adding, however, that 'the infrastructure is not there', that these still represent 'small changes', and that there was a lack of guidance from funders as to how to facilitate access.

Funding schemes not specifically aimed at the cultural sector but providing funding that supported the employment of people with disabilities in general, including artists and arts workers with disabilities, were also highlighted as facilitative by a small number of participants. These included mobility services and access to work schemes. According to a representative of a Finnish theatre company that includes people with and without disabilities, employment services, and mobility supports enabled the theatre company to work with performers living at some distance from the venues, and while it created some bureaucratic challenges, it was also very valuable, and most of the actors with disabilities in the company use it (FI A&D). According to a UK participant (UK A&D), again from an inclusive theatre company, the Access to Work fund from the UK Department of Work and Pensions facilitated work by performers and other company members because it could be applied to various access measures such as sign-language interpretation, taxies to work, or having a note-taker.

Although this book does not engage with EU law and focuses on Article 30 CRPD (and the CRPD more broadly) as the legal axis of the book, it is worth noting that participants also referred to projects funded by the EU – both in terms of making buildings more accessible and in terms of funding for specific projects focused on culture.[2] Thus, participants from several countries outlined how EU funding spent on cultural buildings had been used to create more access, especially in heritage buildings. These included participants from different countries that included Italy, Spain, Latvia, and Poland. For example, an Italian participant suggested that 'a lot of innovation within monuments, historic buildings, where there was a need to adapt for accessibility' had resulted from a combination of EU and national funds (IT OPD). Likewise, a Latvian participant highlighted how EU funding has been used to make 'public buildings, including museums, libraries and theatres' more accessible (LV OPD 1), and a Polish participant referred to many cultural institutions that have used EU funds for building renovations for greater accessibility, instancing installing lifts and hearing loops (PL A&D). Several participants referred to EU-funded projects specifically in the cultural sector, which they often perceived positively in the sense of enabling and highlighting work in disability arts or in the sense of raising knowledge and ability around accessibility or enabling learning from other countries. For example, a Croatian participant referred to greater

2 It must be acknowledged that there was also some criticism of how EU funds were spent at a national level in terms of a lack of compliance with conditions and lack of monitoring relative to access to buildings.

visibility of people with disabilities in the cultural sphere in recent decades and attributed this to 'pressure' from the EU and funding (HR A&D) and a German participant referred to EU-funded projects such as festivals that are inclusive and barrier-free as representing 'a best practice example' that can be learnt from (DE OPD). Indeed, a Bulgarian participant (BG A&D) suggested that 'maybe most' of the activities, 'connected with culture and art, of people with disabilities', came through EU programmes and that was also the view of a participant from a Bulgarian association of Deaf people (BG D). Some participants nonetheless stated that the administrative burden of obtaining such funding (for example, from Creative Europe) was challenging or prohibitive, especially for small organisations, or that EU-funded projects did not always have long-lasting effects or, indeed, that accessibility pre-conditions were not always fully realised at a national level, sometimes criticising their national governments in that regard. For example, a Slovakian participant welcomed funding conditions linked to accessibility in relation to projects and activities ('it is a positive aspect for sure') but also added that accessibility requirements are not always 'fully followed' (SK A&D), and a Maltese participant referred to the fact that there have been 'many projects in the disability sector which have been funded by the EU', some of which 'have had long lasting effects' while others may have resulted in the employment of people with disabilities only for the duration of the project resulting in 'limited effects' (MT A&D).

Overall, the findings just discussed suggest that funding schemes that incorporate accessibility and other disability criteria, especially if supported by detailed guidelines or related capacity-building measures within cultural sectors, should be regularly embedded in cultural policies and deserve to be more widely employed by cultural agencies, governments, and funding bodies. This would support the implementation of the obligations laid out in Article 30 CRPD.

### 3.2. *Meaningful Consultation and Engagement with Organisations of People with Disabilities*

To improve accessibility for audiences, to enhance the availability of cultural content in accessible formats as required by Article 30(1) CRPD, and also to improve the participation of people with disabilities as artists and creators, advocacy of OPDs is key, along with their involvement in shaping the cultural offer as well as cultural policies. Indeed, the work of people with disabilities who are active in the arts was perceived as being significantly facilitative. This aligns with the ethos of the CRPD and with the obligations laid out in Article 4(3) CRPD and, more broadly, with the general principle of participation.

Especially with regard to access for people with disabilities as audience, a key facilitator was meaningful consultation with organisations that could advise cultural institutions about the diverse accessibility needs of people with disabilities. A consultative process engaged in within the museum sector was described by an Estonian participant (EE OPD) as follows:

> [There are] some good examples about museums that focus on the topic of accessibility. . . . They have gathered the experts from these organisations [of people with disabilities] together [at] the start of the process, they have thought out how the exhibition, how the rooms in the museums are built up also. . . . And together they have made these exhibitions, thought out how is the most accessible way to build them up, to set them up in the rooms. And the final outcome has been quite fantastic and has met the needs in the terms of accessibility.
>
> (EE OPD)

They also suggested that the impacts have been positive for other groups, including children and older people, suggesting that the organisations have come to see 'accessibility' in terms of 'this lifelong meaning' (EE OPD). They also added that the processes could be improved by introducing auditing for compliance and that a national-level expert group that cultural organisations could consult with for practical guidance would be a key facilitator of further change (EE OPD).

Participants in the study pointed to the advocacy or support given, or actions taken, by OPDs, or organisations of Deaf people – whether by way of direct advocacy or by way of informing, training, or consulting with cultural organisations or by taking up with them the importance of consultation. For example, a Slovakian participant suggested that what helps to promote cultural participation is 'effective interaction with professionals of specific cultural area[s] and support of organisations of persons with disabilities' (SK A&D), and a representative of a Deaf organisation from Lithuania made a similar point talking about extensive 'inter-institutional co-operation', aiming to provide opportunities for Deaf people to get involved with cultural activities (LT D). Several participants instanced ways that they had contributed to improvements in the field of culture. This included influencing guidelines on accessibility of cinemas (FI OPD) and helping organisations to spend their finances available for accessibility more efficiently (PT A&D). A participant from the Netherlands linked the need for advocacy, awareness raising, and networking by organisations working on disability to the fact that laws were not always enforced ('the legislation part is weak'), which is a point discussed in Chapter 5 (NL OPD). This participant highlighted that museum and theatre directors, for example, had to be made aware through advocacy of the potential to attract new audiences by making venues more accessible (NL OPD). A Spanish participant instanced work done by their organisation in the area of culture (including lobbying public officials, organising an influential cultural event jointly with a municipality and advocacy to address inaccessibility of a third-level college in the area of cultural heritage), and also referenced the work of several other OPDs in the area of culture, suggesting that this was 'the determining factor' in change (ES OPD). Similarly, a UK participant suggested that the social model of disability had proved a great basis for advocacy and change in general, and they linked the supportive policies pursued by Arts Council England (discussed previously) to advocacy by artists with disabilities over three to four decades (UK OPD). Likewise, another UK participant talked about the advocacy happening in the UK, to which they felt that the arts work of their organisation contributed: 'there is so much fantastic stuff happening . . . and I think the disabled community is growing in confidence and it is brilliant because that means there is more of us to share the advocacy and keep pushing' (UK A&D).

Specific trainings targeting people working in the cultural field and led by persons with disabilities or OPDs were also highlighted as facilitative. This training was considered important in dismantling stigma, fear, and prejudice as well as in addressing lack of knowledge on the part of people working in cultural arenas around engaging with people with disabilities or Deaf people. As Hadley, Rieger et al. (2022) argue, prevailing understandings of disability as a medical problem remain hard to shift and are associated with projections by able-bodied people based on unquestioned assumptions about the lives of people with disabilities. In the cultural sphere, these represent a barrier, 'to productive working partnerships, no matter the access infrastructure in the institution, and would-be allies need to be educated and engage with disabled people to develop respect for their identity, culture, and community' (Hadley, Rieger, et al., 2022, p. 6). Consistent with this, an Estonian participant talked about organising accessibility trainings for cultural organisations aiming to increase their engagement with people with disabilities as audiences, as well as sharing information on good practice examples that 'are really working for our target group' (EE OPD). Similarly, a Portuguese participant considered training and sharing information as 'very important', linking it to the need to challenge negative attitudes and contextualising it as follows:

> [L]ack of awareness and knowledge . . . keeps people away and afraid of dealing with certain new things . . . and [training] makes them feel more comfortable and conscious of what kind of services they need to provide, what is the best way of providing them, how they can better deal with people. Front-of-house staff, for instance, they are very, very worried of offending, of not receiving [people] properly. So training is very important. Sharing information, you know, making people feel that they have the knowledge necessary.
>
> (PT A&D)

Sometimes participants highlighted the efficacy of consultation and links in the context of recruiting audiences. For example, a Slovenian participant (SI OPD) emphasised the need for links between cultural organisations and different communities of people with disabilities, suggesting that it worked well when people with disabilities could act as 'ambassadors', which could 'motivate the co-members of a certain organisation to participate'.

On the whole, faced with the prevalence of negative or ableist attitudes, several participants perceived that the work of OPDs was a key facilitator, not only of improvements in general for people with disabilities but of reframing cultural perceptions about them and of enabling or supporting them in efforts to access and contribute to cultural opportunities as well, of course, as opportunities in other areas of life.

### *3.3. Employment of People with Disabilities Within the Cultural Sector*

As discussed in Chapter 5, and noted earlier, participants often perceived that a lack of knowledge on disability or accessibility on the part of staff of arts organisations constituted a barrier to participation. In that regard, one factor that supports improved knowledge and that may in turn result in disability-inclusive cultural goods, services, and institutions is consultation and engagement with persons with disabilities. However, a key facilitator of cultural participation in all its facets is also the employment of professionals with disabilities as workers in the cultural sector (e.g. curators, librarians, archiving experts, technicians, backstage professionals, and so on) and as artists, which was perceived as engendering trust and engagement amongst people with disabilities (or amongst some groups of them). With regard to workers in the cultural sector, for example, a German participant (DE A&D) highlighted a change to a festival that focused on disability arts once it was led by a director with disabilities:

> It made a massive difference. There were also two disabled curators organising the symposium for the festival and . . . there were more and more smaller projects popping up.
>
> (DE A&D)

Also concerning employment but relative to libraries, a Bulgarian participant discussed a library where two people with disabilities were employed, and which consequently provided a service that 'accounts for differences' and attracted visitors that included people with disabilities but also others. They broadened out from this example to say that 'having disabled people on the staff in such places like libraries or cultural clubs or movie theatres – that makes a difference. . . . And that makes a difference in service, in accessibility and in attracting clients including disabled clients' (BG OPD). They went on to say that, while the employment of people with disabilities in that library 'made the difference', there were some prerequisites 'in order to reach this point'. These included the physical accessibility of the building and a library director who was 'open' enough to employ the two people and to put them in a position to influence other staff (BG OPD). However, this participant also perceived that the employment of people with disabilities in cultural organisations was extremely rare in their country, and that it depended on the knowledge/interest of key decision-makers. Thus, as signalled earlier, the employment of artists and cultural professionals could depend on the interest or enthusiasm of staff as allies.

Some participants highlighted the impact of a few theatre and cinema directors who have come to routinely cast people with disabilities even when disability is not the focus of the work. Amongst them, a Portuguese participant (PT A&D) mentioned a major theatrical production featuring actors with disabilities alongside actors without disabilities and also including a Deaf actor speaking through sign language. That participant characterised this as one of a number of 'small steps that are making a big difference'. Crucial to arriving at this point in their perception was the involvement of staff who have been working on these issues for decades, including an artistic director, 'who made a choice – otherwise it wouldn't be this kind of production with these specific conditions' (PT A&D). In a similar vein, another participant discussed connecting to create joint work with mainstream cultural bodies, which they felt led to more knowledge about disability and more hiring and casting of artists with disabilities (NL A&D).

The employment of people with disabilities as artists and performers was considered critical to the quality of a performance. For example, a participant from Germany referred to a film made in collaboration with a Deaf person and with Deaf actors. In the opinion of that participant, 'this way the film appears more authentic, and the topic of Deaf culture and sign language would be treated and described properly' (DE D). Thus, making art was a way to develop and communicate 'new accounts of what it means to be disabled' (see Hadley & McDonald, 2019, p. 2).

However, most of all, the visibility of artists with disabilities was perceived as capable of challenging negative attitudes and also as facilitative of participation, with instances cited of artists becoming role models or influencing amateur groups or groups of younger people with disabilities. Amongst them, a Finnish participant mentioned classes run by professional artists who are people with disabilities, which they felt provided role models: 'they can be quite a good example for someone who hopes to be [an artist]' (FI OPD). Relatedly, a participant from Luxembourg said that it was important to see Deaf people participating, asking: 'how else should people get the idea that culture is something they can really participate in?' (LU D). Another participant stressed the importance of the integration of people with and without disabilities in performance companies (CY A&D), perceiving that this kind of integrated approach was vital in their country where participation in cultural events by people with disabilities, and especially professional engagement, was very limited. Linked with this, several participants working in disability arts felt that though the primary aim of their work was artistic, it also constituted advocacy. For example, another Finnish participant suggested that 'doing good shows' changed attitudes, as a show that was artistically good meant that a 'new audience' would see it and 'that sort of changes attitudes and expectations and everything' (FI A&D). Furthermore, a Romanian participant indicated that, in their country, there was a lack of acceptance of people with disabilities, but went on to suggest that this was countered when self-advocates are present in all aspects of life, including in culture, and are producing 'quality work' (RO OPD). That participant added:

> We have the biggest success in this domain by being present in almost every important event which involves the general public: music or cultural festivals, wine fairs and wine events, student festivals, or big events organized by the municipality'
>
> (RO OPD)

In connection with the importance of employing persons with disabilities, participants sometimes pointed to the need for mainstream arts organisations to be made aware of the availability of performers with disabilities and there were some examples of registers or lists being created that promoted knowledge of them.

In addition, some participants perceived that cultural identity can develop through arts practices developed amongst specific groups of artists with disabilities. For example, a Finnish participant distinguished between mainstream cultural offerings that translate performances into sign language and ones that 'maintain sign language culture' and that are created in sign language from the outset, saying:

> It is highly important to make a difference between performances that are produced straight to sign language from those performances that are first produced, for example, in Finnish and then interpreted into sign language. These organisations [led by Deaf people] maintain sign language culture and enable people whose native language [is] sign language to express themselves in their own language
>
> (FI D)

This collective and identitarian aspect links to Article 30(4) CRPD and it is notable that such a collective element was raised particularly in the context of experiences of Deaf people (who are in fact singled out in the CRPD) creating art or contributing to the creation of mainstream productions.

### *3.4. Changes to Professional Training and Education to Include People with Disabilities*

When it comes to the implementation of Article 30(2) CRPD and the right to be actively involved in culture as an artist, creator, or performer, as discussed earlier in this book, many participants identified a lack of access for people with disabilities to professional training as a serious barrier. As a participant from Luxembourg said, 'to make Deaf people participate in culture themselves, they need to have the opportunity, ideally from childhood on, to participate in cultural workshops and trainings' (LU D). This was the backdrop to perceptions on the part of a small number of participants that there were some examples of good practice, especially regarding third-level education. For example, a Finnish participant talked about working with a performance academy doing training on access and disability, characterising this as 'a first step' towards change in relation to the overall access of people with disabilities to such training, adding that this area needs 'huge changes' (FI A&D). In that regard, educational policies need to ensure access to third-level education and that children with disabilities can access education that includes a focus on the arts, and cultural policies should not only foster contributions by artists with disabilities but also leverage and foster advocacy, as well as ongoing engagement with awareness raising and training provided by OPDs.

Education more generally was also seen as key in relation to supporting accessibility. An Estonian participant pointed to some 'good examples' of change starting to take place in relation to the education of people working in cultural sectors, instancing librarians and cultural managers, who, they felt, would now sometimes be exposed to modules on accessibility, and which they characterised as 'one way to raise the awareness and the importance of the accessibility in the field of culture' (EE OPD). Findings discussed here, therefore, suggest that a key area for change to start is in training programmes within higher education, 'the pipeline for future creators' (Flys & Amidei, 2021, p. 16).

## 4. Concluding Remarks

Overall, the findings presented in ths chapter suggest that cultural participation has become more central, and good practices are starting to emerge. As argued already, the CRPD, as global standard on disability rights, has contributed to these developments. In turn, good practices related to cultural participation are perceived as beginning to challenge devaluation of people with disabilities in society and to realise the human rights model of disability, even if much remains to be done. However, they also signal the need for embedding disability issues throughout the cultural sphere, through disability-sensitive funding schemes, meaningful consultation and engagement with diverse groups of people with disabilities, and actions to promote greater training and employment of artists and professionals with disabilities. With regard to the implementation of Article 30(2) CRPD in particular, changes to educational policies or virtuous educational policies are viewed as a necessary step towards the more creative engagement of persons with disabilities.

A systematic, mainstreamed approach to cultural participation of persons with disabilities, as is called for by the CRPD, but is yet to be realised. However, in this chapter, we have discussed factors that may contribute to effecting change and to facilitating the implementation of the broad obligations laid out in Article 30 CRPD read in conjunction with its general principles. Facilitators have been described as operating in specific instances which were identified as good practices, but, as yet, neither mainstreamed nor ingrained in the cultural system. Specifically, facilitative funding mechanisms are understood as those that mandate accessibility on the part of funded organisations, that promote knowledge and skills around anti-discrimination measures, and where roles that focus on the inclusion of persons with disabilities are supported and resourced. It is evident that these criteria should be embedded more consistently into all national and EU funding mechanisms and that funding bodies also need to become more knowledgeable about disability and access issues, not least so as to be able to support grantee organisations and to also be able to connect them with representatives of people with disabilities who could contribute to the planning stages of their work. In that regard, another facilitative tool identified was meaningful consultation and engagement with OPDs in all steps along the way. Consultation and collaboration with OPDs are key to realising accessibility and to making accessible events known to people with disabilities and trusted by them. Alongside this, perceptions of negative attitudes and a lack of knowledge on the part of people working in culture continue but could be challenged and sometimes transformed by activism and by OPDs engaging in collaboration, networking, training, and education with the staff of cultural bodies. In this regard, the employment of people with disabilities is key to promoting understanding of the common humanity shared by all people but also in shaping and highlighting disability as a cultural identity. To facilitate the employment of people with disabilities in cultural sectors, especially artists with disabilities, education and changes in artistic education policies and practices are perceived as crucial. An underlying issue in respect of most, or all, of the facilitative factors identified is the usefulness of addressing attitudinal barriers amongst people working in culture. This is consistent with arguments, already mentioned, that prevailing understandings of disability as a medical issue or problem, amongst people working in the cultural sphere, remain hard to shift and are associated with unquestioned assumptions about the lives of people with disabilities (Hadley, Rieger et al., 2022).

On the whole, consistent with the findings expounded in Chapter 5, facilitators identified by people with disabilities point to the need for an approach to the implementation of Article 30 CRPD that includes, but goes beyond, access measures and, in essence, involves a change of ethos (see Reason, 2022). Further, the findings suggest that the cultural participation of people with disabilities triggers a virtuous cycle whereby the expression and visibility intrinsic to artistic creation is facilitative of change, not only in how culture is constituted but in how disability is perceived in society. This points to the fact that, even though the right to participate in culture has been described as the 'Cinderella' of human rights (Xanthaki, 2015) and has been considered less vital than other issues (Disability Ombudsman of Croatia, 2014), it has potential to fundamentally influence how disability is understood and, hence, in the realisation of the human rights model of disability.

## References

Agostiano, M. (2016). The 'compensatory solutions' for an alternative accessibility of cultural heritage sites. In A. Arenghi, I. Garofolo, & O. Sørmoen (Eds.), *Accessibility as a key enabling knowledge for enhancement of cultural heritage* (pp. 131–147). Franco Angeli.

Argyropoulos, V. S., & Kanari, C. (2015). Re-imagining the museum through "touch": Reflections of individuals with visual disability on their experience of museum-visiting in Greece. *Alter, European Journal of Disability Research/Revue européenne de recherche sur le handicap*, *9*(2), 130–143.

Cachia, A. (2013). 'Disabling' the museum: Curator as infrastructural activist. *Canadian Journal of Disability Studies*, *2*(4), 257–289.

Disability Ombudsman of Croatia. (2014). *Parallel report: On the implementation of the UN Convention on the Rights of Persons with Disabilities in the Republic of Croatia on the occasion of the review of the initial report of the government of the Republic of Croatia before the UN Committee on the rights of persons with disabilities*. Republic of Croatia Disability Ombudsman.

Flys, E. S. V., & Amidei, A. (2021). Access and inclusion for students with disabilities in performing arts higher education. *Acotaciones. Investigación y Creación Teatral*, *2*(47), 15–44.

Glow, H., Kershaw, A., & Reason, M. (2021). Leading or avoiding change: The problem of audience diversification for arts organisations. *International Journal of Cultural Policy*, *27*(1), 130–148.

Hadley, B., & McDonald, D. (2019). Introduction: Disability arts, culture, and media studies – mapping a maturing field. In B. Hadley & D. McDonald (Eds.), *The Routledge handbook of disability arts, culture, and media* (pp. 1–18). Routledge.

Hadley, B., Paterson, E., & Little, M. (2022). Quick trust and slow time: Relational innovations in disability performing arts practice. *International Journal of Disability and Social Justice*, *2*(1), 74–94.

Hadley, B., Rieger, J., Ellis, K., & Paterson, E. (2022). Cultural safety as a foundation for allyship in disability arts. *Disability & Society*, *39*(1), 213–233.

Hadley, S. (2021). *Audience development and cultural policy*. Palgrave Macmillan.

Lazar, J., & Briggs, I. (2015). Improving services for patrons with print disabilities at public libraries: Moving forward to become more inclusive. *Library Quarterly: Information, Community, Policy*, *85*(2), 172–184.

Leahy, A., & Ferri, D. (2024). Cultural policies that facilitate the participation of persons with disabilities in the arts: Findings from a qualitative multi-national study. *Disabilities*, *4*(3), 539–555.

Levent, N., & Pursley, J. M. (2013). Sustainable museum access: A two-way street. *Disability Studies Quarterly*, *33*(3).

Lid, I. M. (2016). Access to cultural heritage: A multiscaled approach. In A. Arenghi, I. Garofolo, & O. Sørmoen (Eds.), *Accessibility as a key enabling knowledge for enhancement of cultural heritage* (pp. 77–89). Franco Angeli.

Mesquita, S., & Carneiro, M. J. (2016). Accessibility of European museums to visitors with visual impairments. *Disability & Society*, *31*(3), 373–388.

Office of the High Commissioner for Human Rights (OHCHR). (2020). *Article 30: List of illustrative indicators on participation in cultural life, recreation, leisure and sport*. www.ohchr.org/sites/default/files/article-30-indicators-en.pdf

Reason, M. (2022). Inclusive online community arts: COVID and beyond COVID. *Cultural Trends*, *32*(1), 52–69.

Renel, W. (2019). Sonic accessibility: Increasing social equity through the inclusive design of sound in museums and heritage sites. *Curator: The Museum Journal*, *62*(3), 377–402.

Seale, J., Carrizosa, H. G., Rix, J., Sheehy, K., & Hayhoe, S. (2021). A participatory approach to the evaluation of participatory museum research projects. *International Journal of Research & Method in Education*, *44*(1), 20–40.

United Nations Committee on the Rights of Persons with Disabilities (CRPD Committee). (2018). *General Comment No. 7 on the participation of persons with disabilities, including children with disabilities, through their representative organizations, in the implementation and monitoring of the Convention* (UN Doc. CRPD/C/GC/7).

Vas, R. (2020). Blind and visually impaired visitors' experiences in museums: Increasing accessibility through assistive technologies. *The International Journal of the Inclusive Museum*, *13*(2), 57–80.

World Health Organization & The World Bank. (2011). *World report on disability*. World Health Organization.

Xanthaki, A. (2015). Cultural rights. In *Oxford bibliographies*. Oxford University Press. https://www.oxfordbibliographies.com/display/document/obo-9780199796953/obo-9780199796953-0123.xml

# Conclusion

*Delia Ferri and Ann Leahy*

## 1. Challenges and Strengths of a Socio-Legal Analysis on Cultural Participation of Persons with Disabilities

This book has framed cultural participation of persons with disabilities as a human right, with a focus on Article 30 of the UN Convention on the Rights of Persons with Disabilities (CRPD). Embracing the CRPD as an overarching legal framework, it has provided a novel socio-legal analysis of the right of people with disabilities to participate in cultural life, focusing on barriers to, and facilitators of, its realisation. Essentially, it has embedded an examination of Article 30 CRPD within the social situations in which it applies. Consistent with this approach, the book has built on the study of relevant legal scholarship, cultural studies, and disability studies literature and also combines traditional legal doctrinal methodology with empirical research.

The ambition of the book was that of understanding, bringing together, and integrating diverse disciplinary perspectives on the cultural participation of persons with disabilities. It aimed to blend legal analysis of the obligations stemming from Article 30 CRPD and insights from the fields of disability studies, cultural studies, sociology, and the humanities. In this regard, the book has also endeavoured to re-read the right to participate in cultural life through the lens of lived experiences of persons with disabilities. Without rejecting the usefulness of doctrinal legal research, often referred to as 'black-letter', which plays an important role in understanding the legal framework through which human rights are protected and promoted, this book embraces the view that doctrinal research provides a narrow lens (Gonzalez-Salzberg & Hodson, 2019). In fact, in the last few years, socio-legal approaches appear to have gained traction with normative, analytical, and empirical components coming together. This is particularly so when it comes to human rights of persons with disabilities, whereby the understanding of disability embedded in the CRPD is rooted in disability studies literature (Ferri, 2024), and the reliance on lived experience is crucial in challenging structural inequality, charitable and medicalised models of disability, and in articulating the claims of people with disabilities to personhood and inherent dignity.

DOI: 10.4324/9781032619361-11

This chapter has been made available under a CC-BY-NC-ND 4.0 license.

In legal scholarship, the right to culture of people with disabilities has been discussed only within the remit of commentaries to the CRPD, and other disciplines rarely engage with a human rights perspective and the human rights model of disability. Moreover, the initial literature review, set out in Chapter 1, showed that cultural participation of persons with disabilities has been rarely looked at through a human rights lens and, in this respect, the book has addressed a notable gap in disability and cultural literature. Further, the literature review has also shown 'disciplinary silos' and 'narrow perspectives' that focus on specific impairments or specific art forms or specific geographical contexts, or even specific venues. In this respect, the book has attempted to bridge these silos, to address the still very limited interdisciplinarity, and to stimulate further interaction amongst disciplines – such as international human rights law, disability studies, cultural studies, and cultural policy.

This deliberate choice for a socio-legal approach and a highly interdisciplinary perspective to research has also brought methodological challenges, the biggest of which was that of combining knowledge, skills, and forms of research in a consistent manner so as to advance the understanding and implementation of Article 30 CRPD. In fact, linking legal obligations stemming from the CRPD to the 'narratives' of States Parties and to lived experiences in a continuum of reasoning supported by interdisciplinary knowledge represents the most important added value of this book and probably the starting point for further and even deeper or more detailed research.

Another significant difficulty was that of ensuring terminological consistency when dealing with blurred notions of disability, culture, participation, and also barriers and facilitators. In that regard, the book has adopted a social-contextual understanding of disability, according to which disability stems from the interaction between the individual's impairments and external barriers, in line with Article 1(2) CRPD. Consistent with such an understanding of disability as being socially created, the book also emphasises the concept of barriers and facilitators, whereby the term 'barriers' means 'factors in a person's environment that, through their absence or presence, limit functioning and create disability', and facilitators are 'factors in a person's environment that, through their absence or presence, improve functioning and reduce disability' (World Report on Disability (WHO) & World Bank 2011, pp. 302, 304). It has adopted a broad notion of culture in line with that embraced by human rights law (Chow, 2018), but focused deliberately on arts and heritage as specific manifestations of culture. It has also, by using the human rights model of disability as a theoretical framework, looked at cultural participation as a right, encompassing a twofold individual dimension and a collective aspect (EPRS, 2017, pp. 10, 27). The twofold individual dimension entails, on the one hand, the right to access cultural activities, goods, services and heritage, and, on the other, the right to active involvement in culture, which includes engagement in the creation of cultural activities, goods, and services (Romainville, 2015). The collective aspect refers to cultural communities being recognised, protected, as well as enabled to enjoy their cultural expressions (Jakubowski, 2016).

The book aimed to show that law (in this respect, the CRPD) is the basis on which to build a better world, but it is a paper tiger without a layered understanding of what hampers its effectiveness and supports its success.

## 2. A Circular Path Around the Essentiality of Cultural Participation

The starting point of the book was that cultural participation is of key importance, and, as Tatić (2015, p. 6) argues, it is 'one of the essential dimensions of life, both for persons with disabilities and for those without disabilities'. Without the right to participate in cultural life, individuals fail to develop the social and cultural connections that are important to maintaining satisfactory conditions of equality, which can have consequences for the well-being and even sustainability of the social order (Laaksonen, 2010). In fact, the book started from the understanding that culture has the potential to promote fuller enjoyment of human rights, including by challenging discrimination and stigma (Bennoune, 2018). In this respect, the book has built on an array of disability studies scholarly elaborations that underline the role of disability art and culture in challenging stereotypes and fostering diversity. The work from Sandahl (2018, p. 84) has been fundamental in foregrounding the essence and rationale of the book and in supporting the understanding that artists with disabilities 'challenge, not replicate mainstream traditions' and that, without experiencing disabled artists' differences, the 'mainstream status quo may not be able to imagine the ways it could be transformed'.

The overall analysis reinforces and shines a new light on the importance of cultural participation for people with disabilities to challenge existing medical views of disabilities. On the one hand, the book, in particular the empirical analysis conducted, highlights that negative attitudes remain the main hurdle to cultural participation in both its passive and (especially) its active dimensions. Many participants in our study perceived that attitudes were not so much 'negative', as 'ignorant', 'charitable', or 'medicalised' rather than based on ideas of equality or human rights. This tallies with the reversion to medicalised understandings and approaches to disability identified in States Parties' reports. On the other hand, participants in the study that informs the book did emphasise the extent to which disabled artists can change the way disability is perceived.

Further, the book places emphasis on the small but significant steps made (and that can be implemented in the future) in advancing cultural participation of persons with disabilities and in realising Article 30 CRPD by highlighting good practices across Europe. This is not to say that it is not all 'bad' and to infuse 'optimism' but mostly to allow States Parties to the Convention to build on good practices, to reflect on what can be done, and to look forward. In fact, this book has also emphasised that improvements, and a new focus on cultural participation of persons with disabilities as audiences and artists, can be located within a broader renewed attention to disability rights which stems from the CRPD. The choice of the overarching legal framework of the book is hence particularly meaningful because it not only recognises the CRPD as the global standard on disability rights but takes into account its spillover effects, groundbreaking nature, and transformative cypher (Harpur, 2011; Goldschmidt, 2017; McCallum & Martin, 2013). It is not surprising that some participants experienced the CRPD as a game changer, bringing 'movement', as one participant put it, in the cultural field.

## 3. Progressive Realisation: Dismantling Barriers

Article 30 CRPD is subject to progressive realisation in line with what is generally established for cultural rights and in compliance with Article 4(2) CRPD. Progressive realisation acknowledges that implementation takes time and commitment as well as resources. However, it cannot lead to inaction. In fact, States Parties to the CRPD will need to address barriers to cultural participation, many of which are deeply embedded and represent structural inequalities. The book has identified barriers under specific headings, and many of those barriers are not novel *per se*. For the most part, they are well-known obstacles that people with disabilities face when approaching culture. In fact, the experiences discussed suggest that culture is structured by a range of barriers that operate in disparate areas of policy, many of which are still informed by medical and charitable ideas of disability. What is new is the understanding that these barriers traverse various boundaries – they are commonly experienced across countries and across different art forms and disabilities (even if they can be experienced to different extents in different countries and also to different extents by people experiencing diverse impairment types). The book corroborates the view that making changes to enhance accessibility seems challenging for various reasons, including economic and infrastructural ones, but it has the potential to expand audiences that include people with disabilities but are not limited to them. What is also novel is the fact that those barriers tend to be compounded and prevent both the enjoyment and the exercise of all the dimensions of the right to participate in cultural life.

In that regard, the book also shows that there is a piecemeal approach to ensuring cultural participation of people with disabilities which emerges from the States Parties' reports and was articulated by participants in the study. In fact, our analysis highlighted the rather patchy implementation of Article 30 CRPD with limited awareness of, and especially attention to, social, attitudinal, and financial barriers experienced by persons with disabilities. In this respect, the book aims to be an essential instrument in supporting a more systematic implementation of Article 30 CRPD that starts from an understanding of what 'does not work' and 'what works'. In this respect, the book provides a robust academic analysis which provides an evidence base on which policy and programming can best implement Article 30 CRPD. It also forms the basis for more in-depth queries and recommendations on culture by the CRPD Committee, supporting their relentless efforts in guiding States Parties towards the implementation of the CRPD. The unveiling of States Parties' narratives and the experience of persons with disabilities should direct the attention of the CRPD Committee to all the aspects of cultural participation envisaged in Article 30, including those which have been disregarded or underplayed so far.

Often, human rights treaties do not translate into improved lives for people. However, the book, as noted earlier, demonstrates that the CRPD has, in fact, triggered some advancements in the cultural sphere and directed more attention to persons with disabilities as audiences and artists. There is some evidence of a developing understanding of people with disabilities as rights-holders, as autonomous beings and of participation in culture as an expression of personhood and dignity. However, there is much more to do to progressively realise Article 30 CRPD.

The implementation of Article 30 CRPD must reflect the human rights model of disability that the Convention embodies and must itself contribute to the realisation of this model. The CRPD has the potential to effect a cultural transformation in how disability is understood and is consistent with the emphasis within critical or cultural disability studies on the need to analyse and transform what is perceived as mainstream culture from the perspective of disability. As the former Special Rapporteur on the Rights of Persons with Disabilities argues, neither awareness-raising programmes nor the generalisation of anti-discrimination measures will alone suffice for disability to be embraced as part of human diversity, and a cultural transformation is needed in how society relates to the difference of disability (Devandas-Aguilar, 2019).

## References

Bennoune, K. (2018). *Report of the Special Rapporteur in the field of cultural rights: Note by the Secretariat* (UN Doc. A/JRC/37/55). https://digitallibrary.un.org/record/1473375?ln=en&v=pdf

Chow, P. Y. S. (2018). *Cultural rights in international law and discourse: Contemporary challenges and interdisciplinary perspectives*. Brill Nijhoff.

Devandas-Aguilar, C. (2019). *Rights of persons with disabilities. Report of the special Rapporteur on the rights of persons with disabilities* (UN Doc. A/HRC/43/41).

European Parliament Research Service (EPRS). (2017). *Access to culture in the European Union*. https://op.europa.eu/en/publication-detail/-/publication/66f298ec-6840-11e7-b2f2-01aa75ed71a1

Ferri, D. (2024). The role of disability studies in the advancement of EU law scholarship. In R. Deplano, G. Gentile, L. Lonardo, & T. Nowak (Eds.), *Interdisciplinary research methods in EU law: A handbook* (pp. 39–58). Edward Elgar.

Goldschmidt, J. E. (2017). New perspectives on equality: Towards transformative justice through the disability convention? *Nordic Journal of Human Rights*, *35*(1), 1–14.

Gonzalez-Salzberg, D., & Hodson, L. (Eds.). (2019). *Research methods for international human rights law: Beyond the traditional paradigm* (1st ed.). Routledge.

Harpur, P. (2011). Embracing the new disability rights paradigm: The importance of the Convention on the Rights of Persons with Disabilities. *Disability & Society*, *27*(1), 1–14.
Jakubowski, A. (Ed.). (2016). *Cultural rights as collective rights: An international law perspective*. Brill.
Laaksonen, A. (2010). *Making culture accessible. Access, participation and cultural provision in the context of cultural rights in Europe*. Council of Europe Publishing.
McCallum, R., & Martin, H. (2013). Comment: The CRPD and children with disabilities. *Australian International Law Journal*, *20*, 17–31.
Romainville, C. (2015). On defining the right to participate in cultural life as a human right. *Netherlands Quarterly of Human Rights*, *33*(4), 405–436.
Sandahl, C. (2018). Disability art and culture: A model for imaginative ways to integrate the community. *Alter, European Journal of Disability/Research/Revue européenne de recherche sur le handicap*, *12*(2), 79–93.
Tatić, D. (2015). *Access for people with disabilities to culture, tourism, sports and leisure activities: Towards meaningful and enriching participation*. Council of Europe.
World Health Organization & The World Bank. (2011). *World report on disability*. World Health Organization.

# Index

Note: Page numbers in **bold** indicate a table on the corresponding page.

For Product Safety Concerns and Information please contact our EU representative GPSR@taylorandfrancis.com
Taylor & Francis Verlag GmbH, Kaufingerstraße 24, 80331 München, Germany

www.ingramcontent.com/pod-product-compliance
Lightning Source LLC
LaVergne TN
LVHW021129300926
849160LV00010B/922
*9781032619354*